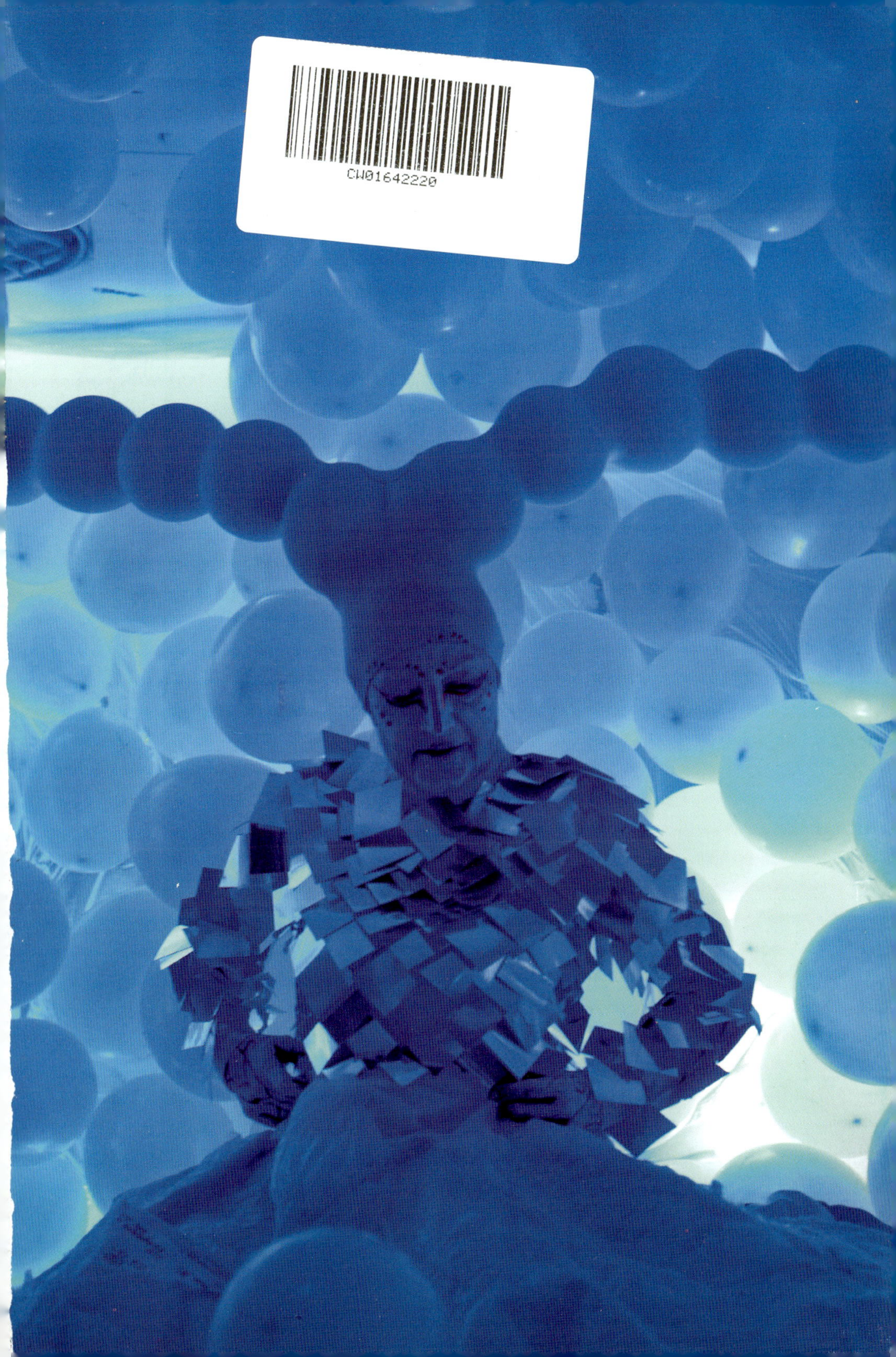

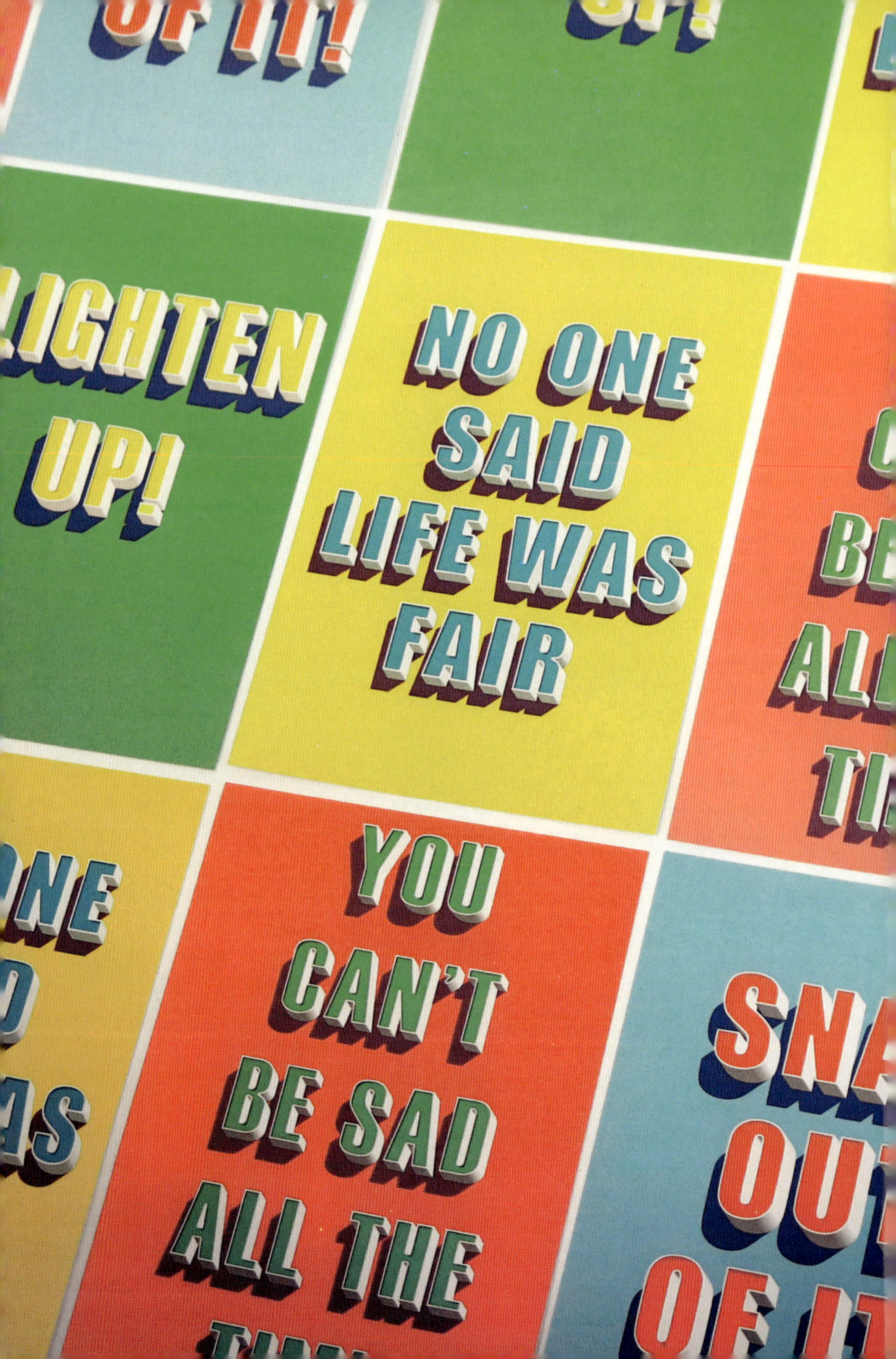
NO ONE SAID LIFE WAS FAIR
YOU CAN'T BE SAD ALL THE
UP!

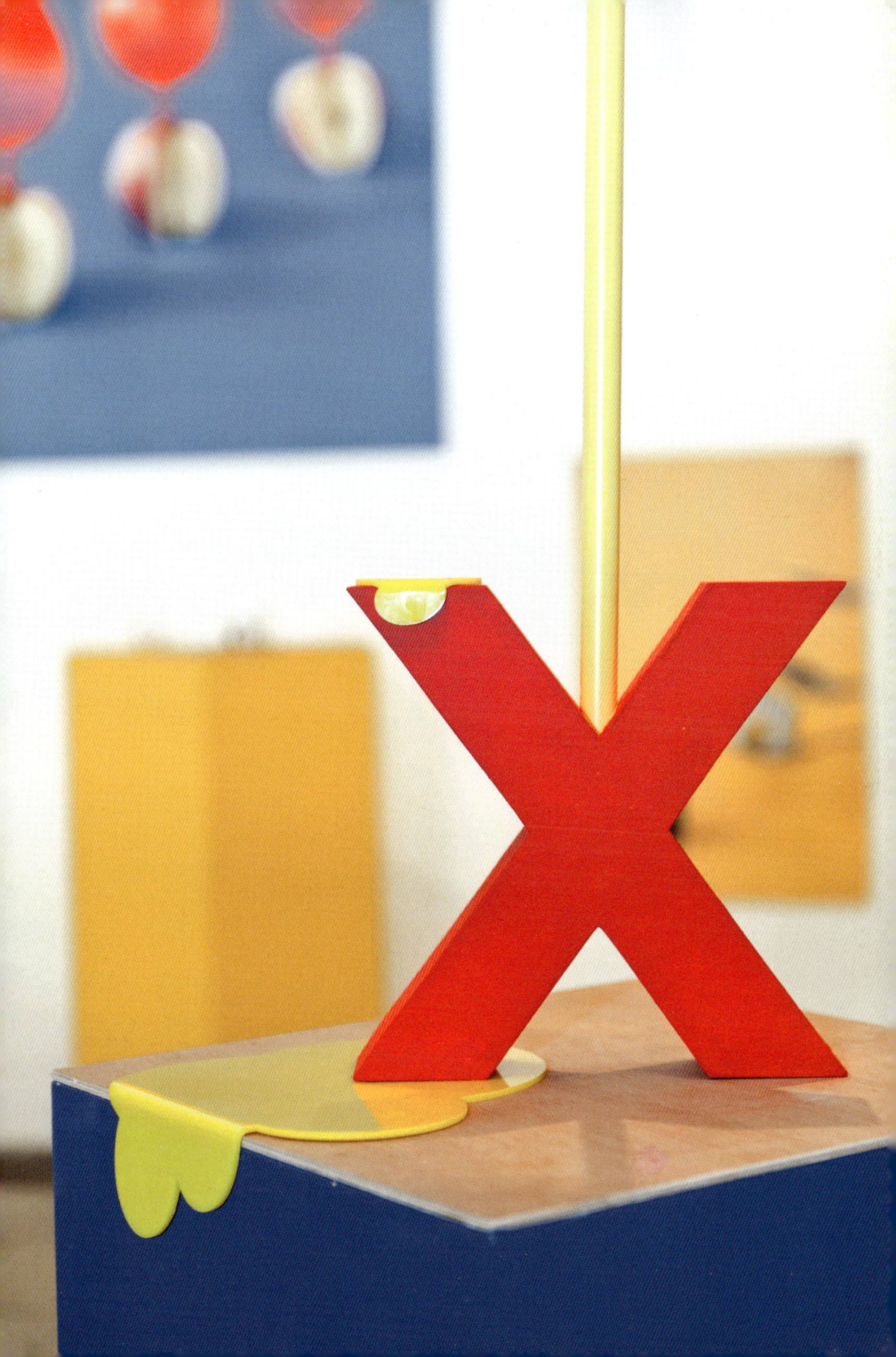

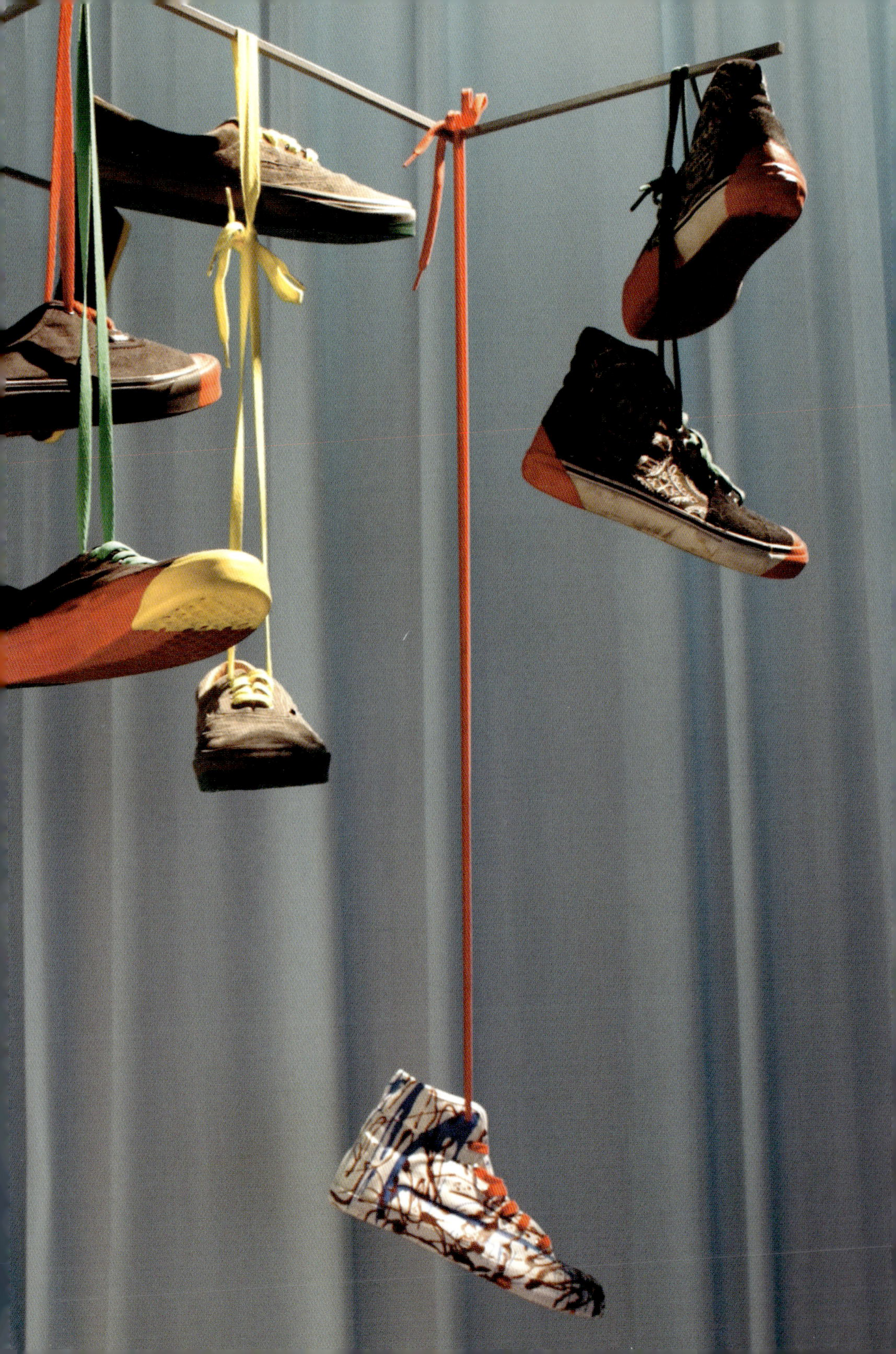

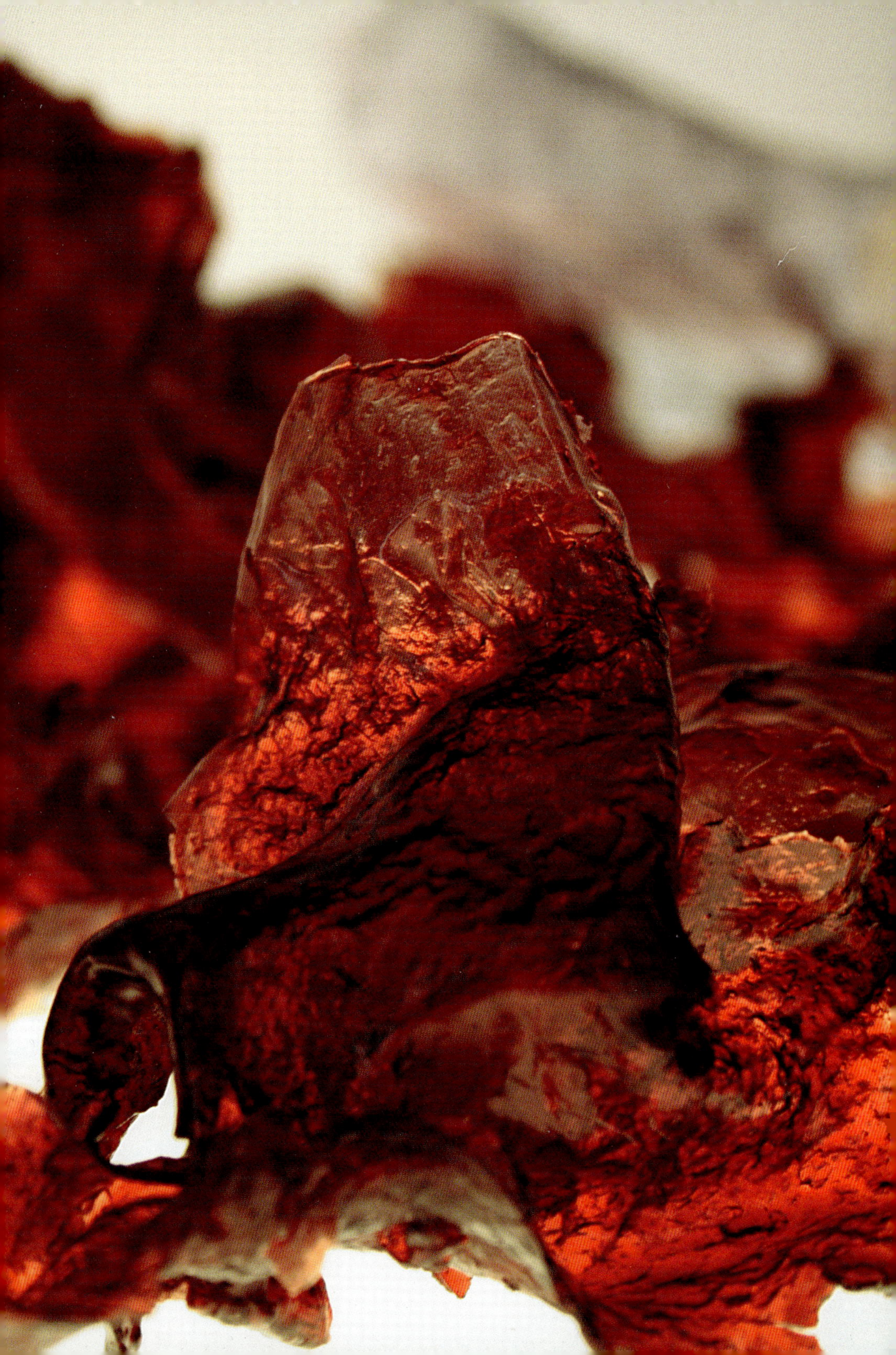

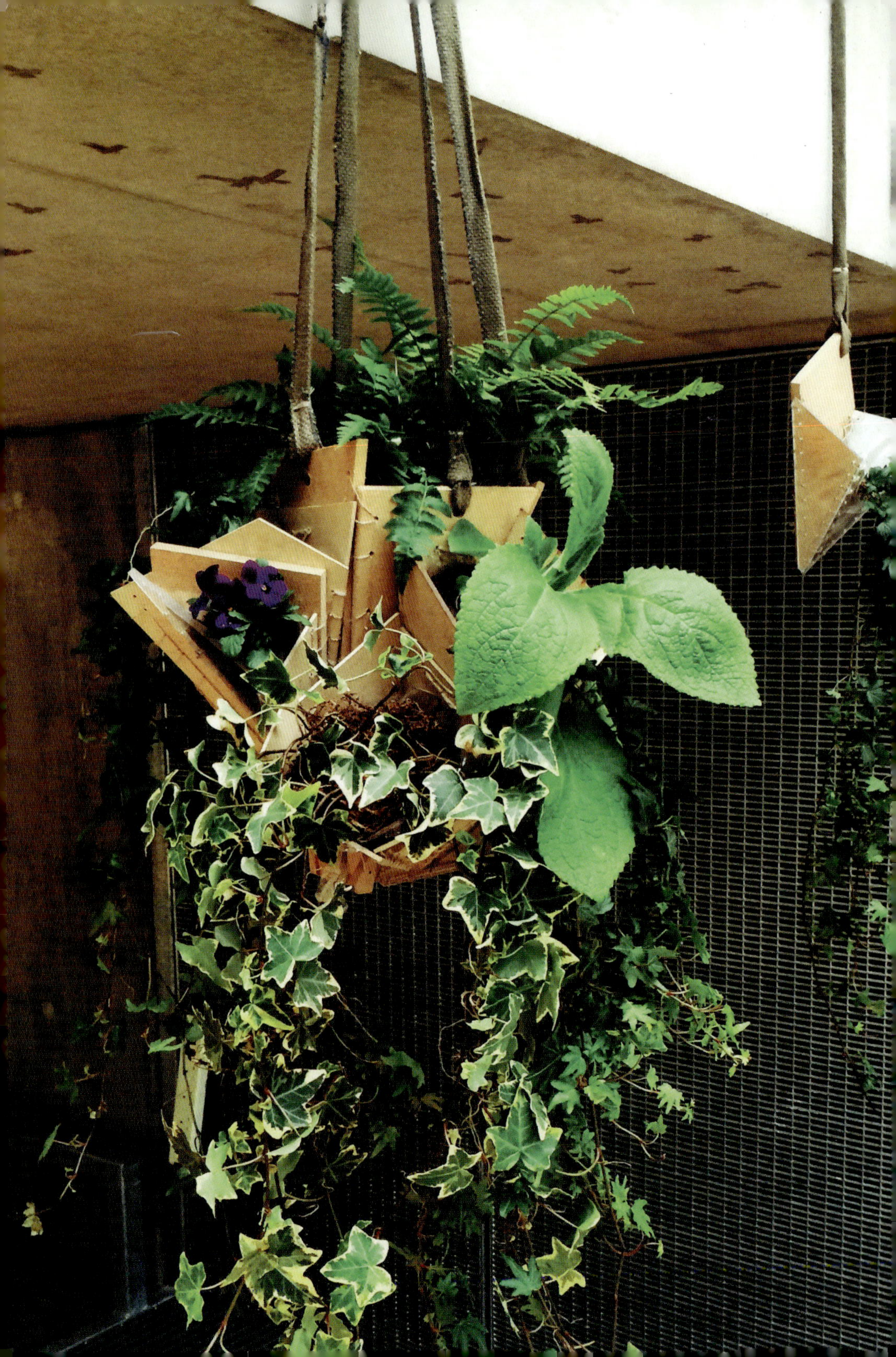

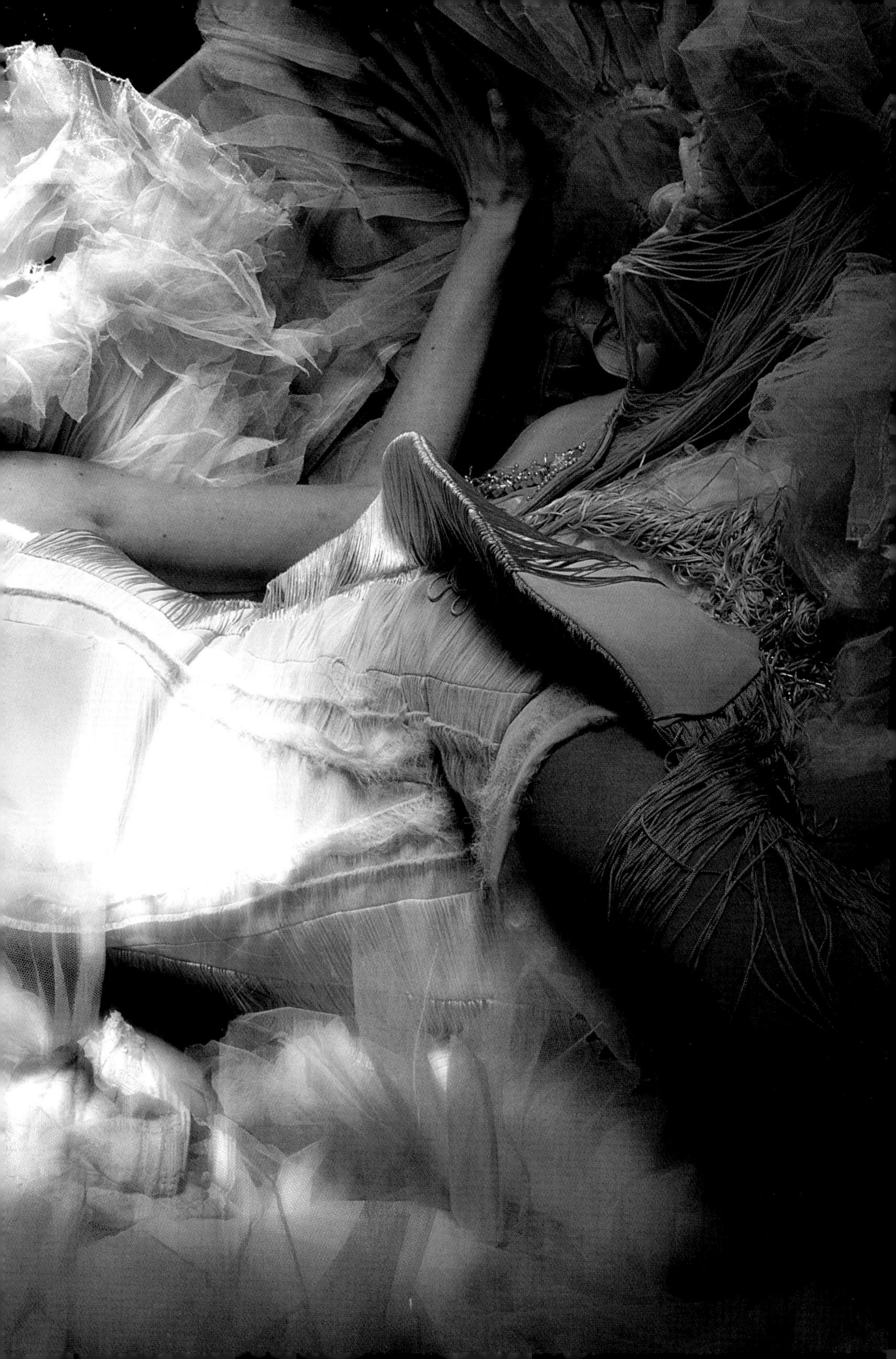

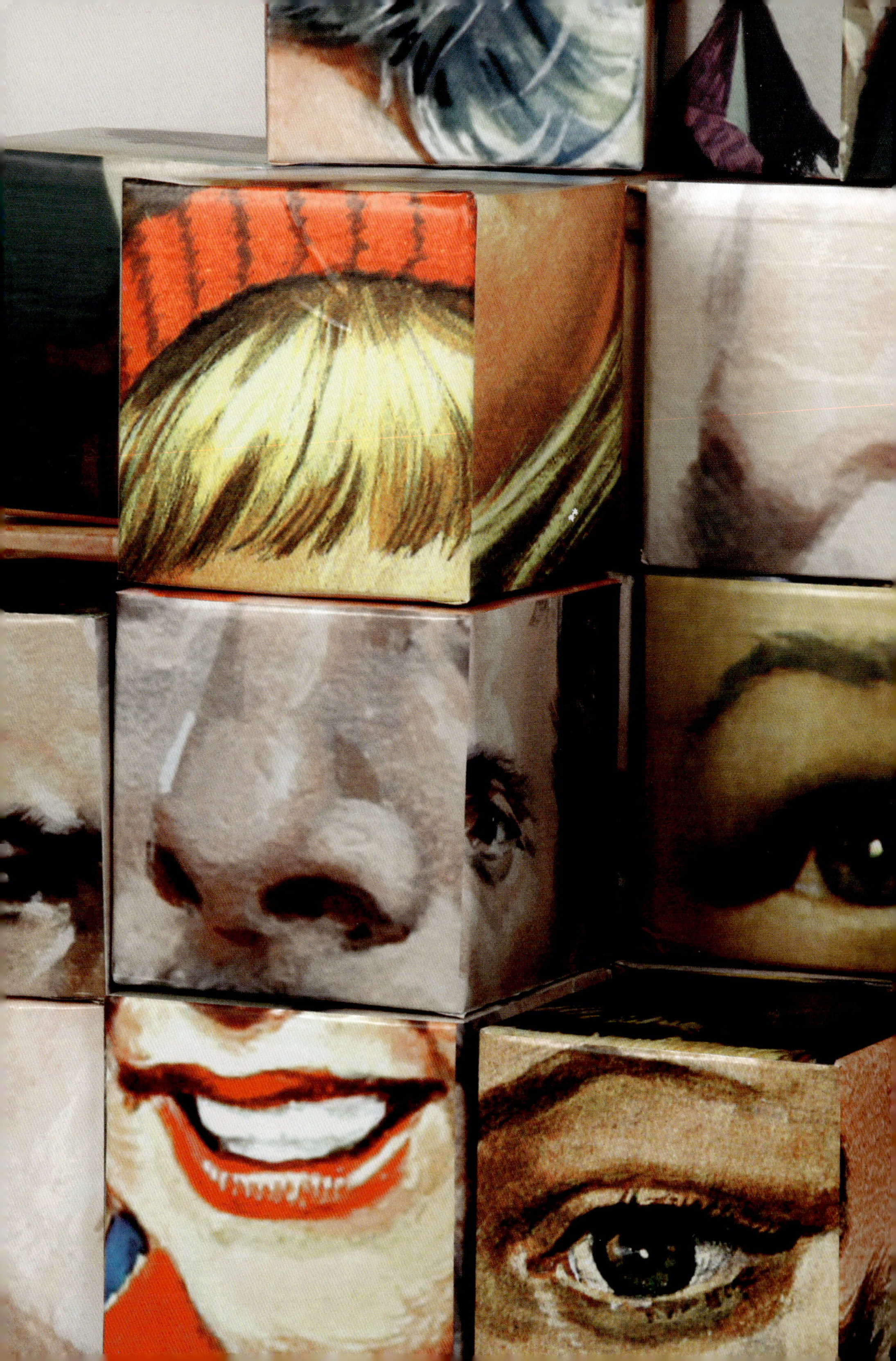

THE CREATIVE STANCE

THE CREATIVE STANCE

COMMON-EDITIONS

Introduction

Nigel Carrington

In a world that appreciates a direct connection between cause and effect, people find it hard to understand how creativity works. Creativity is often thought to be set apart as a quality in business and personal life, and successful creative people are accorded special status, sometimes akin to a prophetic aura. Creativity is widely felt to be innate, something you are born with – in fact, unknowable.

Using examples from British art and design schools, *The Creative Stance* shows that creativity is understandable and can be developed. In the last century, people we think of as creative giants in a number of fields have been taught within the art school tradition. These schools have become a subject of increasing interest and have been emulated across the world, for the value and results of their particular interpretations of creative education. This kind of education is typified by the six famous colleges of University of the Arts London (UAL); by the Royal College of Art (RCA); Goldsmiths, University of London; Ravensbourne; and The Sir John Cass Faculty of Art, Architecture and Design at London Metropolitan University ('the Cass'). Most of these are represented by the voices in these pages.

The Creative Stance examines how art and design schools foster seven creative behaviours: rigour, risk, resilience, ambiguity, agency, imagination and provocation. This list of behaviours emerged from intense discussions among leading educators in this field, who are alumni of the art and design school tradition. They are therefore based on lifetimes spent in creative education in all its complexity.

Structurally, this book deals with the seven behaviours in the same complex spirit, both directly and at a tangent. Each behaviour is unpacked in detail, first in an essay and then in conversation. These texts are interspersed with sample projects of the kind that are typically given to students to help develop these behaviours. We hear many voices – often agreeing, sometimes contradictory. The designer and illustrator of the book are also, of course, art school alumni.

Here we see creativity as an observed effect, the application of a certain type of intelligence; an approach to problems, characterised by the seven behaviours. As Neil Cummings puts it, 'curiosity is the substrate of creativity, overlaid by an appetite for risk, necessarily followed by determination' (see p.64). When we describe someone as creative, therefore, we are describing the manner in which they apply their intelligence to the world around them – what Roger Hiorns describes as 'trying to redesign the way that we're supposed to behave' (see p.171).

This approach is quicksilver – the enemy of your own and other people's certainty. A state of optimistic dissatisfaction, of relentless questioning. A preoccupation with quality without regard for the established order. It is a holistic intelligence and attends, as Siobhan Davies says, 'to the way [the] whole body works as an integrated system' (see p.25). These points of view are learned as much as innate, a point made by Sonia Boyce, who expresses her fascination and dismay at the way that talented black artists fall out of the canon (see pp.160–64). And, at art and design schools, creativity is taught in a collaborative way that shares the 'authentic' experience of 'not knowing where you're going', as Helen Storey says (see p.152).

Through its insistence that we should try to understand creativity, *The Creative Stance* deliberately undermines creativity's special status, and to critical effect. Because, if creativity cannot be fostered, there is no point in funding creative education. And if education is not funded as a necessity, it will be the preserve of those who can afford it as a luxury.

It is as unhelpful to expect all creative people to be geniuses as it would be to expect it of all scientists or all engineers. Creatives may well use their right brain more than their left. Some have a higher order of intelligence than others. Some may achieve flamboyant mastery and achieve mythic status. All have their place within society and the workforce. James Dyson and Thomas Edison famously went through thousands of prototypes before their breakthroughs – where do resilience and rigour start and imagination and inspiration end?

And, of course, creativity is already suspect to those in power. Creative resistance to the status quo inevitably subjects the State to question and attack. Dictators co-opt or silence creative people because they challenge the authoritarian version of the truth. Perhaps for the same reason, Western economies misunderstand the creative industries as 'special' or ignore them as impractical – this is why public debate focuses on subsidised activities such as fine arts and theatre, rather than on product and industrial design or communications. It is why drawing is explained as a line on the page, something that a six-year-old could do, rather than a different way of seeing.

There will never be an accommodation between the State and creativity – if such a thing were brought about, the creative mindset would immediately set about undermining it. Bob and Roberta Smith points out that 'art students look at the world as outsiders and demand change' (see p.137).

Nevertheless, we do need an equilibrium and understanding between the two. There is an ethical dimension to this in an era in which nations are split apart by a knife-edge vote, or when our energy demands store up problems that are beyond science alone to resolve. Creative thinking must be part of this – '"decently troubled" by the attempt', as Pratap Rughani suggests, to make work 'that responds to suffering' (see p.100).

Although its starting point is the British art and design school, *The Creative Stance* makes no claim to exclusivity. This is a manifesto for creative education anywhere in the world, and a manual for those interested in the strange connection between effect and cause made by creative people.

In these essays and conversations, you hear the authentic voice of the art and design school – funny, true, barbed and committed. The authors come from a broad range of disciplines and backgrounds: from artists to graphic designers, brand strategists to dancers, documentary makers to fashion designers. They present evidence from across the creative disciplines, from industry to academia. They celebrate the creative approach in all disciplines and walks of life, and its value to society in areas as far-flung as fashion design and crime prevention. They discuss the principles of creative success. All are leaders in their fields, many are prize-winners.

The book will interest those people who are curious about the creative process, perhaps hoping – as Stephen Farthing says – to gain 'the confidence to make a dangerous decision' (see p.51). It will be relevant to any company interested in harnessing the creative power of its workforce. It will help policymakers to understand why the creative mindset supports innovation.

Above all, it should be read because the creative process is fascinating. This book should help to make it better understood.

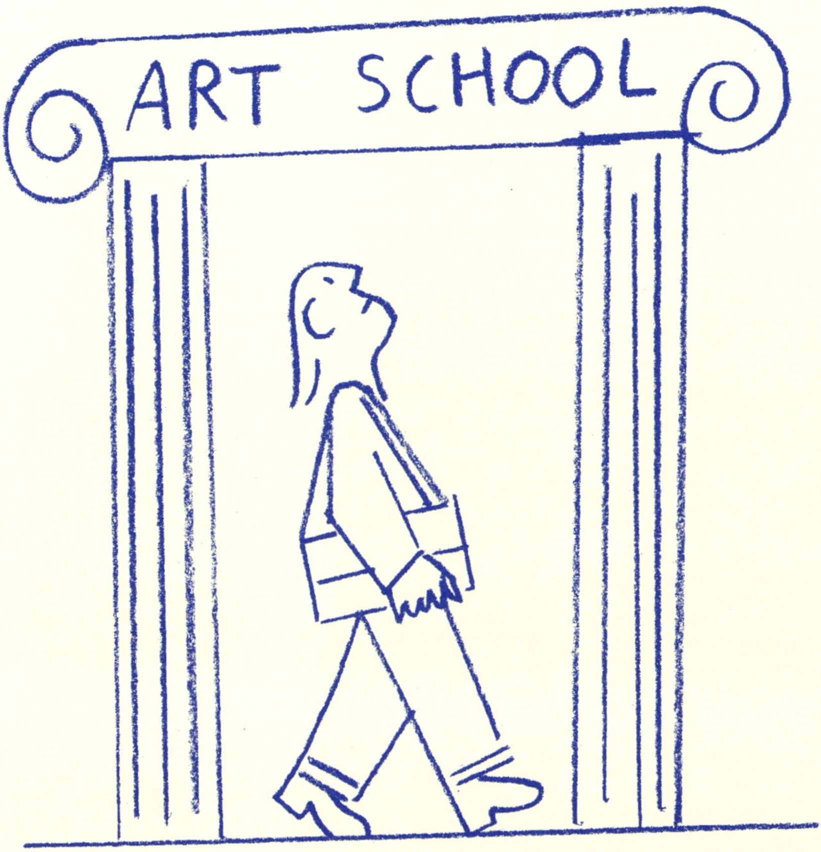

'Tell Us About It' is a scheme that, for nine years, has been asking high-achieving graduates of University of the Arts London, from a variety of backgrounds, to produce creative work reflecting on their student experience. The resulting works – housed in the London College of Communication archive – have taken diverse and unexpected forms, including board games, websites, sculptures and sketchbooks.

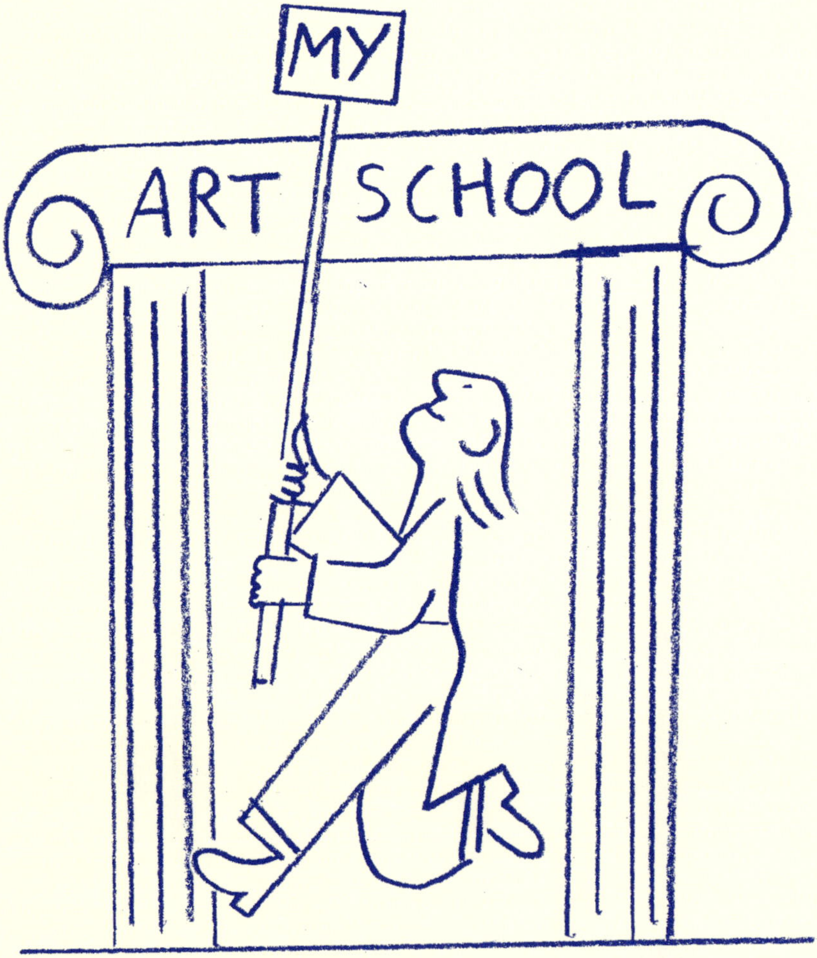

These are presented back to new students and teachers, online and through curated displays, in a creative kind of 'feedback loop', and form a rich mine of information and shared wisdom about the challenges facing students in the arts – including loneliness, financial pressure and the difficulty of finding one's creative 'voice' – as well as identifying positive aspects that link to belonging and identity.

RIGOUR

Grayson Perry

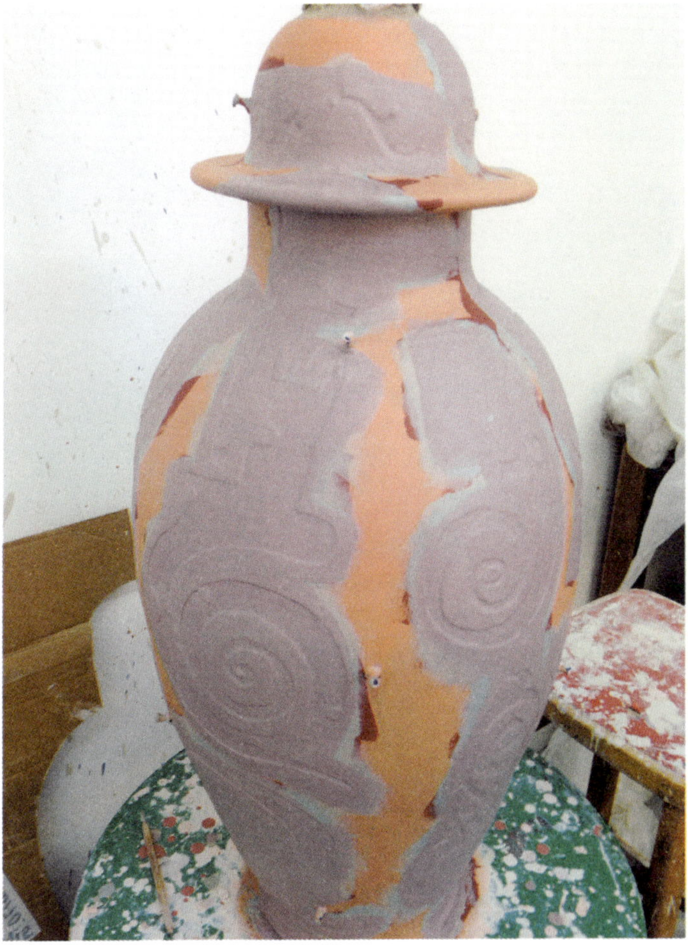

Grayson Perry, *Shadow Boxing* (work in progress), 2016.

Rigour (US rigor)
The quality of being extremely thorough and careful ... severity or strictness ... harsh and demanding conditions ... from Old French rigour *from Latin* rigor *'stiffness'.*
New Oxford Dictionary of English, 2003

I remember once asking a curator of a well-respected modern art gallery what shows he had coming up. He mentioned a Pop artist whose work I liked very much. I wondered aloud why this artist was not more famous and/or more widely exhibited. 'I'll tell you why,' he replied. 'It's six weeks 'til the opening and I have not seen any work yet. He's a nightmare to work with.' Whenever I find myself sitting next to a curator at dinner I ask them which artists are the worst to work with, and hear tales of deadlines missed, tantrums thrown and sloppy work.

There is a lingering myth that artistic success is God-given and that all the artist need do is lounge around drinking absinthe and then, occasionally, in a fit of impassioned inspiration, knock out a masterpiece in a furious bout of divinely prompted creation. Rather, in my experience, most successful artists are pragmatic and work-obsessed; in a word, rigorous. When I am asked, 'if you could give a student one tip about how to get on in the art world, what would it be?', I often reply, 'Turn up on time, be nice and put in the hours.' All the talent in the world can be wasted if an artist struggles with punctuality, good relationships and hard work. This reply I give in a mischievous and provocative spirit, for I know that a lot of art students may find my advice 'oh so square, daddy-o'. That is my style, though – I have long rebelled against the 'rebels'.

The etymology of the word 'rigour' comes through an old French word, *rigour*, meaning stiffness. This I find interesting, as I think rigour in art should be used judiciously. 'Stiffness' is not a compliment in the art world.

I often joke about having two artists in my head, whom I characterise as the 'Hobbit' and the 'Punk'. My personal Hobbit is the one more prone to rigour. He likes obsessive detail and craftsmanship and he will work away for hours on a meticulous task in order to achieve a certain effect. Hungarian psychologist Mihaly Csikszentmihalyi, in his book *Flow: The Psychology of Optimal Experience* (1990), suggested that this state of energised focus was pretty much as happy a state as it was possible to experience. I have a deep affection for the Hobbit style – I love nothing more than dibbing away for hours on a skilled yet repetitive task while listening to the radio. I often apply layer upon layer of clay slip to my pots – sometimes up to twenty coats in different shades, sometimes stencilling out areas that I fill with twenty different coats. Often, I then stamp small images or patterns into the soft slip and inlay these images with yet more, different colours. Then, when the pot is of exactly the right dryness, I very carefully scrape back through the layers, which altogether are only two or three millimetres thick, to create a multi-coloured marbled surface. This process can take tens of hours over the course of a fortnight, only for this surface to be used as the mere background on which the headline imagery of the work will be overlaid – imagery usually suggested by the Punk.

The Hobbit often plays his part in support of the Punk. The Punk, like his three-chord ancestors, likes bold, messy, mischievous gestures – often political and provocative. The Punk in my head usually provides the concepts and the humour. He tests and teases, checks for bad habits, turns things over; he is light on his feet and, above all, flexible. The Hobbit can be a bit of a stick-in-the-mud. On his own, the Hobbit would be a fine craftsman but a rubbish artist. I have seen many beautifully made but hideously ugly objects, particularly in the field of contemporary craft. Rigour in art can often lead to the dead end of perfectionism. Perfectionism is an unlovable trait. It assumes that there is a final state in which everything will be completely correct, beautiful and happy forever. But a happy life lies, in fact, in steering a course between rigidity and chaos, and good art is no different.

These days, I work a lot with digital image-making. I enjoy the vast range of techniques and facilities it opens up to me, but I have noticed that it also murmurs suggestively in my ear of perfectionism. Every mark, colour and effect achieved on the screen is contingent, changeable, perfectible, whereas paint, clay, wood or textiles, by contrast, will fight back, often irreversibly. The diligent pixel will only do what you ask of it. Paint will splash, clay will shrink, wood will split in unpredictable ways. Working with them develops a part of the artist that has to say 'that will do.' Working digitally, I find myself having to ask, 'What is my style? When will this image look like a Grayson Perry image?' With digital, the creative process is much more cerebral. The arguments between the Hobbit and the Punk are more apparent to me. While working with physical materials, the Punk (with his streak of chaos) often has an ally. The paper will tear anarchically, pigment will bleed, glaze will run and the Hobbit's idea of rigour is often thwarted. The Punk will say, 'I kind of like the way this has gone wrong – it gives the piece energy, freshness,' and the Hobbit will reluctantly agree. And I find myself thinking, 'that'll do.'

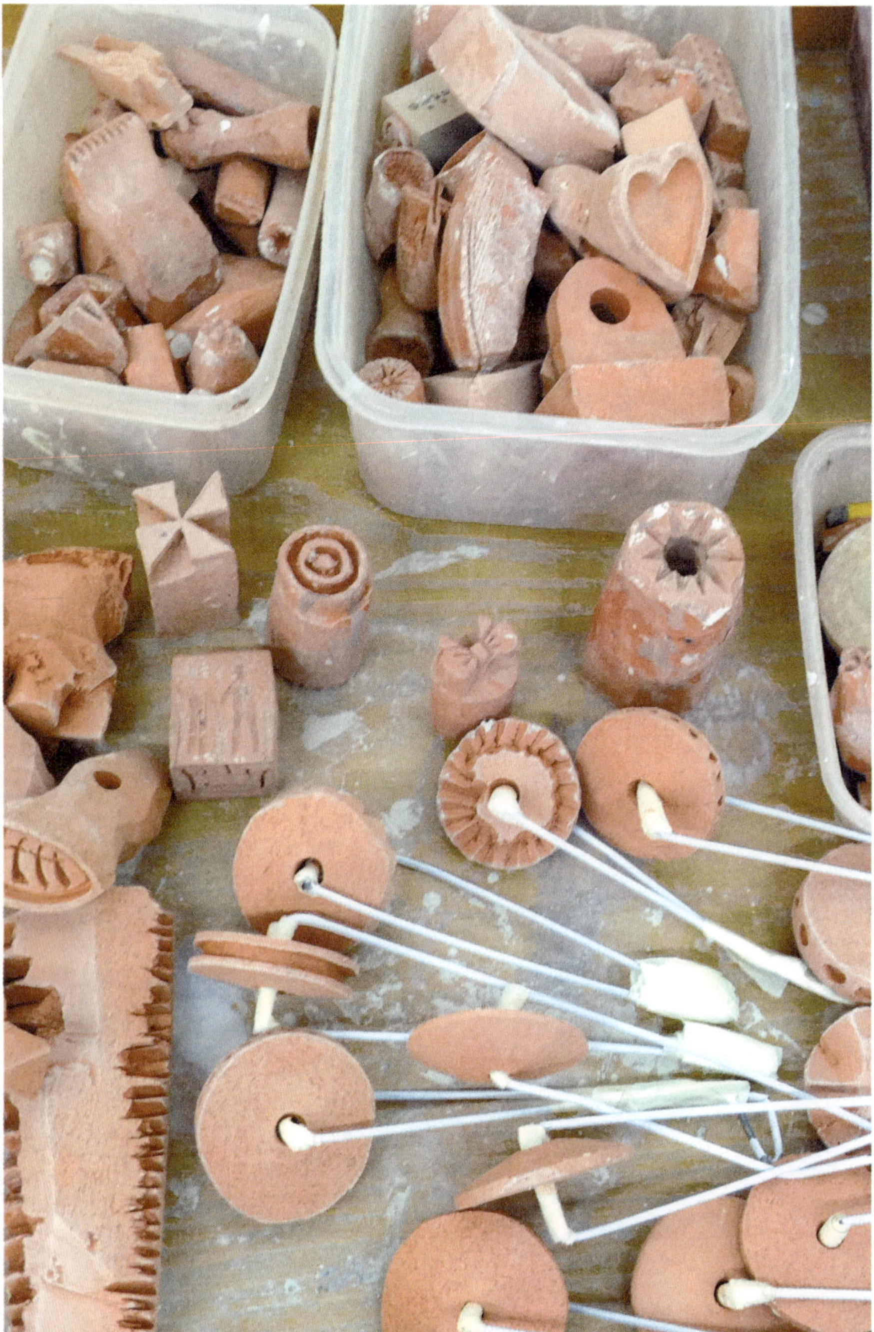

Stamps and 'sprig' moulds, hand-carved in terracotta, 2016.

This is not to say that my Punk does not have his own kind of rigour. I would say that often, in the contemporary art world, the Punk's version of rigour takes precedence, in fact. The Punk has political posters up in his bedroom; he reads books full of ideas; he wants to make a splash. The Punk does not worry that the seams are crooked or that the nail has split the wood and the canvas is sagging, as long as the work has energy and is in the fashionable style and the content is 'edgy'. Rigour, in terms of skills, takes a long time to achieve – 10,000 hours or so, according to Malcolm Gladwell, in his 2008 book *Outliers*. The Punk does not have time to pin himself down, learning how to sew a buttonhole or carve a marble bust – that's for drones, and the Punk is a 'revolutionary'. He is rigorous, though, in his loyalty to the art school ethos: to experimentation, observation, provocation, intoxication. He is hypersensitive to bullshit; he is extremely observant; he *notices* things – an absolutely core skill for an artist. He will turn things over in his mind and not rest on his laurels. The downside of the Punk is that poor craftsmanship can distract from his good ideas. Things get left unfinished. I need both my Hobbit and my Punk rigours to make good work.

Many contemporary artists now outsource the 'skilled' element of their art production to studio assistants or fabrication studios. Because I hand-build my ceramics on my own, I am often used as the poster boy for craftsmanship in arts practice, but I am happy to seek help. I use print workshops, digital-production expertise, foundries and all sorts of craftspeople – from dressmakers to custom-motorcycle builders – to help create my work. One thing I have always been most rigorous about, however, is that every aesthetic decision – the shape, colour, texture, size and material of everything – is mine, usually made by making many detailed drawings and overseeing tests and production. I look at work that has been fabricated for an artist and it often seems a bit lifeless, like an idea efficiently carried out. I joke that I could never let anyone else make my pots for me, because they would be unable to make them 'wrong' in the right way.

As my career has thrived, I have become very anxious to avoid a trait I have noticed in some successful artists. As demand for their work, from dealers, collectors and museums, increases, their work becomes less rigorous and more dilute. This dilution manifests itself not just in the decreasing man-hours they personally put into each piece, but also in the richness of their ideas. This thin-ness is emphasised by the fact that their works become larger, to fit the vast acreages of polished concrete that are today's contemporary art galleries. Concepts are spread thinly; an idea that would have justified a single work becomes the theme to a whole show of pedestrian variations. The 'upside' is that every museum or collector can buy a 'typical' work, because they all look the same.

Just as every artist develops their own style and writes their own career plan, they also need to notice where a degree of rigour is important in their work. Is it in managing a huge staff well and getting those expensive surfaces beautifully polished? Or does it lie in keeping their output small, so as to maintain a personal touch and good quality control? Are they rigorously making sure that their judgement does not get dazzled by the cult of their own celebrity, and are they listening to an advisor who suggests that branching out into figurative painting is a bad idea? All artists need rigour.

It is not without irony that I find myself agreeing to write about rigour when I am feeling under stress, diligently trying to complete a number of projects to my satisfaction. I feel as if I am suffering from rigour. I say yes to too many things and then find I cannot do any of them half-heartedly, so end up agonising over the preparation of every college lecture and every charity postcard drawing. I find it hard to just toss things off. I suppose I have been asked to write about rigour because my work looks like it takes loads of effort, care and skill to make, which it does! I suppose I am a pretty rigorous person, except when it comes to researching essays – then I just make things up.

There. Finished. That'll do.

In conversation on 'rigour'

Siobhan Davies

Fred Deakin

Edmund de Waal

Siobhan Davies
(SD)

Choreographer and Artistic Director of Siobhan Davies Dance

Fred Deakin
(FD)

UAL Chair of Interactive Digital Art, founder and director of Fred & Company, and half of band Lemon Jelly

Edmund de Waal
(EdW)

Ceramicist and author of seven books including *The Hare with Amber Eyes* (2010)

The participants were asked to discuss the topic of creative rigour, with particular reference to their respective fields. They begin with their definition of 'rigour' in relation to creativity.

FD:

There's a common stereotype of the artist as someone who swans around and gets struck by a lightning bolt of inspiration occasionally, and I think, actually, rigour is the proverbial iceberg, with the finished work only constituting the tip of the iceberg. I think that's one of the reasons why the creative industries can be undervalued, because we're not very good at exposing that rigour. Or if we do, we talk about it purely in terms of craft. The public doesn't really care or doesn't think about all that rigour, about all that sweat, and, in turn, we tend to hide it because it's not really necessarily the core of our offering. I think about people attracted into the creative industries, into creative education, by the notion that they'll just be sitting in a studio making nice things, and perhaps they get a little bit of a wake-up call in the end.

EdW:

What a terrific start for us, because that idea of how much work there is to do before the work happens seems to me to be absolutely at the heart of pretty much every artistic practice I've encountered, and certainly the two practices which I have in my life: making and writing. And there is still a huge, painful fallacy about inspiration. One of the things about getting older is discovering that the 'out of nowhere' moments, when they do happen, come from decades and decades of being, and thinking, and working. Actually knowing which extraordinary idea is an extraordinary idea, and not just a piece of inconsequential nonsense, is work in itself. It's profoundly countercultural, within the arts, to talk about that. It is not part of the story to talk about discipline, to talk about craft, to talk about structure or 'turning up', but everyone I know who I admire, whether they're a poet or a choreographer or a musician or a film-maker, seems to have some kind of shared language of work.

SD:

I wonder if this shared language needs more exposure, not only among artists, but others. I know that I can feel more included when watching a work by another artist if I am given clues about what occupies that artist or how a work came into being. I like to feel the grit rather than the polish of what I am experiencing. But at the point of offering the work to the audience, that rigour, as you've said, is not always seen. When we are making a new dance work in the studio I have the opportunity to see the performers layer up knowledge in their body. I can see how they build up useful experiences, strategies for finding movement, and use the neverending-ness of learning as their ground for performing. Part of the live-ness of a performance is how the performers and audience are making decisions. The audience use their background and the performers need to use theirs, but honed for the particular work they are doing. All of the investigative stuff that has supported them to get this far is a resource to be called upon in the doing of it in the present, then called on again, and again, each time with a potentially different but relevant outcome.

FD:

It's interesting: as a child, I was educated as a classical musician, I played the cello, and the Western classical mode is one of daily practice and rigour, with a kind outpouring of performance at the end of the process. I'm very grateful for that, but one of the things I have had to unlearn is this notion of performance as a practised repeated act. There's also the notion of performance as improvisation – the other side of the jazz-classical dichotomy, if you like a musical metaphor. When you hear a concert pianist, they have played those notes a hundred times in exactly that order, and perfected every exact nuance and, my God, the rigour that is manifested in that performance is very clear. When you listen to a jazz musician improvise with another jazz musician, by contrast, there's no doubt that you're hearing a lifetime's work manifested in the moment, but it merges with the performance completely. So I think you're absolutely right; it's slightly more complicated than we work hard and then dance or perform looking like we haven't.

SD:
What I think we – myself and other dance artists – are doing is using years of curiosity and investigation, turning that into knowledge. This is why I enjoy including research, physical exploration and compositional structures during all work preparation. We are often the makers and the performers within the same process. As we perform the work more, we can also feed that physical information back into the longer-lasting structure – the choreography of the work. We have some kinship with the improvisatory nature of jazz, making 'in the moment' decisions about how we are 'playing' the movement; we also want the choreographic ideas to have the strength to let the performers work into them during a live performance but without pulling away from the core of the choreographic intent. When thinking about making a work I sense some kind of state of animation at the edge of my mind or in my body – it's not yet verbalised. My work is finding out by what means can I reach this place. I understand that the routes that worked in the past cannot be directly repeated. No circumstances are the same. Instead I have to create some kind of diagonal, stepping-stone path and, on my way, ask myself questions that matter to the moment – ones I can cope with, deal with, which intrigue but also surprise me.

EdW:
I would think that's an absolutely fantastic definition of rigour. And it's not an ethereal practice.

SD:
It's not an ethereal practice at all. I need to be very clear about that, because I sense that this pre-verbal state can sound fanciful. I am trying to get across that solutions are not always in front of you. They need to be found, and, when found, may need to be thrown away in order to clear the ground for better ones. I recognise in my own behaviour, how I can talk about something, and then talking is covering up what I actually feel. The talking then becomes part of the uncovering, like losing skin. Gradually I come face-to-face with something that I can believe in.

FD:
But this is your rigorous process. I'm in the digital sphere – I'm working a lot with people who are incredibly binary in their thinking. If I'm collaborating with engineers or business people, who are very used to thinking, there's the goal, we are here, and it's very clear that we have to do so-and-so and get there, I have to say to them, look, we have got rigour, we have got a process, but it doesn't look like any process that you are familiar with.

The problem I encounter time and time again in these relationships is that our rigour, as creative practitioners, is not as well respected as their rigour and,

Siobhan Davies Dance (performed by Charlie Morrissey), *Table of Contents*, 2014.

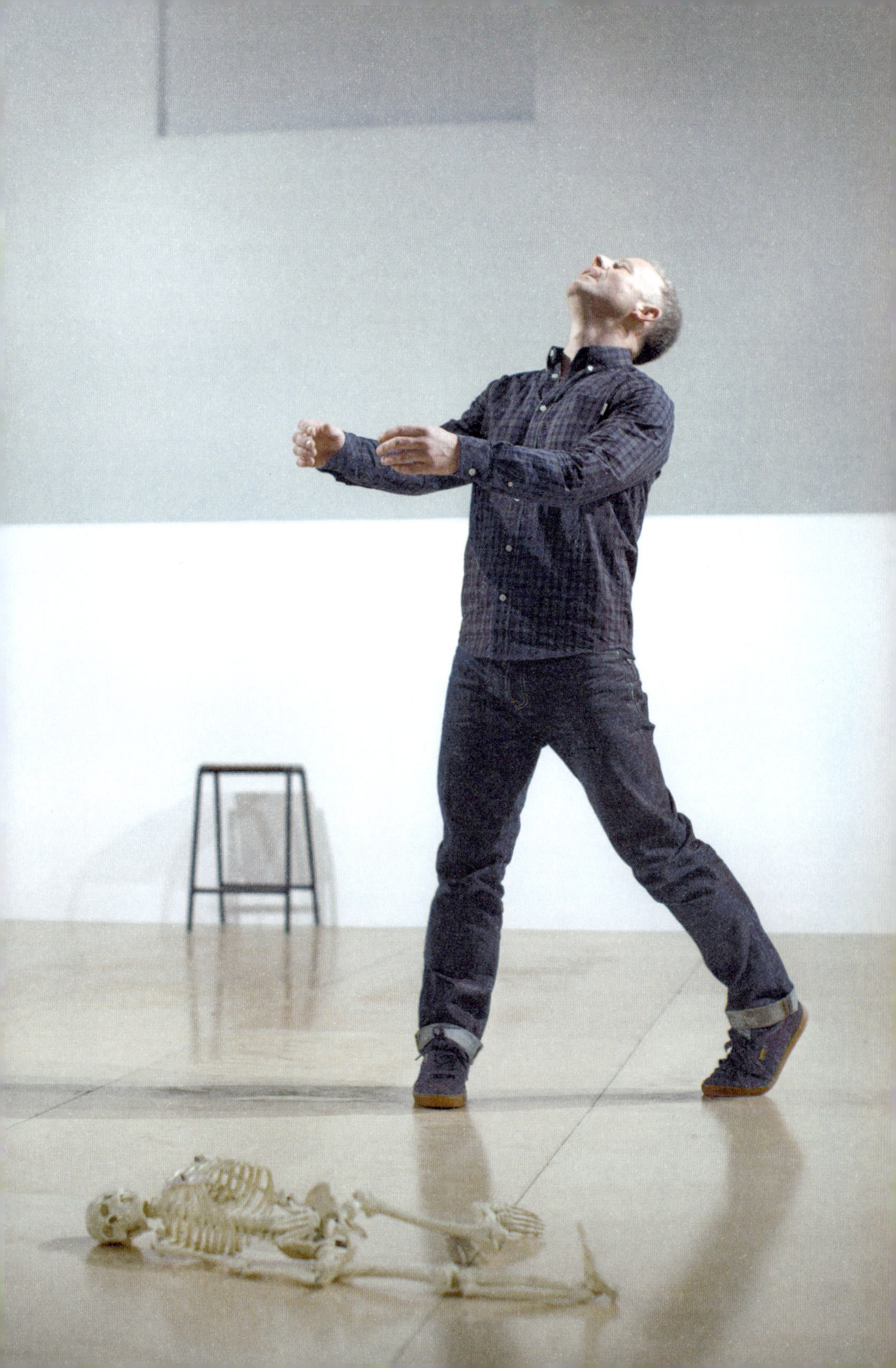

to be fair, we do not respect our own rigour as much as we respect theirs. There's a need for more of a reciprocal understanding of process but, in order for that to happen, you have to understand first and then seek to be understood afterwards. We need to be able to express our rigour in those conversations, if those are conversations that interest us.

I think that understanding our practice and having that self-awareness is a big part of creative education, because most people who come into it have an inkling that they're good at something, but, a lot of the time, they just want to do it and not examine it.

EdW:
Yes, the iteration of doing and examining as part of the language of our practice is absolutely fascinating. John Dewey, the wonderful philosopher, talked about it as the flight and perching of the bird; you're in the moment and then you stop, you're immersed and cannot stop and then there's the moment of reflection. Both are absolutely essential. The extraordinary thing that I have learned is how and when to stop, and also just how much time it takes me to reflect fully on what I've done. For me, the stopping is writing books. So I have this practice of making things, and making art, sculpture, and then every few years I spend time writing a book, which is my 'perching'. That's a rather ridiculous way of doing it but that's my way and it allows me to start a whole new kind of work again as an artist, takes me into a whole new landscape.

FD:
I don't want to get hung up on justifying our practice, but I do think writing is a brilliant way of reflecting because it makes it visible.

SD:
Rigour has a sternness attached to it. I'm not sure I would use the word. I am more drawn to the energy of finding something out. It might begin with a single-cell idea, but then the multiplication of cells leads to more information being generated. For instance, if I take a physical step – one pace in a walk, even – every part of my body has to adjust at a minute level. The orchestration of each action is a response to and has an impact on another movement. I am using this as a metaphor for the process of making, which requires consistent adjustments throughout.

EdW:
There are all kinds of learning that we do. One of the kinds of learning that isn't shared enough, perhaps, is, of course, bodily learning, somatic learning. I had a formal apprenticeship and the guy, on the first day of the apprenticeship, he said to me, you know, the first 30,000 pots you make are the worst – after that it gets easier. Now that's an old-fashioned rhetorical tool about putting the hours in, but there's a kind of truth about bodily learning. I hate that 10,000-hours rule about learning – that's just the beginning, it doesn't even scratch the surface – but bodily learning, bodily rigour, developing a language of movement, of touch, of response, that has to be talked about.

SD:
Well, we certainly privilege intellectual output – in education we privilege it. I think our Western society does.

FD:
I think arts education is a response to that to some degree, although it could go further, in my opinion.

SD:

As a dance and choreographic practitioner, I *know*, because I have tried to attend to the way my whole body works as an integrated system, that it is one of the wonders of the world. Every one of us has a natural access to this knowing – after all, we live by it – but we don't choose to be conscious of it, sometimes for obvious and good reasons, but it gives those of us involved in dance and choreography a very rich terrain to work with. If I speak about it too much outside a dance practice, however, I feel there's a sense of distrust, or a sense that I'm saying something secondary, less intellectual. Maybe there is still a fear of the body?

FD:

I do think, in Western society specifically, that we worship the brain. One of the real problems with the digital shift, and this is a slight digression, is that it has turned us all into very static people, who just go click, click, click, click, click. That's not what I wanted to do when I started out being a creative practitioner. And when I teach workshops for my students, I make them move. I teach a very open creativity platform and there's room for all sorts of practice to come out of it, but I do make them move around, and they go, why are we doing this? How can it possibly serve us in any way, shape or form to move? Pre-computer, of course, virtually all artistic practices had an element of physicality, of movement. How that is manifested in the digital world is perhaps another conversation for another time.

Dyslexia is a really good example though, because we know, as people who are familiar with creative education, that, for decades, incredibly intelligent and talented kids with dyslexia have been funnelled into arts education because they've been deemed surplus to requirements in more traditional education. I think it's an indication that an arts education is not about purely intellectual learning.

SD:

But it's not as if thought and action aren't embedded as a combination already. Our society still separates them out, without noticing how living beings actually function. The practice of a dancer or choreographer includes revealing how physical intelligence can be put to work. We can explore this with great variety and it is a useful tool for everyone, regardless of their chosen medium. Movement is a form of thinking and communication.

FD:

Absolutely.

EdW:

I used to teach as well, and part of my practice in teaching was to try and help both staff and students in art situations who were frightened of writing, terrified about words, but needed that space to be able to reflect and communicate. It's an appropriate ask, within arts education, to ask people to reflect with rigour on what they've done, but we have to find ways of doing that that begin somewhere with *them*, students, rather than positing a model of how it should be done.

FD:

A model that is often imposed on them, from above.

EdW:

It's not asking them to justify what they're doing; it's about them communicating for themselves in public.

FD:

I think our responsibility as art educators, if we share this opinion, is to make sure that that communication is on our own terms. We need to develop our own academic rigour, our own intellectualisation, which manifests our thoughts and shows the excellence of our thinking but does it in a way that we're good at, that's grounded in our practice. Speaking of practice, when you're starting out, there is a certain amount of craft that's got to be acquired; there're no two ways about it. I run these workshops that pull practitioners together from across the university to create cross-disciplinary groups and we explore innovation [the 'Modual' workshops; see opposite], but they can't walk through the door without some skills. And in terms of self-awareness, if we want to be collaborative practitioners, it's good to identify who we are in terms of a really deep profound practice – for example, illustration or playing the cello or dancing. We also need all the other stuff that we've dabbled in, where we're quite good, so that if we meet someone who is a deep practitioner in one of those skills, we can have a conversation with them.

But there is also a process for innovation, and that, I think, is deeply personal and is sometimes not analysed. I pretty much know that if I put the hours in, I can master a whole wide range of practices, but it's about how I then personalise that and evolve my own path up the mountain.

EdW:
For you, is innovation a moment of crisis or is it a moment that can come out of an iterative process, gently? From the outside, it looks like you've had some very substantial changes in your practice, or additions, so what does it feel like?

FD:
I'm sure you've been through phases in your career where you got to the 'end of the row', so to speak. I don't think it's about crisis so much as the feeling that the moment of mastery in a particular area is the time that I need to start thinking about moving on. Sometimes I don't get my act together to move on fast enough, but I think that's the knowledge experience gives you.

SD:
I can identify with that. A few years ago, I made and was co-director of a film (*All This Can Happen*, 2012), and needed to trust that my choreographic knowledge would support me while using completely different material. This was unknown territory, but a place where I hoped I could rely on my hard-won skills – to test them in a new context, enjoying what I knew while also knowing I had huge amounts to learn.

EdW:
So the innovation, it doesn't lessen the need to have done all that other stuff in the first place.

FD:
No, absolutely not.

EdW:
You see, one of the things I would argue is that putting in the rigour in a practice enables you, later on, to develop extraordinary, innovative skills in something totally different. I learned to make pots, which helped me write books, you know, and who would have known that learning to make casserole dishes for five miserable years would enable me to write 100,000 words of narrative nonfiction?

FD:
I often compare it to extreme sports – somebody who gets their kicks out of throwing themselves off a mountain. I get my kicks out of throwing myself into

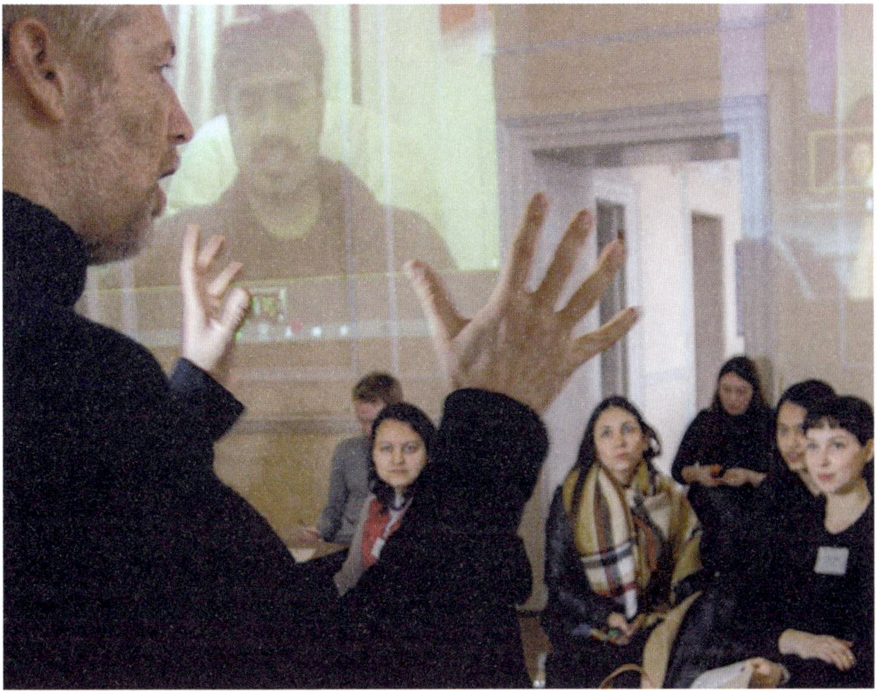

The 'Modual' workshop, a 'creative industry incubator' led by Fred Deakin, London, 2014.
Overleaf: Edmund de Waal, *Lichtzwang* (2014, left) and *black milk* (2015, right), *ten thousand things* (installation view), Gagosian Gallery, Beverly Hills, 2015.

a new creative area, and with absolutely no idea whether I can pull it off or not. And, a lot of the time, I wish I didn't. I sit there going, I don't want to risk all of that, but you know you've got to.

SD:
Is it something to do with evolution? The incremental additions that seem to cause some kind of shape-shifting and draw us into new patterns of doing? Fred, you touched on meeting people from other disciplines at your workshops. I feel curious about what might be 'over there' in other disciplines. I imagine a kinship and want to go and explore.

At [Siobhan Davies Dance] we have been speaking with neuro-cognitive scientists, as they, like us, pay attention to how the whole body works, albeit in very different contexts. We can share some information on what it feels like to have a body, the feedback from bodily perceptions. The first conversations are shocking in the sense of how little we know about each other. Then each of us peels back a little in order to find some common ground. Recent conversations have been centred on proprioception, synchronicity, robotics and human consciousness. Of course we were concerned when we first imagined these conversations, but in reality we enjoyed them and have put some findings to use. Also, both groups come away with a usefully expanded language and one

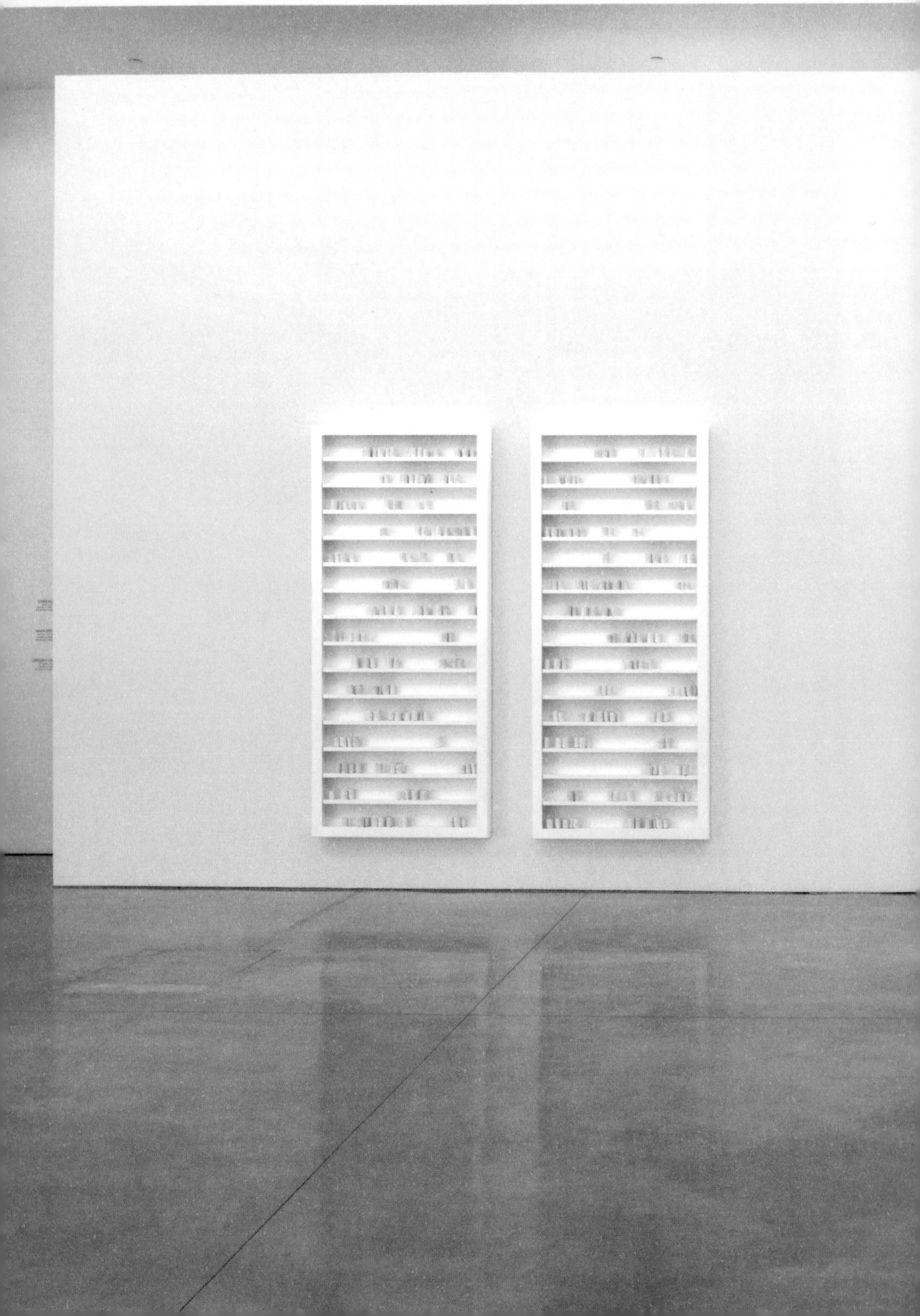

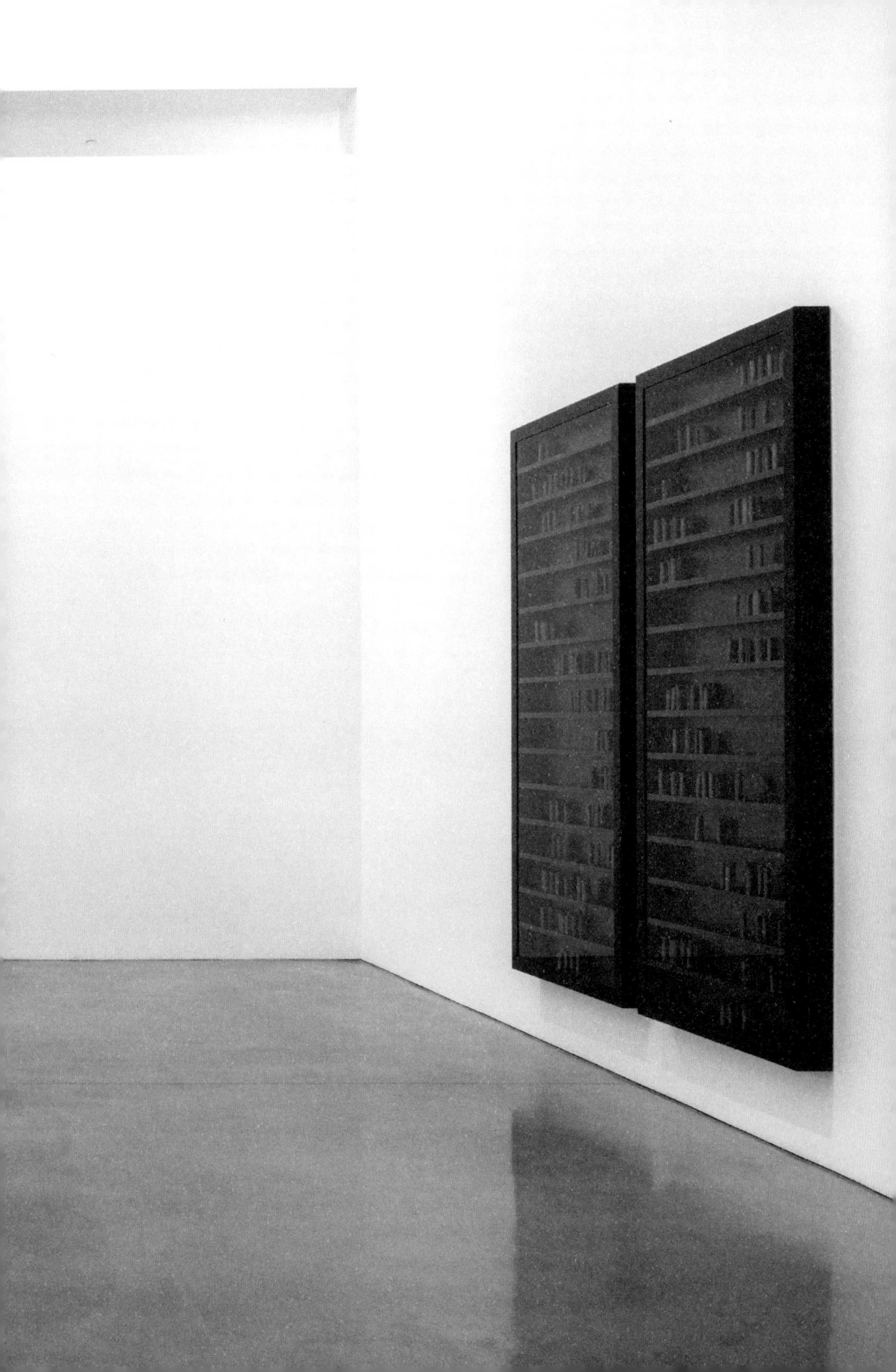

that gives us more room to think. These little, unorthodox grains of knowledge have arrived in the space between us, and we can enjoy what they bring.

EdW:
It's beautifully said. This last autumn, I was working with Aurora Orchestra – a good, young, innovative orchestra. We did a long project together about the colour white. Just spending time doing that programme together and spending time in each other's spaces was extraordinary because I am passionate about music but I don't know nearly as much as these extraordinary people, and they know nothing about ceramics. But actually, we found a shared space.

FD:
A friend, a colleague of mine, Professor Rob Kesseler, worked on an exhibition on art and science [*Lens on Life*, Lethaby Gallery, Central Saint Martins, UAL, 20 January – 27 February 2015]. He's passionate about the arts and sciences combining. There was this panel (see p.33) and on one side, it said artists do this and, on the other side, scientists do this. The processes could be described in exactly the same words, which was a surprise to everybody coming to the exhibition because you think of that as the ultimate right brain-left brain split.

I think that what we're describing is a practice for innovation. The rate of change in the modern world is so extreme now – there is nothing certain any more except change – but change is something that we, as creative people, are really skilled at, because we serve that change in our own practices all the time.

EdW:
So then, Fred, how do we talk about perpetual change and the longevity of disciplines?

FD:
As creative people, I think the news is good, because we're natural innovators by definition. A lot of creative people think they're no good at change, especially digital change. I say to them, the Internet is the most creative space that there ever was and it's being co-created by the world's population as we speak, and they go, but I don't understand JavaScript! It's nothing to do with JavaScript! It's to do with manifesting something innovative, which you do every day as your practice.

EdW:
But we need to be able to articulate that there are people whose practices don't appear to change, or for whom the change happens over a lifetime.

FD:
That's very true.

EdW:
I've gone back a few times to the Frank Auerbach exhibition at London's Tate Britain [*Frank Auerbach*, 9 October 2015 – 13 March 2016], and there is an artist who has been in the same studio since 1947. He spends every day working, doesn't leave his studio, often spends two days painting and then scrapes it all back and begins again. The stylistic change in surface between paintings from the 1950s and this year isn't enormous, but, in fact, in terms of what he's been doing, I think it's extraordinary and provocative, but also very beautiful. But in no sense could he be described as someone who has reached out to other practices or embraced the digital landscape or been involved in any of the other kinds of catalytic change that we might identify as exemplary elsewhere.

FD:
Clearly, he occupies a space that no one else could occupy, and has had the guts to claim it, and that, to me, is innovation. So yes, I don't think we should all necessarily be experimenting wildly.

SD:
Maybe there are as many art forms as there are artists. All the materials, mediums, ways of thinking and doing are out there. Auerbach keeps a focus, a plumb line running down through his work. That magnetic line is a real force for me, but I know that I am more wayward. I want to know what isn't there yet! And I have to combine that with trying to hold a steady course. The making process is very active. Whatever discipline artists choose, we also seem to be required to keep explaining what our potential is in the world. In order to evolve as artists, could we better articulate our other skills, such as dealing with the unknown, negotiating and being willing to learn continuously?

FD:
There is a point of view, which I do not necessarily agree with, but which I think needs to be expressed, which is basically, 'fuck off, don't ask me to justify what I do as an artistic practitioner. I do what I do and I have my practice and I have my rigour and I don't feel I should have to explain or defend that.' Graduates coming out of arts education, and I'm also talking about resilience here, need to have that self-possession. Otherwise, we're just saying, well, Mr Abramovich, would you like this part of my rigour, which costs you about £10,000, or the deluxe rigour, which costs £100,000, where I do this, this and this.

EdW:
I think you're hard-pressed not to encounter people who are making wonderful, lyrical, grounded cases for what they're doing at every level, actually. I keep coming across people and fora where things are expressed. If you look at the situation a decade ago – this was a particularly pernicious time within arts education, where there was an appalling need everywhere to borrow particular kinds of academic language and force kids to read French philosophy in order to say why they were making pots or dancing – I actually think we're in a totally different space now.

SD:
Artists are now working in expanded fields, which gives us mobility. We can grow links with people who know different stuff. I sometimes step outside that expanded field, however, and look at politics or education, who are looking back at us, judging us but not necessarily for what we are offering right now. I want to feel I can contribute more, but through being an artist.

FD:
Yes, and it's very problematic to say to arts educators and to the artistic community, you need to put a financial value on what you do and show very clearly your economic worth. Once again, we're forced into defending ourselves in other people's language, which I don't take too kindly to.

Are you familiar with a guy called Stewart Home at all? He's a punk author and, about ten years ago, he proposed an art strike. He said that everybody involved in the arts should stop making art for a year and see how people liked it! It would be fascinating, if the Victoria and Albert Museum shut down, if all pop music stopped, all performance stopped, if you weren't allowed to watch films or anything. It ain't going to happen, but it's a lovely piece of science fiction. I think the best way to prove our worth, at the end of the day, is to make great work and to produce fantastic practitioners.

SD:
Just going back to the first thing we said, I think that if information is somehow present either in the work we produce itself or somewhere else, then somebody outside of our respective disciplines can look and see the journey of the making – the adventure of gathering, disseminating, choosing and throwing away all those pre-existing ideas that are present in most disciplines. Instead of justifying ourselves, it could be possible just to open up what we do.

FD:
Documentation is what we're talking about here, and going above and beyond the performance. Without wanting to come back to the digital too much, there is so much opportunity now to share work that way. But it has to be done sensitively and collaboratively, and with skill. You know, that's a whole different set of skills from the ones we're actually embarking on in practice.

EdW:
With respect to education, if you're asking students to come in and learn, experiment, innovate and reflect, I don't think it's too much to write and document and to articulate all these things with passion and integrity and rigour. I think it should be above the door when you come in, that there is a huge level of expectation on you if you cross this threshold.

FD:
Do you know a book called *Daily Rituals* [Mason Currey, *Daily Rituals: How Great Minds Make Time, Find Inspiration, and Get to Work*, 2013]? It's a guy's blog and it's been turned into a book. He's just gone through history and found as many accounts of famous artists' daily rituals as he can. Ninety per cent of them have a daily ritual: I get up in the morning, I go out for a walk, I eat this meal, I sit at my desk. It's fascinating, this commonality of daily practice, and I really believe in the daily practice although, again, I struggle sometimes to actually implement it myself.

Someone once said to me, do you do what you do every day or do you just do it when you feel like it? Because the first one is practice and the second one is a hobby. When students hear that they go, okay, I've got to do it every day because I don't want to do it as a hobby. Hobbies are great, there's nothing wrong with hobbies, but I think that element of rigour, that's a journey undertaken within arts education. You probably do come in as a hobbyist. You think, oh yeah, it's great when my mum drives me to dance class or cello class. Really embedding that practice in your being is one of the things that we give students. It requires discipline – discipline is kind of a given, isn't it?

SD:
Yes, though I have some concerns about the word 'training', especially in the study of dance, which should also include choreography, a very different discipline. Many dance institutions teach particular techniques, initially brought into being by choreographers in order to shape their dancers for their work. I understand that use of pre-formed techniques, and that such disciplines can be a good foundation, but if we're not careful, the body can become more of a recording device than a site for encouraging questions around choreography and the reasons to study movement in this decade. I feel that across a range of art schools there is more room for students to question and imagine how they might shape their artistic future. In dance

THE ARTIST

THE FIRST THING ARTISTS DO, IS ONLY *SIMILAR* TO WHAT THEY MAY HAVE IN MIND. ARTISTS SEE THE SIMILARITY AND THE DIFFERENCE, AND FROM THIS PERCEPTION SOMETHING FURTHER EMERGES IN THEIR NEXT ACTION. SOMETHING NEW IS CONTINUALLY CREATED THAT IS COMMON TO THE ARTIST AND THE MATERIAL ON WHICH THEY ARE WORKING IN A CONTINUOUS *DIALOGUE*.

THE SCIENTIST

THE SCIENTIST IS ENGAGED IN A SIMILAR *DIALOGUE* WITH NATURE AND WITH FELLOW HUMAN BEINGS. A SCIENTIST'S IDEA IS TESTED BY OBSERVATION. WHAT IS OBSERVED IS ONLY SIMILAR TO WHAT THEY HAD IN MIND AND NOT IDENTICAL. THROUGH SIMILARITIES AND DIFFERENCES COMES A NEW IDEA, WHICH IS IN TURN TESTED.

Wall graphic using original text by David Bohm, from *Lens on Life*, Lethaby Gallery, Central Saint Martins, UAL, 20 January - 27 February 2015. Curated by Marina Wallace, ArtAkt.

schools, the rigour has been more about gathering techniques, although there are some institutions, primarily in Europe, that adopt more investigative strategies for their studies. As dancers, we are both the decision-making artists and the actual material, both reflecting on each other at the same time. That requires tough self-assessment. There are also so many possibilities and knowing what to let go of becomes a discipline. Let go of some of the old supports, patterns, rules and see what actively remains.

FD:
It's often said in the world of graphic design that you have to know the rules before you can break them - and that's another one of the rules. It's a good point, and you can also invent your own rules.

SD:
That's the important thing - how you can invent, over a period of time, the rules that apply to you, rather than always adhering to the rules made by somebody else. That takes practice.

EdW:
It's difficult, I find, to talk with integrity and passion about the sheer amount of learning you have to do without becoming dogmatic. How do you talk about discipline or disciplines without it sounding - well, I don't really mind

what it sounds like – but without it being phoney, and being about authority and power and the normative, and keeping people in one place in the classroom for a particular length of time? How do you actually embed people in discipline so that it then becomes their own discipline? I struggle to find the right ways of talking about it, because it matters.

FD:
It's almost parenting we're talking about, and as difficult. At a certain point, you do need to say my way or the highway, I think. You need to be able to say, you may not want to do this but you will do it or you will leave this course. That's appropriate. Yet, at the same time, there is, especially at UAL, a real tradition of anti-authoritarianism and rule-breaking. It's a fine line to tread and it's a huge responsibility as well. Whenever you have a student and see them making what you think is a mistake, you have to think quite carefully about how you intervene.

EdW:
I've dealt with materials all my life and it's about making a mess, about untidiness, which there's no space left for now. Without mess, it is, in my experience, very difficult to put the world back together again.

SD:
It's the state we enter the world in; even within the womb, we are exploring the world through movement and mistakes, failures and feedbacks. It's embedded in us to explore, at first using our selves and the materials to hand, making sense of the world for ourselves. Working with objects and materials can be conceived of as thoughts extended outside the body.

FD:
I think we need to make a case for it, absolutely – the notion of rigorous mess, the notion of a boundaried space for mess. I think demonstrating is probably the best way to make that case. Rigorous mess, maybe that's our innovation in terms of process, and we have to make sure that we have the tools to cope with it – to really harvest a mess as opposed to just unleashing the pure anarchy of childhood.

SD:
I would challenge the idea that it's anarchy in lots of ways because, if one just takes movement, it's built into all human behaviour. Every single movement that a child makes feeds into the next; every instance of a child's play with words is keeping the mind and language alive. I think we call it anarchy because grown-ups have to tidy up after them, but actually it really is learning. This is what makes us human, that we make, that we reflect, that we play, that we know through doing.

<u>CHELSEA JAM</u>

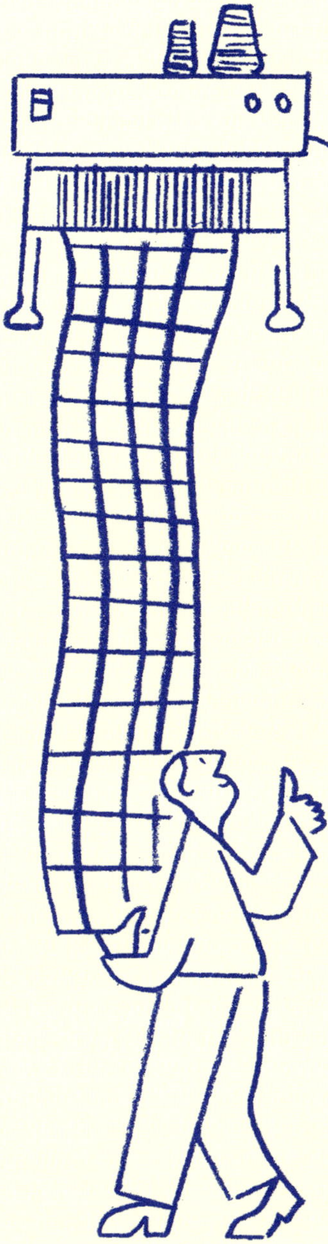

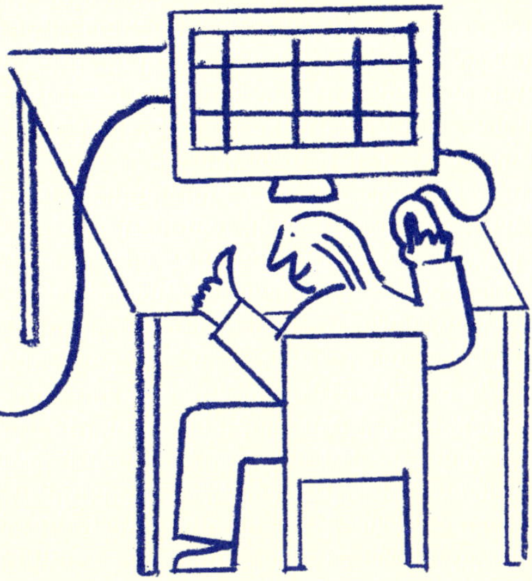

CCW Digital MakerSpace is a cross-disciplinary community working across Camberwell, Chelsea and Wimbledon Colleges of Arts, UAL, exploring the place of emergent digital technologies in arts practice. Formed partly in response to the growing popularity of non-institutional ‘makerspaces’ – well-equipped workshops in which those with shared interests, usually in physical computing, digital fabrication and prototyping, can learn new skills – the group held its first community-building event, the ‘Chelsea Jam’, in May 2015. Demonstrators included Isabella Mackenzie, operating an electronically controlled loom using weave-design software on laptop and iPad, and Chelsea Research Fellow Athanasios Velios, who showcased the applications of open-source software to conservation. With an emphasis on collaboration and emergent tech, in 2016 the event expanded into a week-long festival, its outcomes to be taken forward by the newly formed Digital Maker Collective. This initiative exemplifies a new definition of ‘rigour’ in creative practice.

ACCESSING THE ARCHIVE

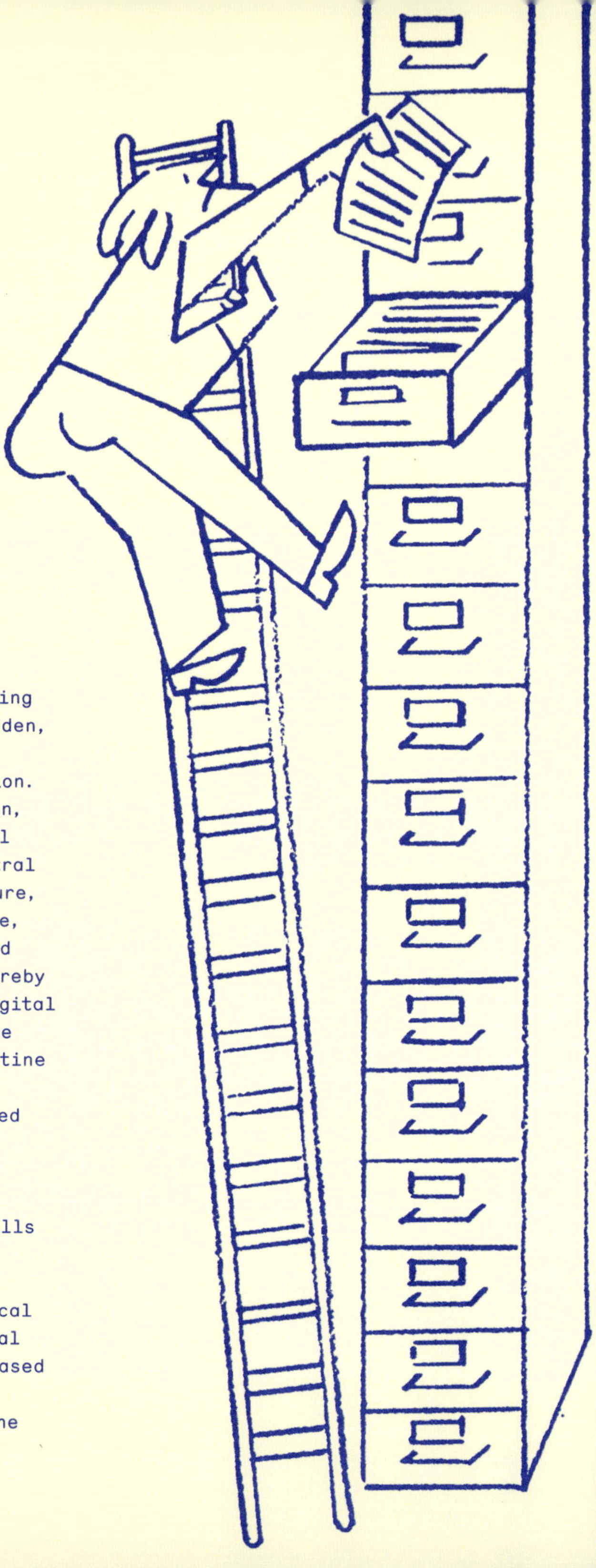

Creative yet rigorous archiving practices can help bring hidden, or simply under-researched, collections to wider attention. When Southbank Centre, London, loaned four boxes of archival material to students on Central Saint Martins' (CSM) MA Culture, Criticism and Curation course, they can hardly have expected the innovative response, whereby social-media accounts and digital platforms were used to create an online presence for Christine Wild, a Royal Festival Hall exhibitions officer who worked on innovative programming on the site in the mid-1960s. This fresh application of research and cataloguing skills democratised and enlivened archive material, allowing users to engage with historical material digitally and in real time. The results were showcased at both CSM and Southbank Centre, London, as part of the 'Web We Want' festival.

RISK

Cécile B. Evans

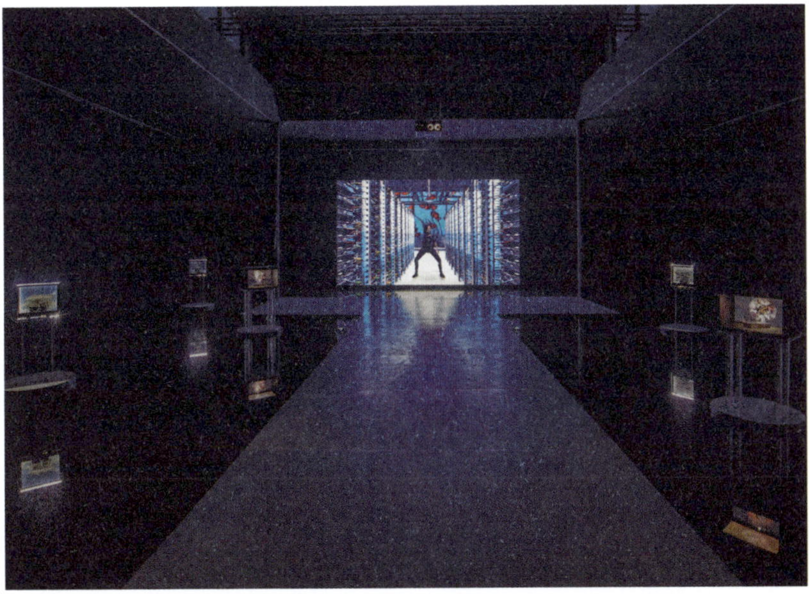

Cécile B. Evans, *What the Heart Wants* (installation view), Berlin Biennale, 2016.

The installation took place in a 500-square-metre room, flooded thirty-five centimetres deep with water. It apparently takes only five centimetres of water for someone to be able to drown. There was a T-shaped walking platform, three metres wide at the base and eight metres wide at the top, where people were meant to seat themselves in front of a large, forty-minute video projection. The only light in the room was coming from the screen and five electronic sculptures placed on islands throughout the watery space. We had placed warning signs and guards, and word had already started to spread about the flood.

People still fell in the water. Every day for the first three weeks of the exhibition. I watched as one person confidently walked off the platform and shouted as they hit the black lagoon. Every few hours a person soaked up to their knees would squeak out of the space. I tried to approach as many of them as I could: 'I'm the artist. Tell me what we can do to keep you from falling in the water.' Many of them replied that they simply hadn't believed the water would be real.

An existential risk is defined as an irreversible threat to the survival of our species. An existential risk's cause is almost always linked to manmade technologies. Most identified existential risks – things like superintelligent AI, a prolonged galactic war, or climate change – are viewed by the public as 'not real'. In fact, much of what has been presented to us as progress and change by way of technology has been sold to us as a virtual (read: not real) experience. From Steve Jobs's presentation of handheld devices with a magician's 'Boom!' to the specially patented screws that keep us from opening said devices to see their inner workings. It still surprised me that people wouldn't be risk-averse enough to prevent them from walking off a platform and into a pool with live wires.

Both the art and technology industries talk a lot about 'the real world' and 'the public'. Both like to speak about and for this public, about what they need and what 'we' could be doing for 'them'. There is a dangerously high value put on anything deemed to be 'authentic', a word often strangely coupled with the use of inverted commas, which deny an attempt to truly define any of the words in between them. Subjective expression and emotions have become such a financially and politically viable resource that there is an infinite amount of channels carefully built to keep them circulating.

The risk as an artist is to accept that at my best, I am similar to everyone else. I do not have any solutions to mitigate existential risk.

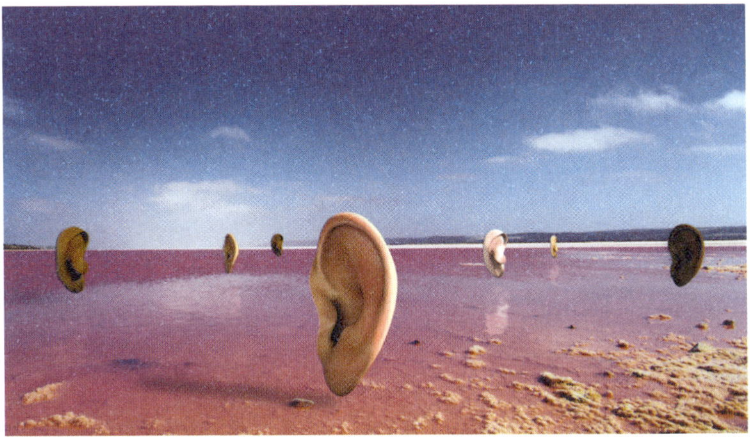

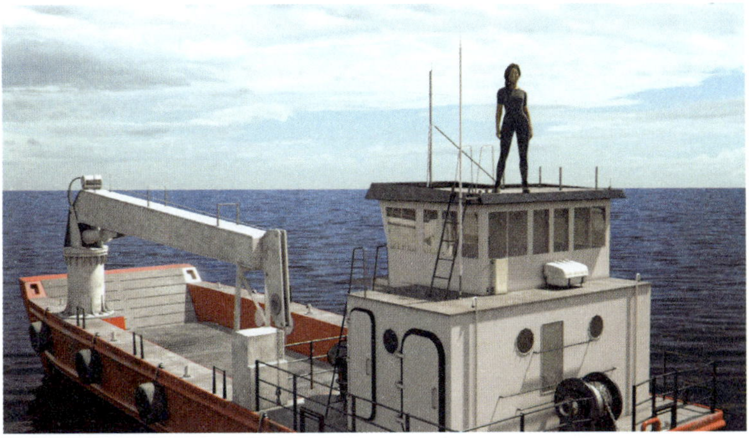

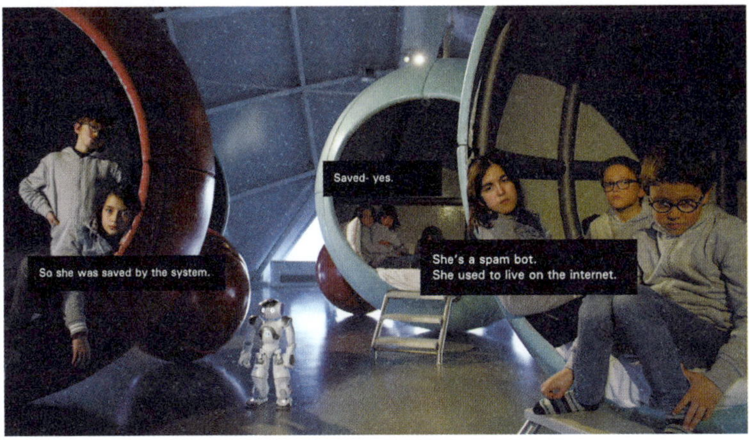

Cécile B. Evans, *What the Heart Wants* (video stills), 2016.

I'm terrified of existential risks, but, annoyingly, my concern quickly slides towards more immediate existential problems, like my own death. One of my favourite lines from Sally Potter's adaptation of Virginia Woolf's *Orlando* (1992) is when Sasha says 'I think you suffer from a strange melancholy. Which is, you suffer in advance.' I can't help but get most depressed about a future that I won't be a part of, which isn't very productive. How can I accept and use my own failures as a human being? I am a part of the public that participates in electronic commerce, that cries after watching (probably) sponsored content, and uses free email and data storage services. I could be part of the problem.

I find it necessary to live in real and unreal spaces, accepting that they are part of the same world. I want to confront the realities of those who I work with and around, their very physical needs, and simultaneously accept the surreality that everyone must be witnessing as nothing short of legitimate. I'd prefer to listen to and live in the time I exist in, rather than just comment on or try to be a part of its history. At risk is not being able to quantify an authoritative position over the public – something seen as a virtue in both art and tech. I can't confirm I have a clue about what's 'going on'.

The production manager for the exhibition (*What the Heart Wants*, 2016, presented at the Berlin Biennale) apologetically informed me that they were going to have to put a railing system around the platform. I, of course, said that the most important thing was for people to be safe. A week later she wrote, 'We have good news: actually our guests are not falling into the water any more. We have no clue why, but we hope of course that it stays that way.'

In conversation on 'risk'

Richard Deacon

Mark Dunhill

Stephen Farthing

Richard Deacon
(RD)

British sculptor and Turner Prize winner

Mark Dunhill
(MD)

Dean of Academic Programmes, Central Saint Martins, UAL

Stephen Farthing
(SF)

British painter, writer and Rootstein Hopkins Chair of Drawing, UAL

The participants were asked to discuss the topic of creative risk, with particular reference to their respective fields within fine arts practice and education, and to the work of students and staff on the 'A' Course – a radical three-year degree programme in the Sculpture Department of Saint Martin's School of Art, London, inaugurated in 1969. They begin with their definition of 'risk' in relation to creativity.

MD:
I've been interested in creative risk-taking in relation to art education for quite a while. You could say that all art practice engages with risk at some level; the very endeavour, right from the word go, involves testing something out, testing yourself, and, as a student, exposing your successes and failures in the company of your peers. While the job of a fine art course is to create the conditions in which creative risk is supported and encouraged, we seem to have put some hurdles in the way. Coupled with a greater emphasis on assessment, taking out a loan of £27,000 to undertake a degree could understandably be seen as an inhibition to risk-taking. The 'A' Course was an extraordinary example of the ways in which a group of staff and students could challenge the prevailing model of fine art teaching at that time - question it, and play with the idea of what art and education might be, in a very serious way. The word 'play' is an important word, I think, because playfulness, perhaps more than risk, characterises how students become aware of what might be possible. As a teacher, a great deal of time is actually spent giving students permission to do something that they feel they either shouldn't do or couldn't do, or that might fail.

RD:
I'm having difficulty with the distinction between risk and uncertainty. I think that risk can be managed and I think the 'A' Course did an enormous amount to manage risk from an institutional point of view. The staff were extremely attentive to the students in their care, and today's students would be quite jealous, I think, of the amount of time that was invested in us [Deacon was a student in the first 'A' Course intake of 1969]. The staff were unfailing in their commitment to being present while, at the same time, being very good at maximising uncertainty for us. So, we didn't know what was expected of us and we didn't know when it would all end. Although we knew what the rules were, at no point were the desired outcomes ever revealed. Actually, there never were any desired outcomes.

Managing risk is something that all institutions have to do, whether they're teaching climbing or bricklaying, and, in most educational institutions, uncertainty isn't desirable either. You might be trying to project excessive uncertainty into the situation - in a military situation, for example - in order that people become dependent upon some form of authority. But I don't think that's how the 'A' Course worked, though I accept that some people did interpret it like that.

SF:
Richard, do you think you could briefly describe the 'A' Course? Because I'm not sure many people really know what it is.

RD:
Some time ago, I wrote down a description of my first day at Saint Martin's [School of Art, now Central Saint Martins (CSM), UAL], which describes coming in on the first day. We had no prior knowledge that there was going to be something particular going on, although we were all very enthusiastic to be accepted at Saint Martin's, because we knew that it was a high-profile institution and that competition for places had been intense. So, anyway, I wrote this in the mid-1970s, I think, and edited it later:

On arrival at St Martin's, the incoming sculpture students were directed to the A2 studio. One end of this large and – at that time – empty studio was closed off by a barrier of wooden screens. In the centre of this screen wall was a locked door with a notice pinned to it saying 'Project area. Knock before entering.' The sculpture students from all three years of the diploma course assembled in the room: those returning talking; those new sitting or standing, mostly silent. At about 10:15, two men came to the studio, both wearing name badges: Garth Evans and Gareth Jones. The first-year students were told to return to the studio at 11:20.

At the appointed time, the new students gathered in the studio. Garth Evans and Gareth Jones reappeared. Gareth held a small box of name badges. He picked these out one at a time, reading the written name aloud and giving it to the responding student. All having received badges, Garth read from a piece of paper that he held in his hand – an introduction to the project. In this statement he emphasised that the project would be demanding and require self-discipline on the part of the students to make it successful. His hand shook as he read. The door to the project area was then unlocked. Garth and Gareth entered, followed one at a time by the students. As each entered, they were handed, from piles on either side of the door, a cube of about 20 inches on each side, wrapped in brown paper.

The project area was bare of furnishings, save for notices pinned at various points to the wall, saying 'no drawing or writing materials to be used', 'punctuality is essential', 'no verbal communication except between individual student and member of staff', 'the project area will be open 10:00 to 11:00, 11:20 to 1:00, 2:00 to 3:00, and 3:20 to 4:30'. Pieces of card pinned at various points to the floor each contained the name of an individual student. I took my cube, placed it by the card containing my name, and sat down on it.

So, that's how the project started and, by the end of the week, we'd all more or less worked away on our blocks of polystyrene – unwrapped them and started doing things with them. One student continuously sat on his block throughout the whole week and continued throughout the rest of the year to be present but a non-participant in activities.

MD:
A sort of 'conscientious objector'?

RD:
Yes. But he wasn't ever sanctioned. It must have been excruciatingly boring for him to sit there, and that was a radical way of approaching the participation, but perfectly valid. The only rule was that we had to be there.

Anyway, so the next week we turned up expecting to continue where we left off and, when we went in at 10.00 in the morning, the whole room had been cleared. Everything had been taken away and we were each given a roll of brown paper and we had to start again from that. And then - I can't remember the sequence - but the same thing happened the following week. We were given stopwatches for the next thing, but then they disappeared on the third day and were replaced by something else. So, the expectation that you knew the structure was constantly being disrupted.

Throughout the year, with occasional pauses, there were variations, with different rules, different behaviours, different things allowed or not allowed, different materials, different tasks, different controls on the way in which we, the students, could interact with each other. The only thing that remained constant was this timetable and the fact that someone was always there. No one ever said anything or ever evaluated anything; even at the end of the year there was no evaluation, which was cause of some contention the following year when we *were* assessed - the requirement for the assessment was from the establishment, or the administration.

MD:
I was going to say - there must have been that demand from the institution at that time?

RD:
Yes, but, at that point, it was very clear that the 'A' staff were entirely supportive of the students. It was clear that the 'A' staff would never compromise on their 'duty of care'. I mean, the 'A' Course has a slightly dark history - as a place where the students were locked up - which is, to some extent, true. But I think the 'A' Course staff - Peter Atkins [later, Kardia], Garth Evans and Gareth Jones, and Peter Harvey - were taking a risk in trying out a new kind of educational exercise. I never found out what their ambitions were, but I've always assumed it was something connected to uncertainty.

MD:
My sense is that one of the things that Peter Atkins wanted to remove from the curriculum was making 'art'. Whatever you were doing in that first year may have been art, but that was a secondary aspect of the encounter. You had to respond and react and bring whatever you had to bear on the situation. Art and what that might be was removed from the agenda.

SF:
It's the first time I've ever heard anybody describe the 'A' Course. I was in the same art school [Farthing studied painting at Saint Martin's School of Art between 1969 and 1973] and, for the second year, I actually worked in the studio where the 'A' Course was running - we were four painters walled off from the main studio. I can remember thinking: *that* is a very serious course, and that it was amusing sometimes what the students following that course did. One of the things that I observed over time was that the students seemed to know what they were doing, whereas the painters hadn't a clue what they were doing. We were re-enacting a craft in a very traditional way. The other thing I picked up from your description

was the idea of having time; with the luxury of time, I think that we are all capable of going beyond the obvious. I had this described to me by [American painter] Chuck Close when I lived in New York – I met him a couple of times and asked him, what do you think it's like for a young artist in New York today? He said he felt very sorry for young artists who moved to New York, because they only had about eighteen months to make it. It's so expensive to live there, for young people today – the only strategy they had time to use was appropriation. Whether or not that is true I don't know, but I thought it was a very interesting observation, that the lack of time took away the opportunity for taking risks.

RD:
I think Mark and Stephen have made, between them, an interesting point. Mark, you said something about the 'A' Course taking the art out of the equation, and Stephen has made this point about time. In a way, having to turn up on time but without there being a kind of end in sight – it meant you were given a gift of however many weeks. You were, somehow, accumulating stuff in here – in your head – but not necessarily piling up canvasses or unfinished pieces of sculpture; you didn't know where it would end, so you just had to find it interesting.

MD:
I'm not sure that the space and time exists in the same way now. While I know that fine art tutors encourage students to experiment and not become fixated on the outcome or an end product, there is inevitably a certain pressure to perform and impress – even if this is just an internal pressure, being on a time-limited course with a degree show at the end of it …

Richard, surely you must have had some crisis moments during your first year? You must have thought, what is going on here? What am I doing? I mean, where were you getting your confidence from to actually keep going?

RD:
Well, it was clear, and interesting. And yes, there were obviously times when I thought it was hard, or even ridiculous, but there was incredible solidarity among this group of eight or ten students, which was hugely supportive. When we were in our second year, we were pushed a bit more. William Tucker and David Everson and Tim Scott were given charge of the second year and we kicked them out. We said, they're not good enough, and Bill Tucker then went to [head of the sculpture department] Frank Martin and said, Peter Atkins is producing un-teachable students. We weren't un-teachable, but we just weren't willing to take it lying down – we were willing to challenge assumptions.

SF:
Frank Martin was clearly a very confident, clever man – he managed the risk of having a faculty who didn't all agree and who were very strong. He took – I think – enormous risk in letting those parallel courses develop, and in producing, quite possibly, monstrous students!

RD:
Yes. I do regret the Bill Tucker thing, because he was writing *The Language of Sculpture* [1974] at the time and I could have learned a lot from him. I think there was some justice to his saying that, and we didn't really give him a chance.

MD:
My memory of being a student in that period is that we were rather arrogant about our own abilities, and rather

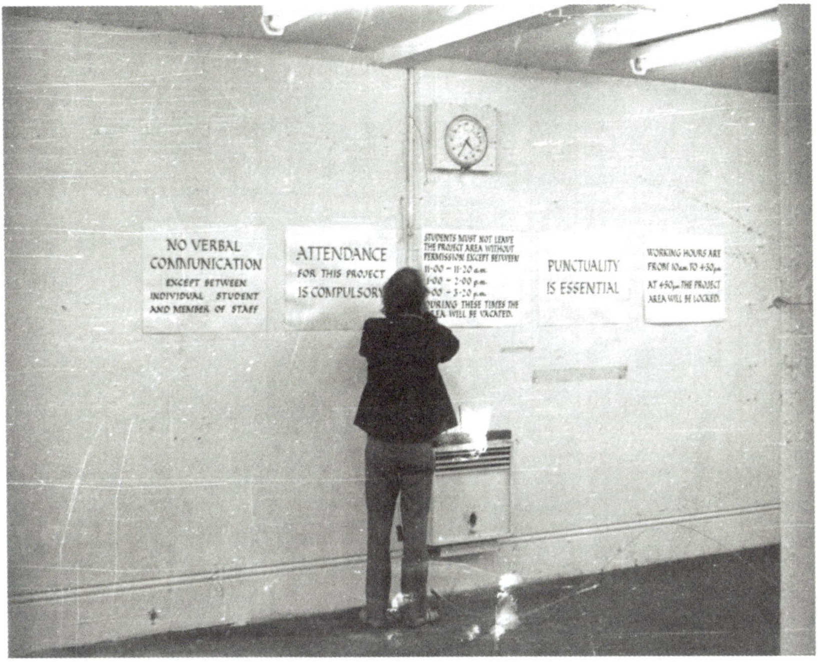

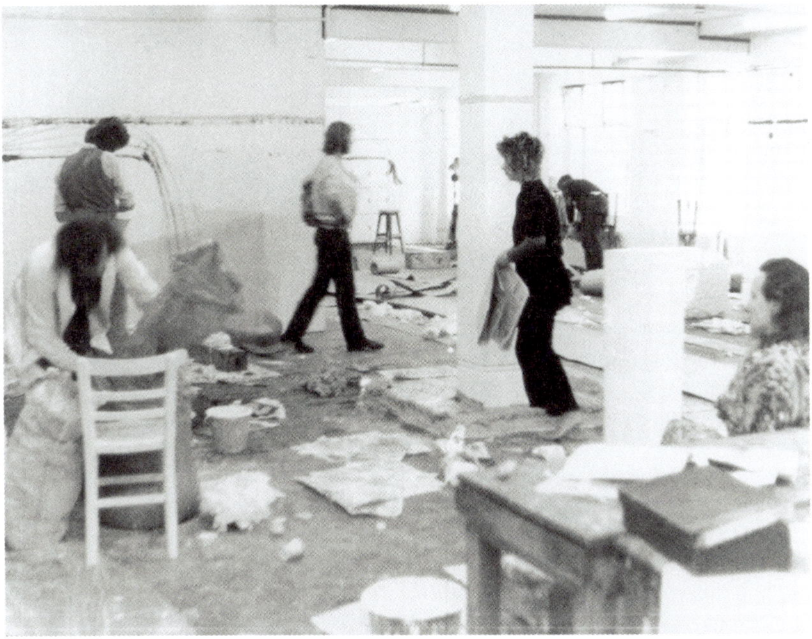

Top: 'A' Course, Locked Room project (instructions), Saint Martin's School of Art, London, 1970.
Bottom: 'A' Course project workspace with students (from left to right: Andrew Rice, Anthony Hill, Richard Deacon, Deirdre McArdle, unknown, Greg Lewis), Saint Martin's School of Art, London, 1970.

scathing about our tutors and the older generation. I am not sure what our confidence was founded on, but it fuelled a certain kind of ambition.

Of course we still see that kind of confidence among students now, and an informed knowingness that is impressive, but equally, I have seen students who are less confident, with conflicted expectations. On the one hand they want the freedom of the 'art school experience', and, on the other hand, they want a recognised, academic university education. Having paid for their fees, their living costs, 'what am I going to get and what am I going to do when I leave?' is a very live question for them and can lead to an understandable anxiety.

SF:
I would say that I didn't know a single student at that time who worried about what they were going to do when they left. The idea of getting a job was not important.

RD:
Well, the idea of earning a living from making ...

MD:
... the idea of making a living from art, at that time did seem completely ridiculous! If we shift the conversation a little bit to the present day – one of the things that everyone is saying now about David Bowie, since his untimely death, is how restless he was, how he was constantly reinventing himself – taking risks with his image, his music, the staging of concerts and the people he played music with. I'd like to look at how we might think about creative risk-taking or uncertainty now. What constraints evolve as careers proceed? Certainly post-art school, there is a whole set of different constraints that start coming into play about who you're making the work for and how that might start determining the kind of risk you will take or you won't take.

RD:
Yes, and I agree, but I also think, on the other side, Lemmy also died and he didn't change in forty years! He wasn't in the same league as David Bowie, but what I'm saying is that it's not that you have to reinvent yourself. He was taking a risk by staying the same. In art, you can think of people who carry on doing the same thing and, by doing so, devalue what they've done before. Then there are other people who, if they ever stopped doing that thing, it would be a disaster. On Kawara's date paintings [1966–2013] got better; they got more and more interesting the more he did them and the more often he did them. There's something about intention involved, but it's really hard to pin it down.

MD:
One of the things I've noticed in comparison with current students, is that we made work for the sake of making work, with very little sense of what we would do with it, because there seemed to be so few opportunities to show it, you just didn't give it much thought. By comparison, students and graduates tend to be much better than we were at making work for an event or occasion; for a site or a place; for different audiences. I think there are probably many reasons for this change.

SF:
It's as though they're commissions and not part of the natural development of an idea.

MD:
Yes, maybe, though I'm not suggesting that it's necessarily a negative thing.

RD:
I think, as a young artist, working for something is very useful and empowering, but there can come a point when the commissions dry up or the opportunities dry up …

MD:
Yes, and you've got nothing to do.

SF:
Going back to something you said, right at the beginning, about students asking permission – it struck a chord with me. When I was in my final year at the Royal College of Art studying painting, [British abstract painter] Howard Hodgkin was my tutor for a term. I'd been in Paris and had made some little collages that were based on a portrait of Louis XV in Versailles; they were kind of crazy. When he first met me, he pulled these out and said, these are really interesting, why don't you do something with them? I can remember saying to him, quite clearly, I think people will think I'm barking mad if I did a great big picture of one of those. And he said, you should.

So, I said to him, I'll do it for you, and he said, yes, do it for me. The next time I met him we talked about the painting, and I ended up winning a John Moores Painting Prize with it. It was purchased by Walker Art Gallery in Liverpool. It actually started me as a serious artist, and it was written about by a number of people. It was 1974, I think, and the beginnings of postmodernism, and this was a postmodernist painting, but I actually asked him if he would ask me to paint it, because I didn't have the confidence to do something so crazy. So, that's something an art school can give a student: the confidence to make a dangerous decision.

MD:
And that made a huge difference to your career.

SF:
Well, at the same time, I was thinking of joining the navy when I left art school! It's what made me carry on. Thinking about risks, they're not things you necessarily take all the time. You take them at key points in your life.

MD:
And you don't always know they're risks when you take them either. I don't think you go into the studio thinking, 'I'm going to take a risk today.' It happens as a process of working on something. As a student, there is a crucial moment when you realise that the work you are making is not all about you; it's about tuning into the work and letting it tell you what to do.

SF:
A couple of years ago I did a book on Derek Jarman's drawing books – there are thirty-six of them in the BFI archive and everything is handmade (see overleaf). What I suppose I learned was that he was trying out ideas in these books and they ended up as films. It was something he did every single day, and I do think that the idea of practising every day and being in a room on your own is a very important part of it. Today, with much easier access to a conceptually much bigger space through computers … I use a computer as much as I sit in the studio, but I do think that the experience of actually being in a studio, touching stuff, and having books around is a very important part of making yourself able to take risks without actually knowing it.

RD:
Have you two edited your own pasts?

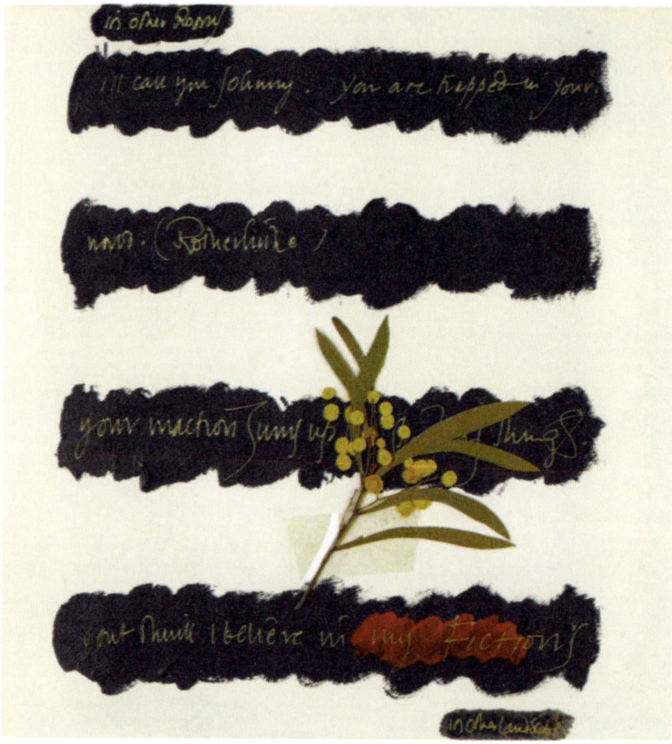

From Stephen Farthing and Edward Webb-Ingall, *Derek Jarman's Sketchbooks*, London, 2013 (detail).

MD:
No.

RD:
Have you destroyed work?

MD:
I have destroyed a lot of work. Yes.

SF:
Yes. I have – not systematically, but wilfully.

RD:
I'm doing an exhibition this year of work I made on my foundation course [at Somerset College of Art, Taunton].

SF:
Have you got it all?

RD:
I've got quite a lot – enough to make an exhibition anyway. I was thinking that there could have been a point when I threw stuff out or edited, and then I started looking after it instead. It could be that that was something to do with the 'A' Course. Perhaps because it was quite intense, somehow precious, and that spilled over into a sense of not knowing where to draw the boundaries or when things might be interesting.

The 'A' Course did seem to disable certain of our editing processes: what I think of as positive was that it encouraged a degree of uncertainty and not-knowing within a secure environment. The negative side was, and I'm speaking personally, that we didn't really get equipped with any ability to edit or to finish; I think I learned those skills at the Royal College and subsequently. I've always been a kind of advocate for the 'A' Course and its intensity, seriousness, commitment and all that, but I think the way in which they tried to theatricalise things towards the end was a realisation that this was an incipient problem: they were producing a bunch of students who couldn't draw the boundaries any more.

MD:
Is this where they put the hoods on? [The 'Mask Project', presented in students' third year, involved staff wearing masks and adopting 'crude, vulgar and unsympathetic' personae – verbally abusing the students, art and artists in general; see p.55.]

RD:
Yes, that's correct, that project was problematic. It's possible that within a more conventional art education you'd have learned that side of things – how to be more self-critical – earlier on.

SF:
I think that's what the tutorial system in most art schools is all about, isn't it? Teaching students to self-edit?

MD:
I still don't think we've got to where risk-taking occurs within our practices now. How, and in what way, does it occur in a mature practice? Does creative risk- taking come more naturally to a young artist, or does the confidence derived from experience encourage you to take bigger risks? To what extent are risk-taking and confidence connected?

RD:
Well, I don't know about setting out to take risks. Some years ago in my studio in Cologne – in the ceramics studio – I began making something out of folded cardboard tubes. I was on my own and I realised that actually there was a lot that could come out of this simple thing. It's not so much to do with taking risks. It's to do with recognising that pitiful little gestures or small events can be immensely profitable and then having the confidence to pursue them. You can think, okay, now I'll put that aside and do something serious, but actually it's the fiddling around that is really engaged. So one answer, I think, is that it's to do with promoting a kind of idleness and boredom that creates the opportunity and pressure for little incidents to happen and things to develop. Whereas if you start with a kind of huge idea – I'm going to take a risk – you know, you're never going to get it.

MD:
And that's a lot about paying attention, isn't it?

SF:
I think that my answer is actually quite different. I believe that if I destroy something that is apparently successful and remake it, it will be more interesting the second time. In about 1983, I moved out of a big house and studio in the country to a little house in town, and I had a lot of work stored there in an outhouse building. When I looked at it, it had mould growing on it and ... these paintings were not in very good shape. I decided to burn them and then, while they were burning in the garden, I got a phone call from the Museum of Modern Art in Oxford offering me a one-person show. At least four of the paintings they wanted were on this fire – maybe five. I was actually standing, with

an old-fashioned telephone with a curly line on it, looking at these pictures burn, and I just said, yes, I've got them all. About a month later I said to Marco [Livingstone] that I was working on remaking four of the pictures for the show and he said, what happened to the others? I said that I destroyed them and the remakes were all so much better than the original paintings, in my view. It's something to do with embodied experience – a bit like the difference between reading a lecture and just speaking it. My big risk is to destroy something and remake it; not to keep it and then do another version. How do you manage risk? Well, I think each person has to work that one out for themself, but you've got to create an environment where you supportively allow yourself to do that. I suppose the 'A' Course was one way of doing it.

MD:
In terms of risk-taking, I think that you have to *find* the work you're making. We [MD has worked in collaboration with Tamiko O'Brien since 1998] frequently have to go through a process of speculation and game-playing, making mock-ups and prototypes in order to establish the parameters of a new work and what it might be. It goes back to your point about being in your studio and playing around with the cardboard tubes. It's often a dumb procedure that unlocks a door. What would an 'A' Course equivalent be now, if you were to devise a radical course? Would it be the same or would it be different?

RD:
Well, it'd be a huge achievement if you could get funding for four members of staff teaching five days a week for an academic year. One thing you'd do is not so much to do with students. It's liberating the teaching staff.

MD:
That's a very hot topic at the moment at University of the Arts London, for example. The relationship between research and practice, and creating a space for speculative and experimental approaches to teaching within a more regulated institutional structure.

SF:
I've been asked to do some teaching this year on the MA Fine Art course at Chelsea College of Arts and I said I didn't want to do tutorial teaching. I said that something I thought I'd like to try was to introduce some new models or paradigms of art and visual culture and to get students to just talk and think about them. The question is, is this of any use as a reference point in thinking how you might move forward? Through my research I'd come across the drawings that [Lakota holy man and leader] Sitting Bull made. He was a warrior and a diplomat, he wasn't an artist by any stretch, but I think that using those really diverse models is a way of going somewhere between, say, the 'A' Course and a good old-fashioned painting course. You start looking at stuff and you ask the question, is it art? What is its function in our visual culture, and how do you handle other peoples' cultures? That's the best idea I've had, to just look in extraordinary places.

How do you involve students in risk? You show them things that they probably haven't thought about before and that aren't necessarily part of that central canon that you'll find in the Tate. I mean, I certainly spend more time reading anthropologists' work now than I do art historians'.

RD:
That's because you know a lot of art history. It doesn't mean that art history

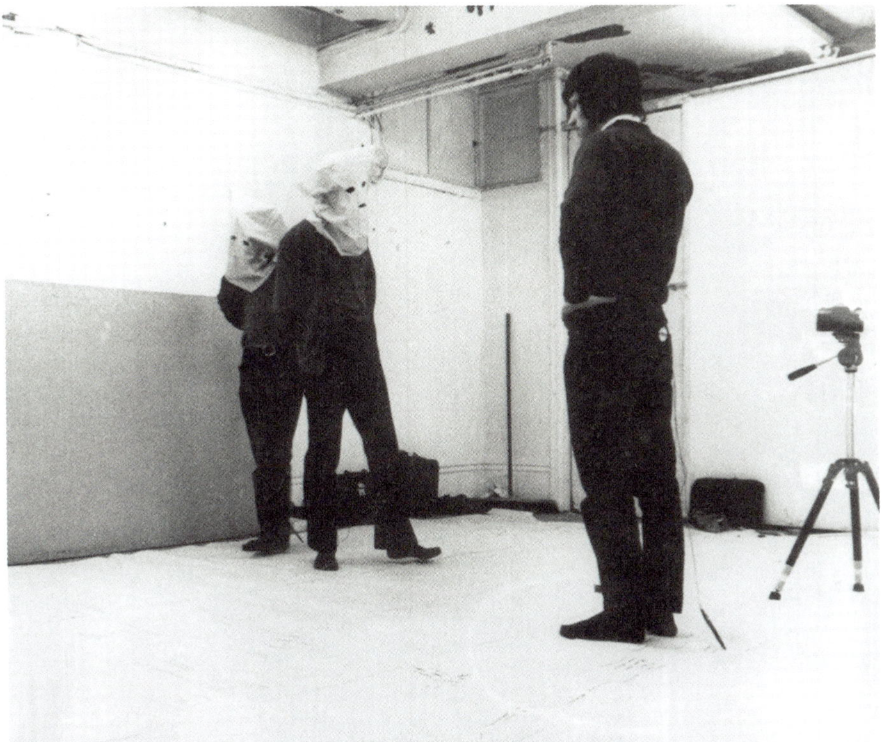

'A' Course, The Mask Project (staff members with a student – David Millidge), Saint Martin's School of Art, London, 1972.

is bunk; it just means you know a lot of art history.

SF:
Yes, and I don't know much anthropology, but I think that, in parallel with this idea of risk, there is intellectual curiosity. What has sustained me as an artist is intellectual curiosity, not a desire to take risk. I would say that good students are the ones with an intellectual curiosity and who make connections between the most diverse sets of circumstances. The ones who are less curious will stay on a safer path, if, that is, safety is the opposite to risk.

MD:
What is, perhaps, not unique, but interesting about an art and design education is that, by working in a studio environment, you're working with a group of other people and what you do is visible to others. In this sense, you have to be prepared to expose yourself and be vulnerable. You may introduce all sorts of tactics to hide and mitigate that kind of exposure, but you will have to step out at some point – and that can be very challenging.

SF:
A lot of students find it very difficult – the things like a life-drawing class, where you can actually see how good your drawing

is relative to your peers. Most students in other disciplines never, ever see that. I was director of the New York Academy of Art in Tribeca, New York – founded by Andy Warhol, of all people – between 2000 and 2004. Towards the end of his life, Warhol invested a lot of energy into building this really quite reactionary academy, because he believed that nobody had learned to draw and that people didn't study the classics any more. My feeling is that it was absolute high camp – it wasn't an old-fashioned academy – but it runs very successfully today. There were two distinct kinds of student who enrolled: there were the ones who are attracted because it offers an absolutely rigid curriculum and that freed them of decision-making; then the ones who sat through the classes and turned the message of the lesson into something that was their own. It's down to the individual in the end.

MD:
Of course the other place that's often cited is Black Mountain College [North Carolina, 1933–57], which is interesting, because it didn't segregate the subject disciplines. It created hybrid synergies and relationships and collaborations between the different subject areas. This is very relevant now, and is something that students are recognising and telling us – we want to collaborate! I don't think they always know what they mean by collaboration, or know what might be at stake, etc., but I think they know that, while they're in this place – this hothouse of creative activity – they want to know how their peers in other subject areas think, and how and why do they do what they do? It seems clear to me that the tribal nature of subject disciplines breaks down and is even less relevant outside the institution now than it was in the past?

RD:
And collaboration does happen. I was interviewed for [CSM magazine] *1 Granary*, which is produced by fine art students but looks like a fashion magazine and has big crossovers between the departments. And I think the fashion students are probably equally interested in the fine art students.

MD:
Yes. They are, and we say to the students, well, go and talk to each other; don't expect us to introduce you. That's your job, you've got to go and introduce yourself and get to work.

MATTER | METHOD | MATERIAL

'Matter | Method | Material' is an exploratory experiment designed to explode habits in creative practice. Participants, working in small groups, create lists under the headings 'subject matter', 'methods of working' and 'materials'. Three randomly chosen terms (one from each list) then form the project brief. Some of the results can be seen in the endpapers of this book.

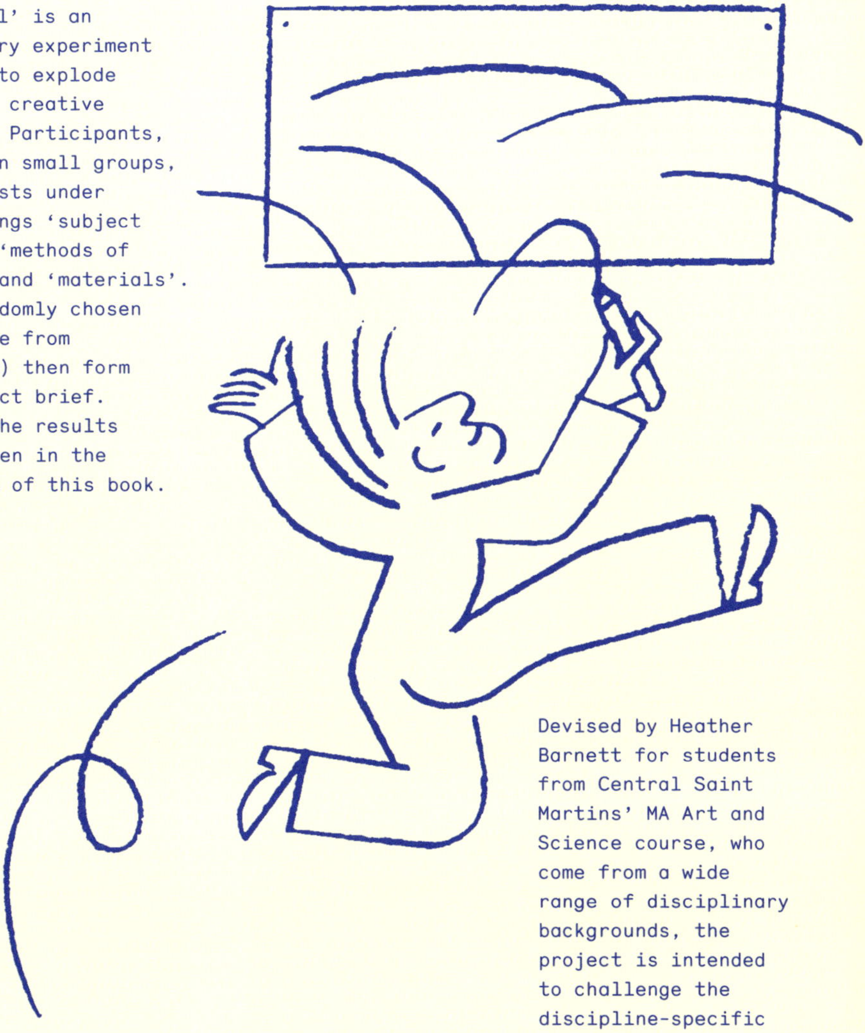

Devised by Heather Barnett for students from Central Saint Martins' MA Art and Science course, who come from a wide range of disciplinary backgrounds, the project is intended to challenge the discipline-specific habits of its participants and open up possibilities for novel approaches and strategies.

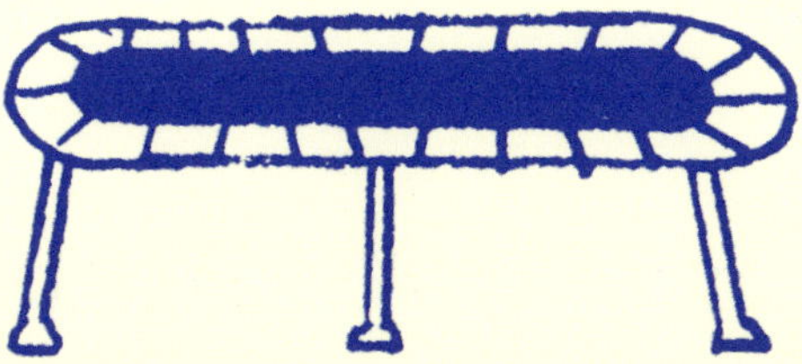

With a focus on exploratory process rather than end product, the creative experiment encourages participants to prototype, test ideas and embrace failure. The randomly set parameters necessitate creative experimentation, risk and invention.

S.O.U.P.
(SOCIALISING OUTSIDE OF UNIVERSITY PRESCRIPTIONS)

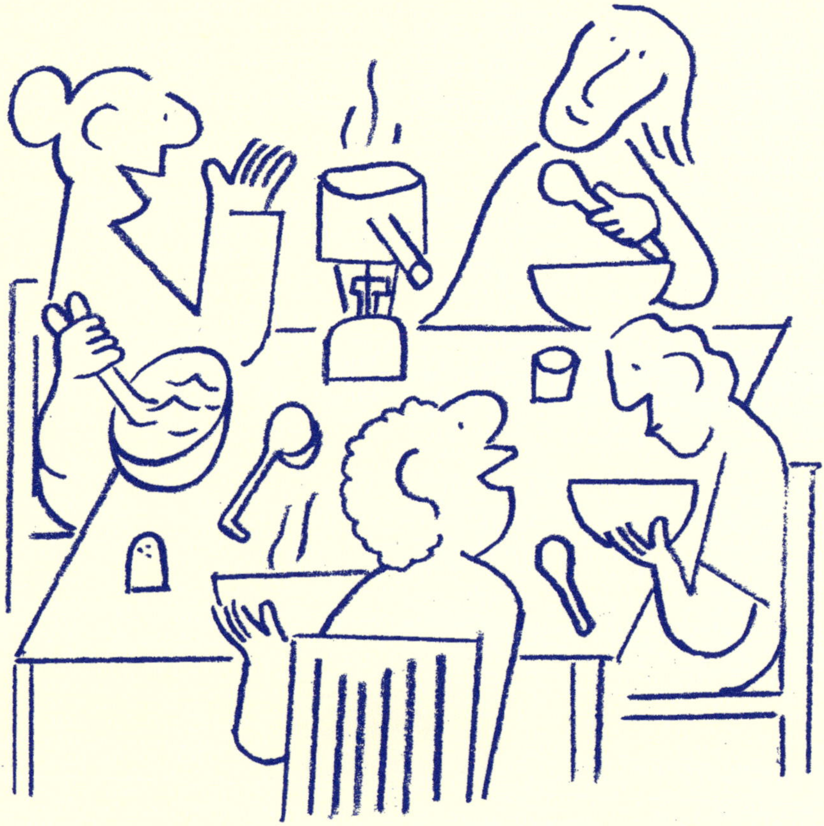

Beginning in 2013, this project, launched by Fine Art students Adeeb Ashfaq, Benjamin Schmechel, Silvy Liu and Tobia Silvotti, was a response to shared dissatisfaction with the quality of education within art schools. Starting with a recycled sink and other furniture, which became a soup kitchen, S.O.U.P. began to host weekly discussions, peer-to-peer tutorials and workshop sessions, with common interest rather than common discipline forming the basis of tutorial groups. The student-run kitchen became a forum for evaluating the art school experience collectively and without inhibition, and for envisioning habit-breaking, even risky, alternatives to the institutional norm: 'In a building where the windows won't open and the only way out is the way you came in … we are surely all healthy and safe but is this a radical hotbed of critical thought? … perhaps we should turn our "criticality" toward our own education.'

RESILIENCE

Neil Cummings

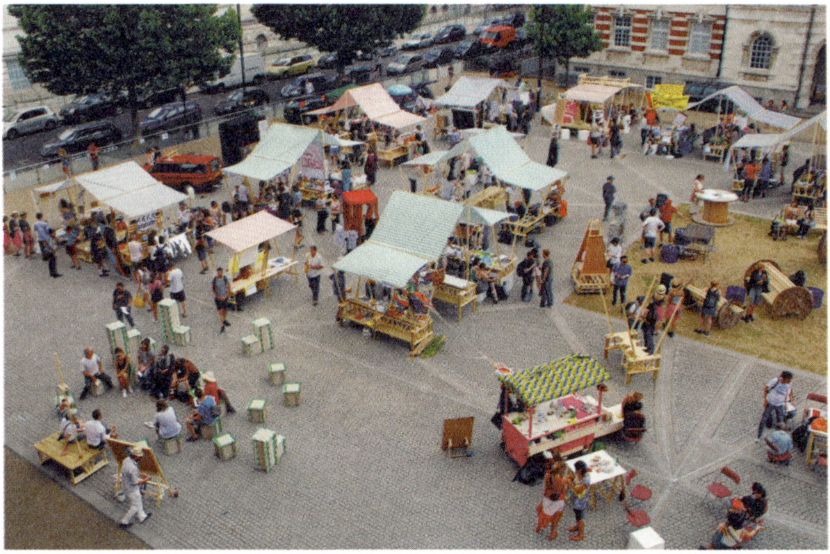

#TransActing: a Market of Values, a pop-up market taking place on the Rootstein Hopkins Parade Ground outside Chelsea College of Arts, UAL, 2015.

Resilience is the capacity of a system – a person, a bacterial culture, a forest, a city or a financial economy – to adapt and continue to survive. It is a creative response to shocks, threats and disruption, and a desire to persist.

And, whether you like it or not, our biosphere, in particular, is changing, and dramatically. Spiking temperatures, rising seas, flash floods and extreme droughts are threatening human infrastructure – our global food supplies, water and energy sources, our public services and even our cities – and our very survival. This more extreme and increasingly chaotic world we now co-produce – our new planetary epoch, the Anthropocene – demands profound structural changes in how we imagine our relation to, and means of subsisting on, our planet; if, that is, we intend to be resilient and persist.

The idea of ecological resilience as a desirable quality was first developed in C.S. Holling's scientific research paper 'Resilience and Stability of Ecological Systems' (published in the 1973 *Annual Review of Ecology and Systematics*). Holling, a Canadian ecologist, studied the interactions between predator and prey in specific ecologies, and realised that such interconnected actors have multiple and dynamic relationships. Individuals die, key resources dwindle, specific populations migrate and, although none of these events is necessarily catastrophic, together they offer an opportunity for adaptive change – for creative resilience.

Put simply, Holling noted that resilience increases with the diversity and the strength of relationships between its actors.

There is nothing intrinsically positive about resilience; it is merely the duration of a described ecology, a set of actors, resources, practices and values, through time. There are many practices and values that are resilient that I would prefer were not, such as the exponential growth of self-referential administration, the Kalashnikov automatic rifle, free-market ideology or fascism. Resilience itself has been subject to ideological capture – it is now used by neo-liberal governments as a justification for reducing welfare, shrinking public provision and deregulating market forces. As a consequence, vulnerable communities will need to become even more resilient, socially, if they are to survive successive waves of crises.

The challenge, then, is to ensure that the values I value are resilient: to *occupy* resilience.

Markets are brilliant bundles of technologies, assembled to distribute things. All kinds of things. The most visible, recognisable form of market, currently, is that derived from the Austrian economist Friedrich Hayek's early theories on the self-organising logic of 'free' markets, which imagine rational individuals pursuing, and markets as being motivated primarily by, self-interest. The forces of supply and demand at play among these rational individuals produce the values - often represented by a financial price - exchanged in any transaction. These fundamental elements: rational agents, resources, supply and demand, and price mechanisms, function in all markets everywhere as if like natural laws. Like gravity.

While this is only an ideological model, art, artists and their art worlds (outside public museums and a small network of public galleries) are principally reproduced through competitive markets, via more or less commercial galleries, dealers, collectors, art fairs, magazines and auctions. A market ecology. Even art and design education is increasingly shaped by 'market forces' and, as the moral philosopher Michael J. Sandel has observed, 'markets mark the things that circulate within them.'[1]

In my experience, competitive markets, whether they distribute contemporary art, financial contracts or Kalashnikovs, are inherently conservative and risk-averse; they value repetition and minor differences. This is why, for example, the secondary art market convened by auction houses loves Andy Warhol's silkscreen prints. Each series is more or less limited, each print is more or less the same as all the others in the series, and yet each can be narrated into singularity, into originality. It's the only one with red lips, for example, or blue eyeshadow, signed on the reverse, printed by his best friend, owned by Jacqueline Kennedy Onassis, and so on, endlessly. Markets value the idea of scarcity, of originality, even where there is none.

We have allowed the values of competitive markets to dominate contemporary art, and the education of those who want to be artists. We have produced and reproduce a virtual monoculture, and monocultures are not diverse. Monocultures are fragile, not resilient.

The glory of British art education, in my experience of teaching at Chelsea College of Arts, UAL, for the last twenty years, is not reducible to the numerous artists who go on to win prestigious prizes, or gain commercial gallery representation and dominate in competitive art markets. While we rightly celebrate their achievements, these artists represent something like 1 per cent of the participants who profit from a creative art college education. No, the glory of British art education is the resilient 99 per cent – artists who go on to produce, often in ways we cannot imagine, the vast creative commons of invention and creativity the world in general, Britain in particular, and London specifically, benefits from.

It often starts with a nagging curiosity. 'I wonder how to do that?', or 'I could do that much better.' Curiosity is the substrate of creativity, overlaid by an appetite for risk, necessarily followed by determination. Through their education, artists learn to cope with the uncertainty produced by curiosity; they come to understand the importance of not-knowing and to be comfortable with finding things out by trial and error (even imaginative error). They create new things by doing, evaluating and doing again, differently. Sometimes by being 'stupid', previously unseen possibilities emerge. This is surely the most valuable form of creativity, producing emergent values, and not the rote, the already sold, or the already known. Instead, the thrill is in finding new knowledge and meanings, embodied in original relations between people and things, between processes and resources.

Producing artefacts for markets is no longer enough; to be resilient, we will need to radically reimagine what art can be, and what it can do. At Chelsea College of Arts, artists are encouraged to be ambitious enough to creatively assemble the very ecology in which they practice. This enables shifting relations to exist between specific people, things, modes of organisation, places, resources and forms of knowledge – it enables an ethics of care, a desire to share, and releases various new funding streams. Creative artists are always enmeshed in networks of cooperation in this culture; even as they pursue their own interests, they're in deep connection with others.

Artists who have graduated from Chelsea, such as Gareth Lloyd at Machines Room, for example, have pioneered skill-sharing networks and maker libraries. Others have produced communal workshops and 'hacklabs'; developed Time Banks – where time replaces money as currency; and, as with #TransActing, explored other resilient economies (see p.61). Some artists have initiated new music-publishing platforms and many, many, many have become musicians – some experimental, others forming groups; some, like Sam Lee, researching disappearing folk traditions. Some compose film soundtracks. The Open Music Archive, which sources, digitises and distributes out-of-copyright sound recordings, was co-founded by artists.

In these fluctuating environments, artists learn to be super-resilient - always alert to chance and opportunity, unruffled by the precariousness of financial rewards or a lack of clear career trajectory. And they tend to be amazing at managing resources, whether material, emotional or financial. Artists frequently wring the maximum from limited resources, and resources are always limited, because, as they increase, so does creative ambition. Artists even squander creatively.

Once assembled, these resilient networks need never dissipate. Of course, they change, but creative artists develop a continuous practice - a lifelong commitment to learning, reconfiguring and sharing the results.[2]

Artists produce crowd-funding platforms, skill-sourcing apps and virtuous communities, where getting personally fit involves doing good for others. Some run independent bike shops, others are personal trainers or lead city-walking tours. In response to the capitalisation of art education, artists have founded and run local, free art schools - such as Open School East in Haggerston, London - Slow Universities, public seminars, screenings, lectures, reading groups, knitting circles and other discursive cells. Some artists teach art to children, others to adults.

Artists from Chelsea run institutional education programmes, public programmes and outreach projects. Some migrate to writing, or publish and build publishing platforms - both analogue and digital - about art, music, architecture, film, digital animation, culture and anthropology, among many other things. Other artists drift into curating and reimagine what an exhibition might consist of; others organise experimental exhibitionary institutions, like The Showroom in London. Others go on to shape the art market rather than being subject to it - they found commercial galleries or, like Francis Outred of Christie's, lead auction houses.

Artists consult and mentor, start start-ups, begin businesses and contribute to various social enterprises. They innovated socially, before the term 'social innovation' was coined. Some are hacking finance, organising money-labs, mining bitcoins or agitating for an Art Auction Transaction Tax. Other artists use food as a creative medium: run urban farms, make cheese, open cafés, work as chefs; many design, build and run restaurants.

Artists from Chelsea, in particular, increasingly self-describe as activists, working creatively with social relations and political structures to change attitudes and behaviours. Liberate Tate champions cultural divestment from fossil fuels; The Carrot Workers campaign against internships and precarity; others are seeking to extend refugee status to migrants, or to resist gentrification. Others join the more formal political structures and represent their peers.

So, we can no longer afford merely to champion and support a niche ecology of artists, artefacts, collectors and select institutions - commercial galleries, art fairs and museums - and a competitive market distribution mechanism. If we are to be resilient, we will need to learn to value and celebrate other kinds of artist, artwork and the ecologies that produce them, including the distribution of art into diverse social networks. We will need to overwrite the production of scarcity with creative abundance, because creativity is one of the few unlimited resources we possess.

Notes

1. 'Markets mark the things they distribute' was a phrase Michael Sandel deployed in the first of his BBC Reith Lectures, in 2009. He used an example, derived from America, in which schoolchildren were paid a fee in order to encourage them to read. By being paid to read, he argued, children were encouraged to believe that reading is a way of earning money. Any good inherent to reading, therefore, would be overwritten by the desire to profit financially. www.bbc.co.uk/podcasts/series/reith.
2. The Latin root of exhibition - *exhibere* - designates the sharing of evidence, specifically within a legal setting.

In conversation on 'resilience'

Mary Katrantzou

Jane Rapley

Susanne Tide-Frater

Mary Katrantzou
(MK)
Award-winning fashion designer and graduate of the MA Fashion course at Central Saint Martins, UAL

Jane Rapley
(JR)
Former Dean of Fashion and Textiles and Head of Central Saint Martins, UAL

Susanne Tide-Frater
(STF)
Brand consultant (and, formerly, external examiner at Central Saint Martins, UAL); currently Brand and Strategy Director of Farfetch

The participants were asked to discuss the topic of creative resilience, with particular reference to the pedagogical culture of the 'crit' as epitomized by Louise Wilson's teaching on the much-lauded MA Fashion course at Central Saint Martins (CSM), UAL, and its implications for students' ongoing personal and creative resilience. They begin by looking at whether resilience is a quality required especially by the art school and the creative industries more generally.

STF:
This term – 'resilience' – it didn't mean as much to me when we started planning this conversation as it does now. In some respects, resilience is a term that is perceived as old-fashioned – it almost doesn't fit into this world any more – but, actually, I think it's very modern and relevant, because the world we're in is about the fast, the new, the more, and we're in total crisis in the fashion industry. Funnily enough, the ascent of the crisis somewhat coincides with Louise [Wilson's] passing. So I think that it is a great term and worth talking about right now, and Louise is the perfect figurehead for this discussion.

JR:
Well, the fashion world is changing, as is the relationship with the customer; it's global and that makes it complicated and expensive – a great deal of investment has to be in place to create young brands. Without umbrella organisations like the British Fashion Council to harbour young talent, it's much, much more difficult now than it was in 1995, 96, to start a business.

STF:
There is a pressure driven by greed; retailers in the States and over here have accelerated their sales cycle and ask for more and more, and that has provoked a profound crisis in terms of the pressures on young designers and how much they need to produce and how fast. Clothes are only on the shop floor a mere, what, six weeks, if they're delivered on time, and then they disappear.

JR:
Some of the intrinsic value has gone.

STF:
Though I think we are at the beginning of a revolution – there is a backlash – and something remarkable will come out of it.

MK:
I think resilience is a term that I'm starting to think about now for the first time because, when you start building your business, you're thinking about work ethic, you're thinking about focus, you're thinking about drive. Then, as your business grows and hits certain benchmarks and you want to scale, you start having all the growing pains that go with scaling up a business in fashion, and that is when you understand resilience. It's not resilience within the changing fashion system, even, it's about resilience within your path and how you find your own way. You find yourself at decision-making crossroads much more than you did at the beginning, when your focus was so singular and razor-sharp.

JR:
Just going back to the initial question – in the creative industries is resilience a more necessary quality? Well, I've never been in another industry, so I don't really know! But I think the nature of what we're talking about in terms of resilience in a design-led business – whether it's fashion or graphics, or if you're a product designer etc. – and we're talking, specifically, about very young brands, is that confidence in your own creativity and decision-making is essential. What Louise was good at was creating a confidence in her students, so that they would go out and want to operate on their own terms.

In terms of the crit, hers was a very specific type – it wasn't the only way of doing it. Group crits, for example, can be very instructive because, in my view, there are many mistakes to be made when you're designing; you can't make all the mistakes yourself and learn from them when you're a student, but you can watch your peers making different mistakes from yours. Because the other reason, of course, why personal resilience is important in the creative world is that there is no exact answer - no right or wrong. So, you can learn just as much from a group crit as from the intense sort of crit that Louise used to do. These were largely one-to-one, or maybe consisted of a group of staff and one student - perhaps with a fit model, who was sometimes a student. It was intense, especially for those students who weren't listening or weren't working. But, you know, sometimes I walked into her office and she was doing a crit, and I would learn so much just by listening to her. The thing about Louise was that she was completely immersed in the fashion world, and what she didn't know wasn't really worth knowing, frankly. And if it was going well, it became a conversation rather than an interrogation.

What she found most frustrating was when a student wasn't giving back, and then she would go in even harder to try and get something out of them. Because, in the end, you only have the person to deal with. I think, in an art school, you're looking for the person all the time and what you're trying to do is to get that student to define themselves and to understand who they are.

STF:
I've thought about this before - I think you [Mary] have a lot in common with Louise. The dedication, for example. I don't know anybody who is as prolific a designer.

MK:
Yes, but she pushed us like that. For the entire first year I didn't even go into her office, I was so scared. I only went with Fleet [Bigwood, Textiles for Fashion Pathway Tutor on MA Fashion] and I had this abstract respect for her, like I know I'm on the course where there's somebody magnificent but I don't want to have anything to do with her. Then Fleet started taking me into the room and, because I started going in at consistent intervals, I felt that I needed to produce enough work so that she didn't feel I was not working.

STF:
Is that why you worked so much?

MK:
I wasn't prolific in this way before my MA, not at all! I felt it was the only thing that you could make sure you were doing, because you couldn't make sure she would like it but you could make sure that you were working hard, and so I did. I'm conditioned now.

JR:
I think her crits were ... you did have to be resilient, but she was most frustrated with students who weren't passionate. If they didn't work and they weren't passionate, she used to say, why are you wasting my time? Even if they weren't necessarily really strong students, but they really tried hard, then she wouldn't be quite as coruscating as perhaps she would with someone who was being lazy. And if you were talented and lazy, she was really cruel, because that would frustrate her beyond measure. You know, when Louise graduated she didn't only work with luxury designers in Italy, she worked on the high street. She didn't go and work in Paris - she worked with Jeffrey Rogers in Hong Kong. I wonder whether there wasn't also a sort of frustration about these people getting a chance that she would love to have had and then feeling that they're going to waste it.

MK:
She did say that, openly, in interviews - I've read a couple of times her stating her frustration at what she'd seen achieved and then the frustration at someone wasting that away.

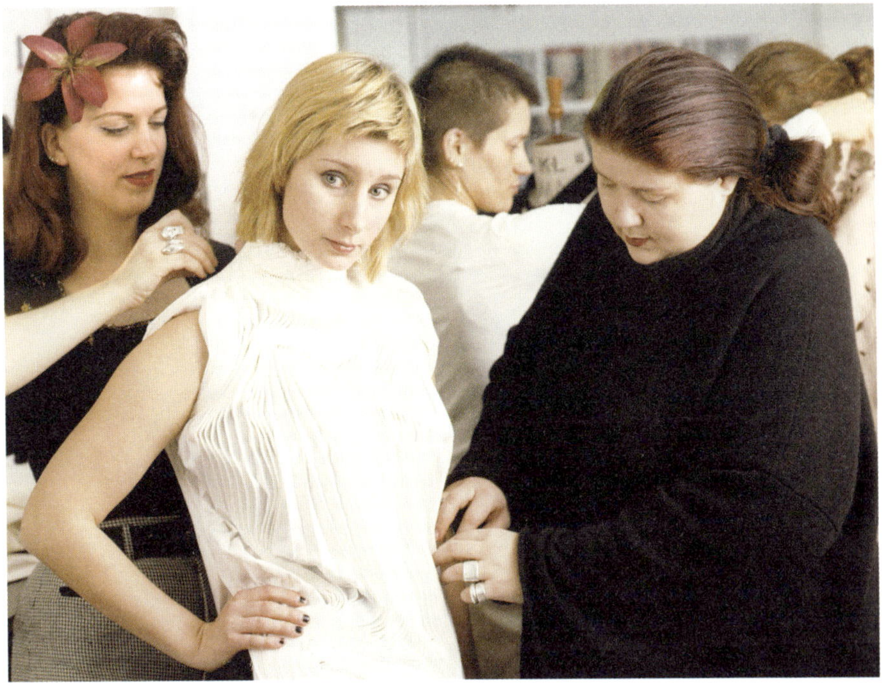

Louise Wilson (right, in black), course director of the MA Fashion course at Central Saint Martins, UAL, c.1990.

STF:
I want to give a perspective on this from the industry side. I've been Creative Director of Selfridges, so I've worked with a lot of the young designers that have come out of CSM, as well as other institutions. Also, as an examiner, I had the privilege of being quite close to the particular course that we're talking about. What they had in common, these graduates, was that they had strong viewpoints, they had variety. They had been so rigorously interrogated - in a loving way, and I will continue to say this about 'love' - that, in fact, nothing could fluster them. They were absolutely resilient. The world of, let's say, a department store - the buyer coming in and passing their opinion, with no love wasted - is tough, but these graduates were prepared. They had opinions, and they were savvy.

From an examiner's point of view, I saw the students at an early stage and then, again, at the end of the two-year course, and they became different people over that period - they all evolved into brilliant, absolutely outstanding, people. It's not an accident, and it wasn't just Louise - it was part of a bigger culture: that tradition of critiquing them one-to-one and challenging them to justify their work.

JR:
There was a process of deconstruction.

Louise deconstructed people. Because they came with expectations; they came thinking, oh, I've got into CSM, I'm it. But a lot of them, in her view, had got bad habits – they all showed their work in the same way, they weren't individual enough.

She got better at it, as well, and the process, particularly in the second year, was the reconstruction of those students into people who understood who they were, what they wanted to do and where they wanted to go. She always said, if you can withstand me, you'll be fine. The business out there is much worse than I am. I'm not sure it was, actually! But, nonetheless, they had that confidence, because they thought, well, if I can cope with Louise I can cope with anyone.

MK:
When I was there, her crits became much more personalised, and she was so intelligent anyway that she could see the type of person you were and what should be used and what shouldn't be used to push you. She had a way about her in which her criticism of your work and of things that were more personal to you built a connection, and built a mentor-mentee relationship – you respect that person so much because you know that they've seen who you are. At that stage, you've never had a tutor or, at least, in my training and upbringing, I had never had somebody, who would talk so deeply in that way about you and your work. Since graduating, I have never been in a situation where I have heard anything like what Louise told me within the course – no one would tell you that to your face – but the industry, of course, is much harder because, at the end of the day, she was motherly.

I remember being in the London Showrooms, doing our own sales, and Jeffrey Kalinsky [Vice President and Designer Fashion Director at US-based retailer Nordstrom] came, and he wasn't responding at all. Then he started being more talkative and warm and, when he left, he said, I hate it when designers show me their collections, but I have to admit that you are a great salesperson – you didn't want to make me uncomfortable and I could tell you everything I didn't like about that collection and you didn't blink once. I was so used to being given feedback about my work that I actually felt it was great, positive, constructive criticism.

STF:
That's resilience, isn't it?

MK:
Resilience is so important nowadays. I do think, especially, in fashion, because of how fast-paced it is – the product you put out is there to create a dialogue and to create an emotional response and to be criticised, and it happens every two months now, every three months. There has to be understanding of who you are because you can't be everything to everyone – Louise always said that – and, as your career goes on, you realise there is a core to your practice and you have to protect that.

JR:
We have to remember as well that her type of crit and this level of intensity is postgraduate. I hated crits when I first went to college; I was so ashamed of my work. I hated showing it, because I felt embarrassed and thought all my peers were better than me. This is particularly the case, I have to say, for overseas students coming into a British system, because the crit is key to nearly all art school education in this country, and I think they find it very, very difficult. So I think that sort of resilience has to be built over time, and staff have to be very skilful about how much they do that and

at what level, because they can destroy as much as they can be constructive.

STF:
I used to be a teacher at Institut Français de la Mode in Paris, and we actually met with Louise, because we had created the European Master of Fashion and Textile Design – an Erasmus programme. The crit, or the technique that CSM had, was absolutely unique – it didn't exist anywhere else – and, in French and European design schools, in particular, crit techniques tend to be a lot more lenient and less intense. There are teaching personalities who are exceptions – I am thinking of [French educator] Franc'Pairon from La Cambre and Institute Français de la Mode, or Linda Loppa, former Course Director of the Antwerp Fashion Academy, both of whom gave a lot, and had to take risks. This is why I always come back to this idea of 'love' with Louise, because it is actually so much easier, in reality, to say, well done, my love, you did so well! And I can see, currently, the pressure that teachers are under at any kind of art school; there are a lot more similar, trend-focused collections coming up, because I think it is harder in the current context for teachers to be able to develop that kind of teaching.

JR:
Yes, and fashion, in particular, is vulnerable across the country because it's so popular – every third sixteen-year-old girl wants to do something in fashion. The pressure on institutions, who now have to pay their way much more, to just start fashion courses – well, it is so tempting, and I think that's part of the problem. When the numbers were fewer – and I'm not saying there weren't problems, or that more people shouldn't have that opportunity – but, then, actually, you had to really want to go to an art school. You often went against your parents' wishes, or at least with their anxiety, because you had a passion to go to an art school; you didn't fit in with the norms of the academic world.

One of the other things, I think, about the crits, just going slightly sideways, is that a lot of people who have a visual acuity are not necessarily terribly articulate, because words are not their métier. I think what the crit does, is that it enables them to practise being articulate about their work. The classic example of that was [Lee] McQueen [p.75] – he was in such a vibrant and complicated visual world and he had to learn, painfully, how to interact in a social, business-oriented way without seeming rude or wanting.

MK:
When I first went to RISD [Rhode Island School of Design], I thought I wanted to do interior architecture. I had applied to both RISD and CSM but, at that stage, CSM wasn't a part of University of the Arts London and my father did not accept that I would not get a university degree. Also, fashion in Greece, by the way, at that time ... there was no fashion, so you couldn't grow up aspiring to be a fashion designer. Because my mother was an interior designer, interior architecture seemed right, or respectable, or even realistic, in terms of having a job when you returned to your own country. So I went to RISD. And then I met my partner and he was going to do his MSc in London, and I was fixated on CSM, because that was where I had wanted to go since I was fifteen, so I applied to an exchange programme, to do a semester on textile design. And I absolutely hated it, at the beginning. You were left to your own devices, whereas, at RISD, every day you had a million classes and would check in with a million different people and different tutors. But that is exactly why, through

my BA and my MA [at CSM], I found a personality within my work, because that independence, as soon as I got used to it – and it probably took me a year – it gave you the space and the time to really challenge your work.

Anyway, my graduation year was the first year I actually went to university [University of the Arts London gained university status in 2004] so I thought, to my father, you have nothing to say, not only did I go to where I wanted, but now I also have the university degree!

STF:
So you were resilient already, with your father.

MK:
So resilient. At that stage it really created a rift – I stayed true to what I felt I wanted to do, but, for two or three years, it was difficult. But it starts giving you confidence in your own decisions, when you realise that you're doing what's right for you.

JR:
You know, we're talking about CSM and I couldn't have gone there as a student – I wouldn't have had the confidence to do that. It does attract a certain sort of student and it is probably the extreme end of the British system, in that people are left to do what they need to do, and they sink or swim. I think other places are more supportive and perhaps cosset students more. The other thing the crit does is that, as students become more mature, towards the end of their BAs and on their MAs, it is good for them to have contradictory advice from different members of staff. They are forced to make decisions for themselves, and take responsibility for those decisions. They should be listening to contradictory advice and actually ploughing their path through that.

STF:
Do you think that the system at CSM is still in tune with what is happening outside the university? Or, to put it another way, do you think that the world has become so shallow in the way that it consumes people and product and 'newness' that, actually, that whole CSM education is a bit anachronistic? It's a provocative question, I know …

JR:
In my view, it's probably even more necessary, because we [in fashion] have to hit a wall sooner or later in terms of pace, over-production and material consumption, etc., and we will need people who have other ideas as to how they want to operate, other business models – people who have the confidence to say, I'm not going to do it like that. You only need one or two of them to be interesting enough, thoughtful enough, convinced enough.

MK:
I have to say, I don't mind the pace, because I think, when you have momentum, to be prolific in that way can be good. At the same time, for me, it's a question of, if you are a designer who has a very strong visual language and you are creating collections that have more thematic, conversational pieces, you don't want to have to drop a new story and a new theme every other day, because there's no consistency. I was saying, I don't want to do this in this way to our new CEO and three days later, literally, Burberry announced that they were changing their model, and [industry website] The Business of Fashion started documenting every time a designer was doing something else. I was relieved and thought, there are other people doing it, we can also do it. It will be interesting to see what happens within the industry.

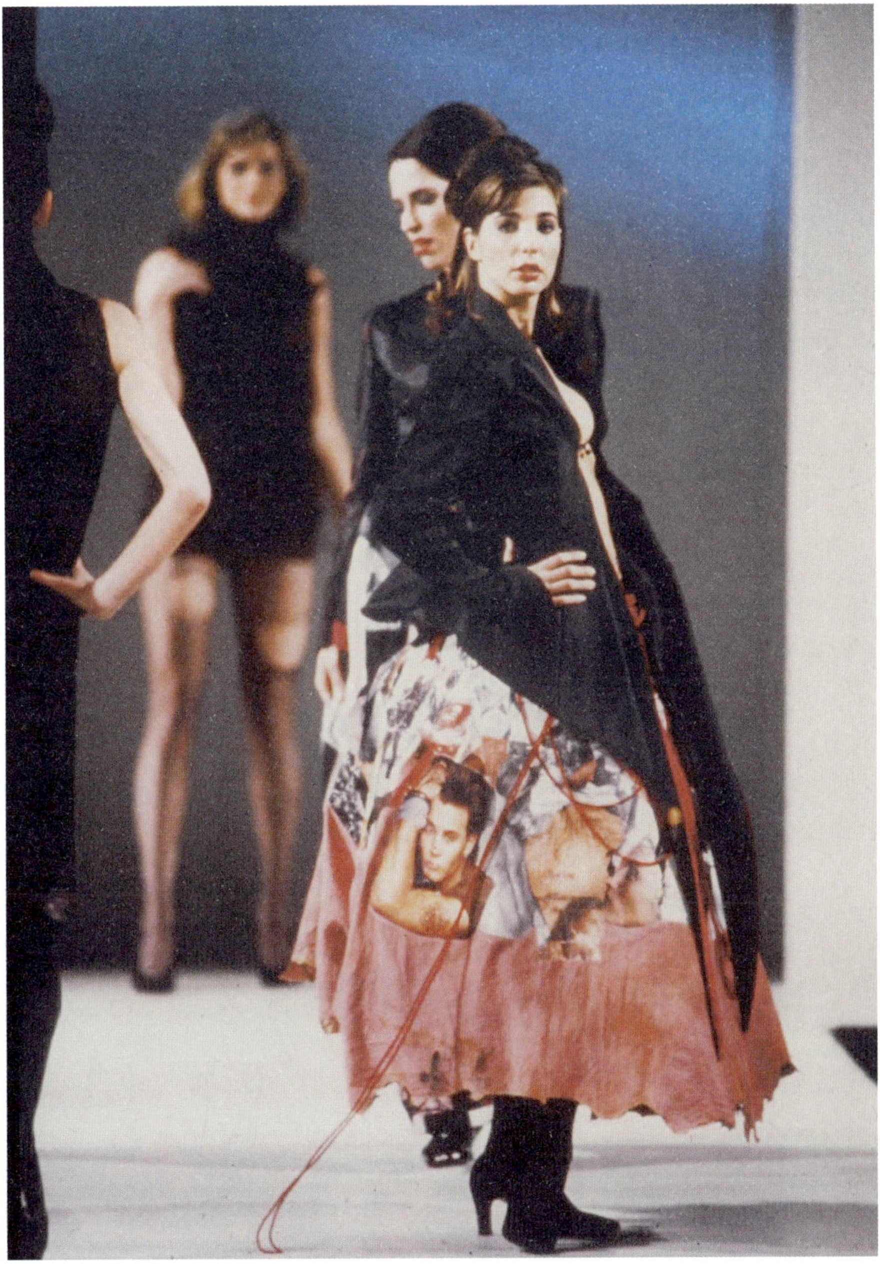

Alexander McQueen, 'Jack the Ripper Stalks His Victims' MA Fashion graduation collection, Central Saint Martins, UAL, 1992. Photograph by Niall McInerney.
Overleaf: Louise Wilson's desk, Central Saint Martins, UAL, 2014. Photograph by Wolfgang Tillmans.

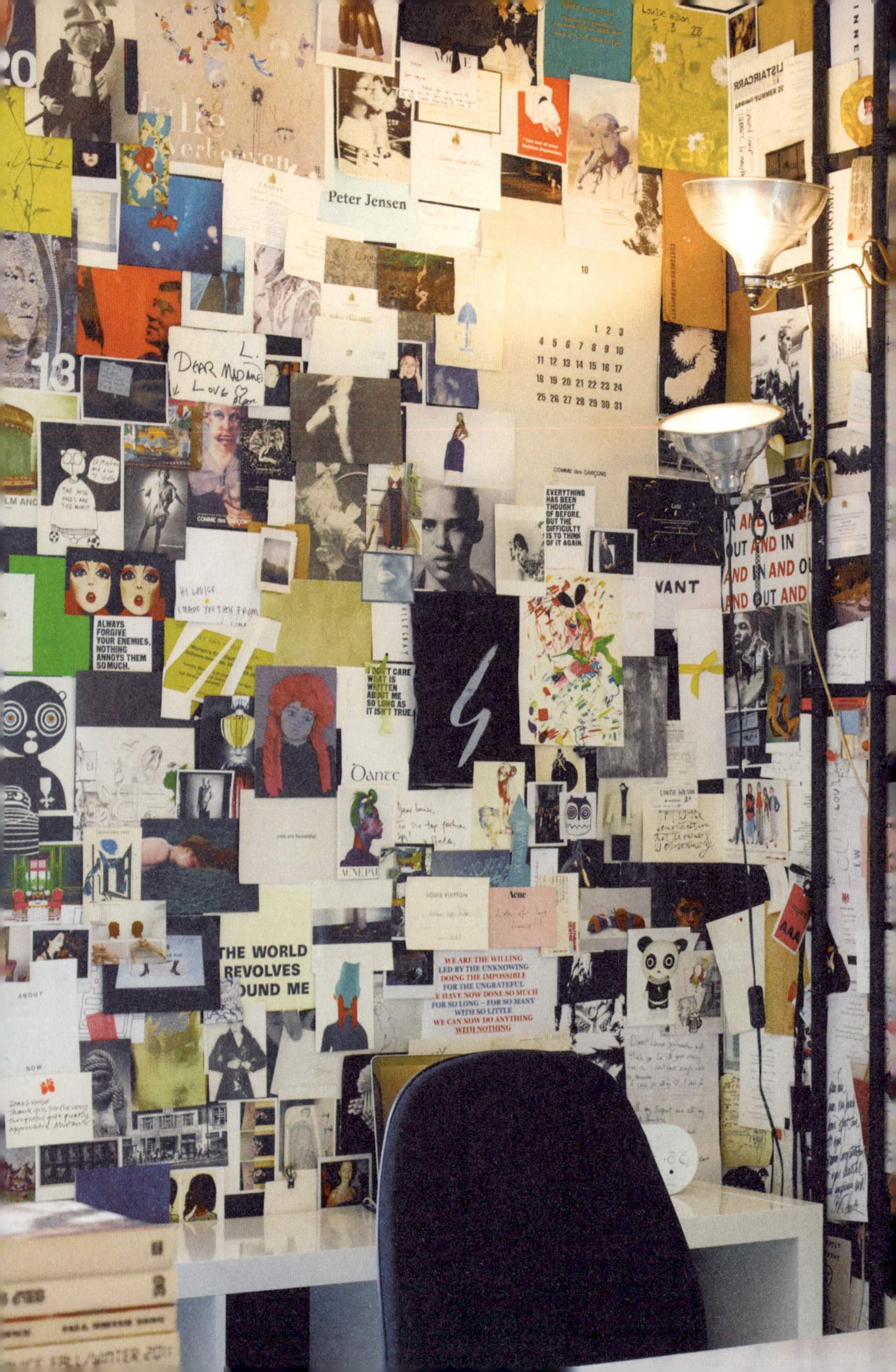
Peter Jensen
COMME des GARÇONS
EVERYTHING HAS BEEN THOUGHT OF BEFORE. BUT THE DIFFICULTY IS TO THINK OF IT AGAIN.
ALWAYS FORGIVE YOUR ENEMIES. NOTHING ANNOYS THEM SO MUCH.
SO LONG AS IT ISN'T TRUE.
Dante
VANT
LOUIS VUITTON
Acne
THE WORLD REVOLVES
WE ARE THE WILLING
LED BY THE UNKNOWING
DOING THE IMPOSSIBLE
FOR THE UNGRATEFUL
FOR SO LONG – FOR SO MANY
WITH SO LITTLE
WE CAN NOW DO ANYTHING
WITH NOTHING

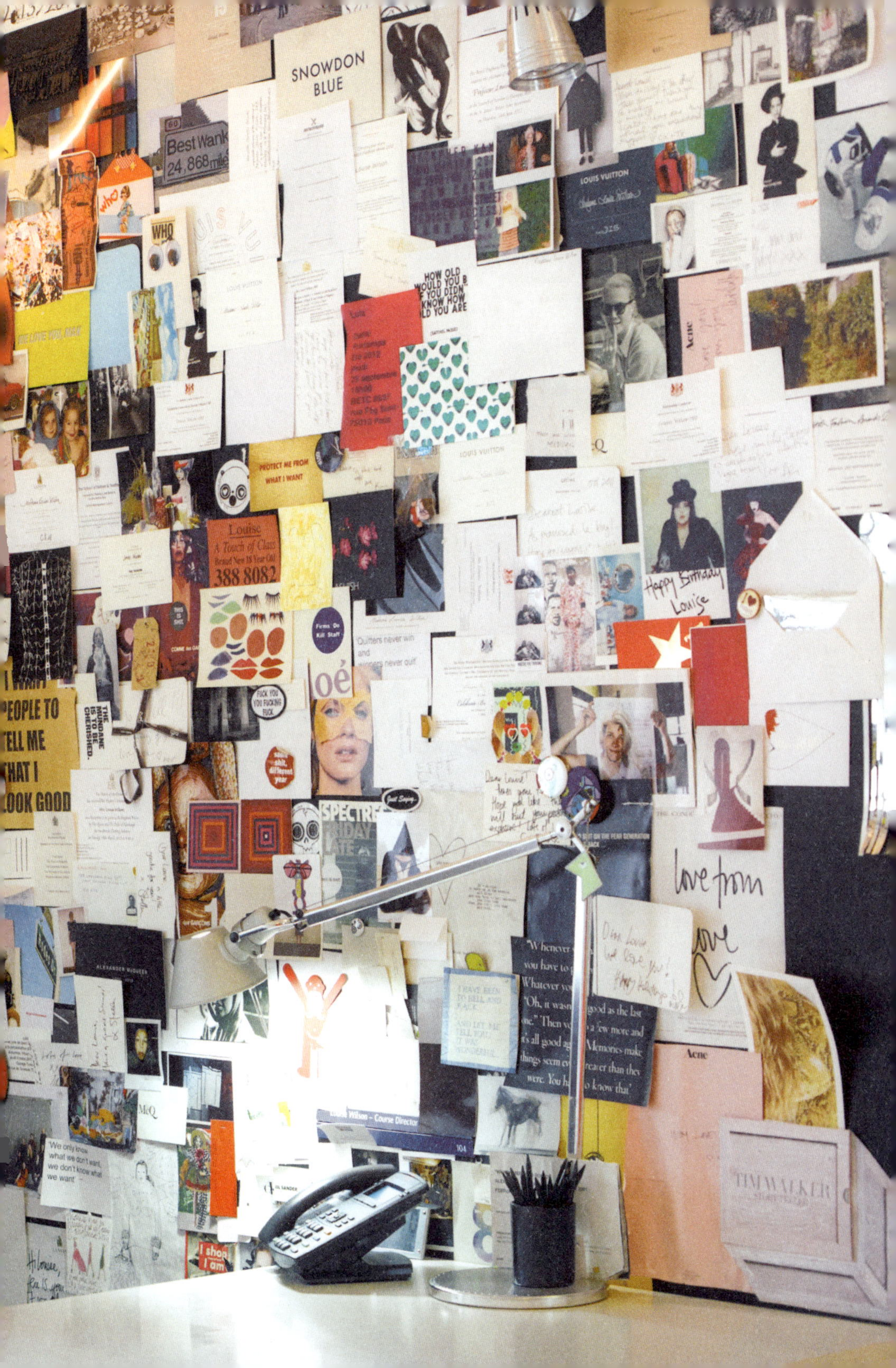

SNOWDON BLUE
Best Wank 24,868 miles
LOUIS VUITTON
PROTECT ME FROM WHAT I WANT
Louise A Touch of Class Brand New 18 Year Old 388 8082
Quitters never win and winners never quit
Happy Birthday Louise
Acne
love from
ALEXANDER McQUEEN
Louise Wilson – Course Director
We only know what we don't want, we don't know what we want
TIM WALKER

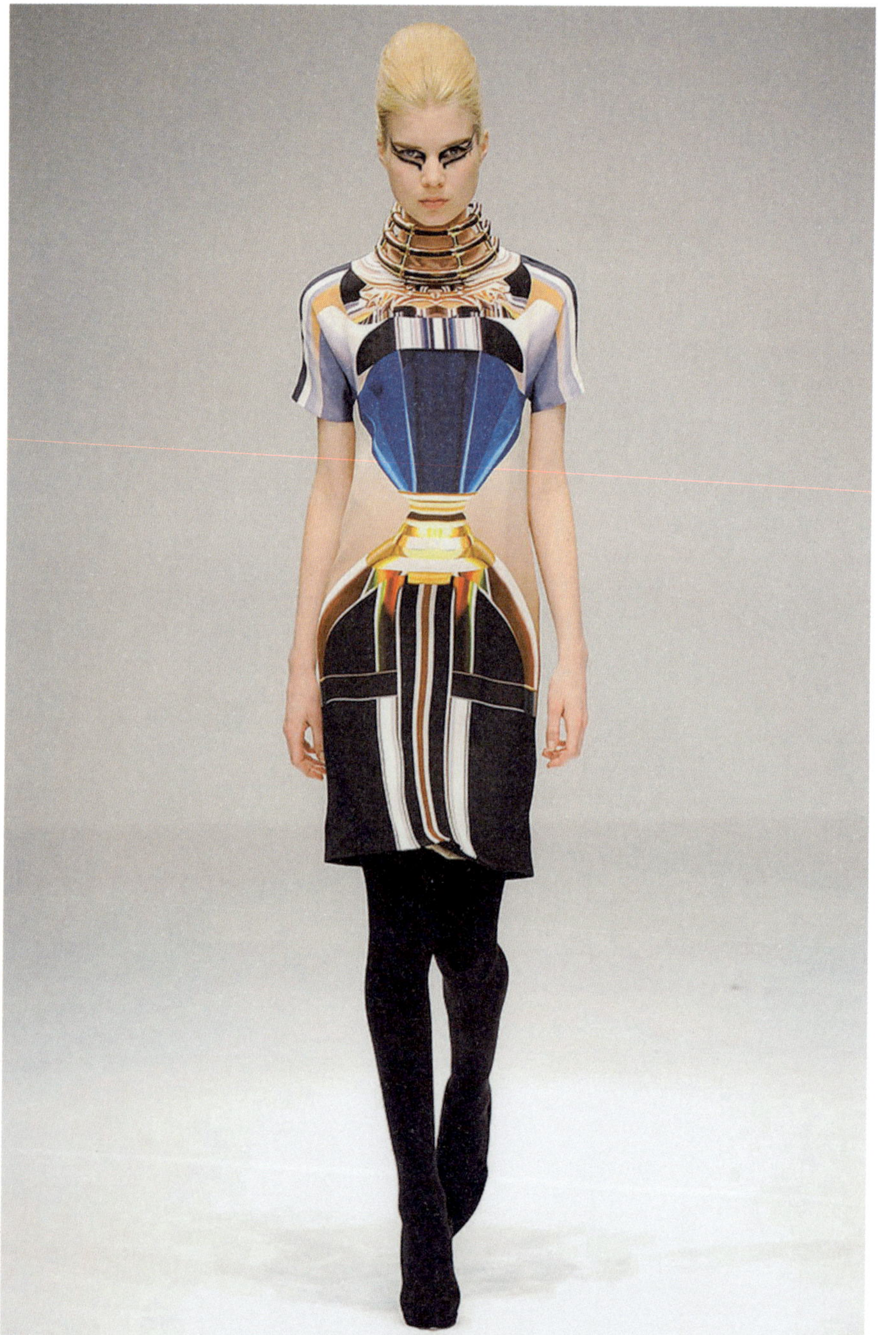

Mary Katrantzou, ready-to-wear collection, Autumn/Winter 2009–10.

I do miss Louise in these conversations. Just having somebody who has been your mentor be there beyond CSM to give you advice - advice that sometimes goes against important things that are happening within the industry - it's something I really miss. I don't feel I have that in my life - somebody who is really independent of everyone. When you talked one-to-one she would tell you what she believed, and that gave you the confidence to make a decision.

STF:
The last time I saw Louise, which was at an exhibition, she talked to me about a certain designer, and she was saying, if you have created an iconic product - say, the Chanel No.5 perfume bottle - why would you want to abandon it and do something totally different? She said that it was important to be careful that you don't, for the sake of a trend or for other people, get rid of your 'Chanel No.5'.

JR:
Though I think there're dangers in that as well. I think she's absolutely right, of course - you don't do a 360-degree turn, because that's not being true to yourself - but students graduate with an identity from college and you can think, third collection out, that looks like what you did at college, that looks like what you did before - please, God, just take another step, you can't just keep repeating yourself! I'm sure that's not quite what she meant, but I remember the pressure when you've got a business to repeat yourself when something is successful. That is an enormous pressure for a young creative coming out - again, whether you're an illustrator, a graphic designer, or whatever. It's like an actor getting typecast, and finding it quite difficult to move on creatively without being scrutinised, criticised. What Louise was talking about is being true to where your own creative life is taking you.

MK:
Yes, the essence. For me, what's important here, and she did say that, is for every designer to find their own 'bandwidth'. It's not that you shouldn't continue experimenting, because she was never against you moving forward, it was about not forgetting who you are.

STF:
From my experience, building brands and selling brands, it's actually about both, and this is the point. It is about the 'signature' and the changes inherent to fashion, and how you tell your new story - how do you move your 'No.5' on? Even the Levi 501 moves forward every season because, if it doesn't, it begins to look old. By the way, I think that what Fabio [Piras, current course director of MA Fashion at CSM] has done this year is wonderful. There is a lot of variety and Fabio is a bit more eclectic, but there is still a strong character inherent to the collections.

I'm not a designer, but I'm a creative professional and I have worked in very many places. My resilience had to be learned; after a while, over the years of hard work, I learned to trust my creative judgement, and my intuition, formed through years of experience. Then, you follow that 'North Star', and the quality that has to accompany that journey is courage. I always work in companies where I have to be the 'disturber'; it's an uncomfortable role, but I'm always hired as the person who will keep saying, let's push on, we can go further.

JR:
It's the grit, it's the grit in the oyster. You also have to maintain a curiosity and you have to be greedy about how you grab moments when you can indulge your curiosity. A metaphor I use, when I'm

talking to students, is that your imagination is the most precious thing you've got as a creative, but it is a bank, and if you keep spending it without putting money in, you go into overdraft and then, eventually, the money stops. You have to ensure that you keep feeding it, and with 'primary' source material, as well – that's how you discover yourself.

We come back, yet again, to this idea of confidence. In the fashion world, you can get criticism from [fashion journalist] Suzy Menkes or from the buyer or from the consumer, and somebody will love it and somebody will hate it, and you will also have the cultural commentator or the art critic stating their opinion. People will project their preoccupations or their particular tastes on the product. There is no 'resilient' product, in that sense.

MK:
What you're trying to find is a product that will last in time, but I think it has to do with being in sync with your times in such a way that people want to project something on to it, and as long as people are projecting – negative or positive – it's giving it a value, and when there is a value to it, it does stand the test of time.

When I started out, it was at the time when [British fashion designer] Phoebe Philo had gone to [French label] Céline, and it was all about minimalism, and I was coming out with digital print and colour. Everyone was saying, it's so niche, no one will buy it. Susan Foslien of the Susan stores in Burlingame came to the London Showrooms with her assistant, and she didn't realise I was a designer sitting there, and she said, who would ever want to wear a perfume [bottle print]? The next year I did a collection based on blown glass and she passed by again but she spoke to me and said, it's very difficult with so much colour, maybe you should look into doing your beautiful shapes in block colour. Then the third season she came, three seasons later, she said, I think what you're doing is brilliant and we want to pick it up. She's very opinionated, and in the moment she was reacting to what she saw, but it interested her enough to repeatedly follow it, because it was different, and eventually to engage with it. It's just that sometimes it happens at different times. On a global scale, when we're tired of something, sometimes it hasn't even reached certain parts of the world!

JR:
That's the point of what you're expecting good graduates to do. There are thousands of designers out there already doing what they're doing and making the clothes that I'm wearing or you're wearing; this is the moment when you have the opportunity to say what you would do if you were in their shoes, which is not repeating what they're doing!

MK:
As long as we do it with conviction.

JR:
With conviction, yes.

MK:
I was asked to judge a graduate fashion week and I knew who I felt I wanted to support, though it was a bit crazy and unconventional. In the end, we decided to give [the award] to her because her book and the way she talked about her work were very convincing – that conviction was there – so it wasn't a matter of taste, it was that her journey was consistent. Whether you liked the end product or not, you had to admit that what she was doing was new; it created conversation, and that was enough.

JR:
I have seen, in my career, some students, though – I would've given my eye teeth for

their talent – and they hadn't got the resilience of personality or character to actually cope with their talent or potential. There is an increasing level of mental health instability in students generally, I think, and in art schools in particular. You have to be very careful that you don't get too involved, because teachers are not necessarily experts – there's always the temptation, particularly as it's such a personal relationship, to think that you can help students, and sometimes, of course, you make matters worse. Often there are complex life problems that students have brought with them, so you have to ensure that those students are supported by people who really know what they're doing. I think the crit can sometimes exacerbate these issues, but experienced staff can usually manage not to do that.

STF:
I have also, as an examiner, been present at the meetings where we have to decide on marks and witnessed how they affect the staff. It is a huge responsibility, and I have felt for everyone in these situations, especially people like Louise, who put themselves on the line. But then, art and creative professions do tend to bring that out even more.

JR:
You also have to remember that students can't get on with everybody, and the staff can't get on with every student. I've always said that if you've got one member of staff who works for you, that's all you need – as long as you can get on a wavelength with them, they can get on a wavelength with you.

STF:
I would also say that a resilient person, overall, is the opposite of one who victimises others or themselves.

MK:
Yes, totally. Being a victim or victimising yourself is the exact opposite of being resilient, absolutely so, and I think it is very important to try not to create a blame culture around yourself anyway. I hate if somebody says, oh it's so-and-so's fault. I don't care about that – it's your responsibility and I want you to come to me with a solution. I don't care who's to blame, I care how we fix it, what we do next. And I think that starts from education, definitely – giving yourself the authority to make those decisions and feel responsible, and it's character-building. I feel that that part of my personality changed in the course under Louise, a hundred per cent. I was shy, I didn't talk, now you can't stop me! My mother didn't even recognise me! It unlocks certain things, certain parts that are important, I feel, for this industry.

In terms of mental health, there is a lot of pressure. Speaking personally, when I feel I'm doing a lot of things socially, I feel drained – but it's not that I don't enjoy it or I don't like connecting with people, because I do, but somehow when I get home I feel absolutely drained. I think you have to know when you're going too much against your own grain and when to protect yourself.

And I always had, amid that independence, a lot of self-doubt. We were out for dinner – [British fashion journalist and editor] Sarah Mower, Louise Wilson, my partner and I – and, at some point, Marios, my partner, asked Louise, how is it that Mary has achieved everything she has achieved and she's still not confident in herself? She gave me this amazing quote from [art critic] Robert Hughes, which goes 'perfect confidence is granted to the less talented as a consolation prize.' And there's so much truth in that, in the sense that creative people are often full of fragility and doubt.

JR:

Yes, and you need it. As long as it's not crippling, you do need a little bit of self-doubt, because it gives you a bit of humility, and it also enables you to recognise when you've done something wrong and recognise why it went wrong. Otherwise, you don't self-examine or analyse what's happening.

STF:

I was going to mention Sarah Mower myself, because I had a meeting with her a couple of weeks ago and we actually talked about this. I realised that Louise created a community of like-minded, resilient people, and that resilient people are not tough, as such – they are actually quite open and vulnerable.

JR:

I think it is actually an intrinsic part of being resilient – it's not about being rigid and protective, it's about being flexible, because the world changes around you all the time: your circumstances change, the people you meet change, the industries change. If you are creative, whether you are an artist or a designer or a musician or a writer, part of your role is that you are reflecting your society and therefore you have to have that adaptability because everything changes around you.

MK:

To me, being adaptable is a huge part of your intelligence as a person, to be able to be adaptable. I think it's an important strength in a person to be able to adapt.

JR:

Everybody has to find a balance, depending on their own temperament, as to what adaptability means and how much you resist adaptability – as you were saying, about not being knocked off your track because it's not you, not your bandwidth. I think that is a really good analogy. Designers have to be somewhere in between, where they do know where they are going but they can be flexible enough, pragmatic enough, about what can and can't be achieved.

There's an element we haven't touched on, which is family. Family is significant, whether it's parents or siblings or a 'family' of friends. I think it's about emotional stability and the sort of sense of self that parents can give their children, or that children steal for themselves, from wherever.

MK:

It's true – it's not as if I'm sharing the business with my parents or my partner, but, definitely, because both of my parents also had their own businesses, I grew up with that, and the work ethic that I was taught came from my experience of living with my parents. I say I didn't believe in myself, but if I didn't believe in myself at all I would never have applied to RISD; if I really didn't believe in myself at all I wouldn't have gone to CSM.

The relationship that I had with Louise – because she was so supportive I wanted to prove to her that she was right in being supportive. It is important to find certain people who become your extended family – people that you look up to, that you want to prove yourself to, people that you know you can take advice from. You may only have one or two, and that to me is, not as strong as family, but a very important support system to have.

WHITTINGDALE RESIDENCY

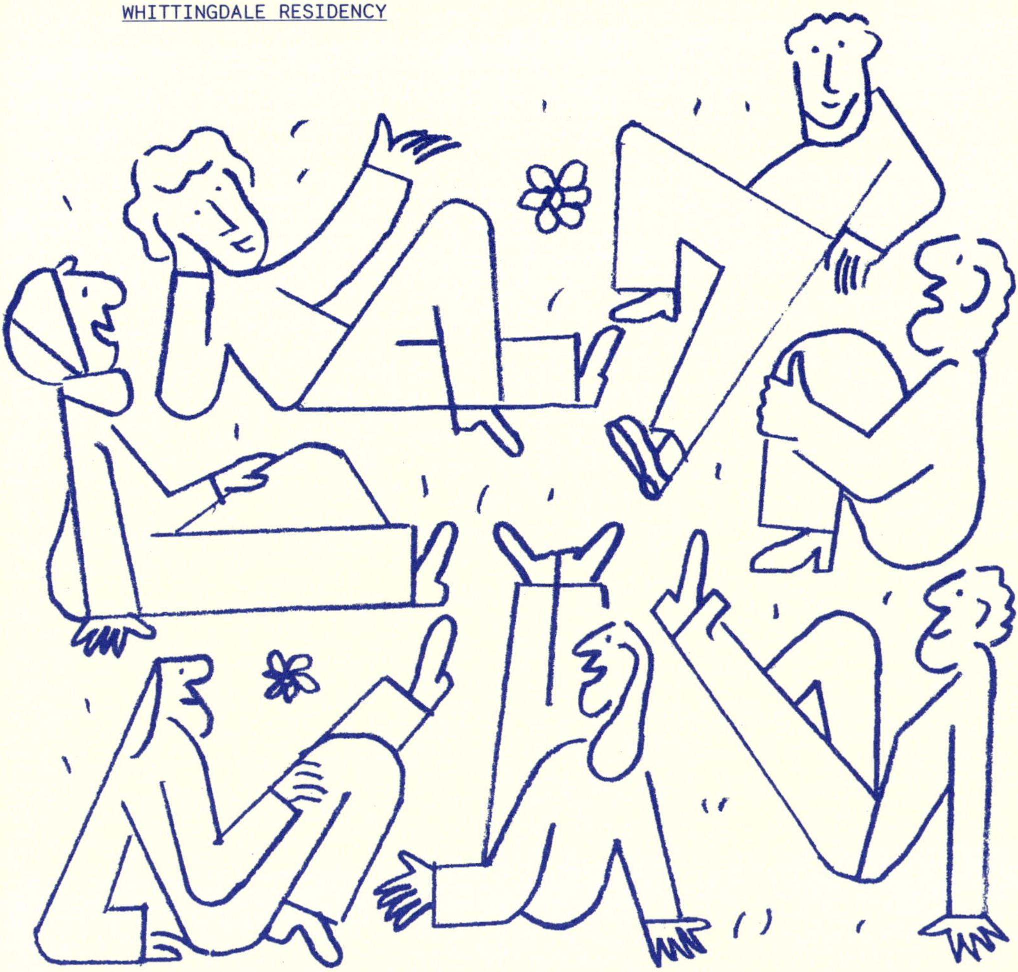

Since graduating from university, the members of artist group CaW (derived from 'CoR' or 'Cultures of Resilience') have continued to discuss and perform strategies for sustaining a 'resilient' art practice. The latest such strategy was the 'Whittingdale Residency' (2015), named for the then Conservative Secretary of State for Culture, Media and Sport, John Whittingdale. This 'nomadic' residency was open to any recent art graduate and championed 'the kind of brilliant useless activity that you cannot monetise'. Participants read, sang, swam, performed and engaged in informal 'crits', all the while discussing the challenges facing emerging artists, including a lack of affordable studio space and time outside their day jobs. Over the final weekend, residents built their own, public 'pavilion' from scrap materials.

DESIGN AGAINST CRIME

How do we, as a society, help both criminals and victims become more resilient to crime? How can we develop designs resistant to criminal activity, while also tackling the root causes of criminality? These are questions explored by the innovative Design Against Crime Research Centre (DACRC), founded by Lorraine Gamman (Professor of Design at University of the Arts London) at Central Saint Martins

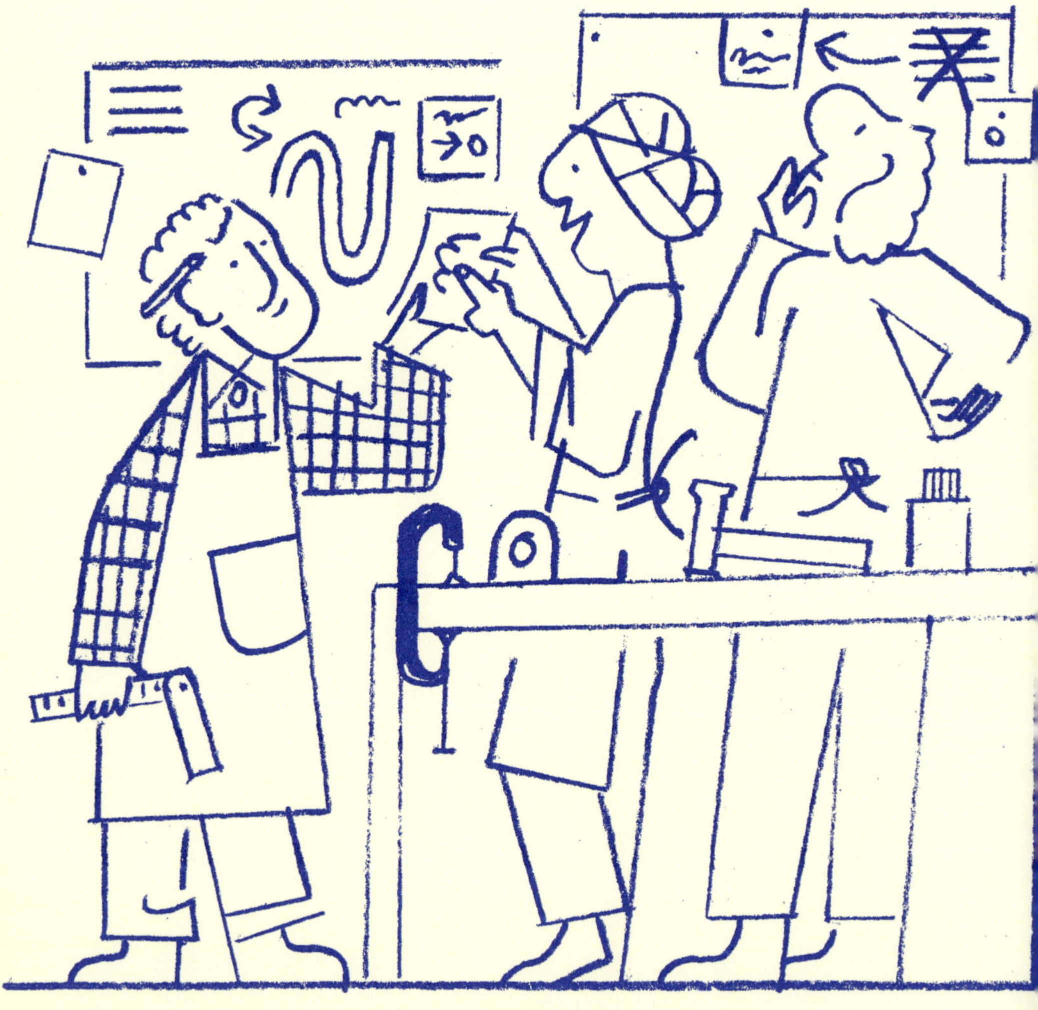

in 1999. From 'Bikeoff' – a four-year research project addressing bike theft and promoting crime-free cycling ('M'-stand designs, co-created with the London Cycle Campaign, are now on the streets of Britain) – through to recent programmes that bring rehabilitative, 'design thinking' education to prison industries, all DACRC projects understand that collaboration and building empathy are key to finding out why crime happens, and what to do about it.

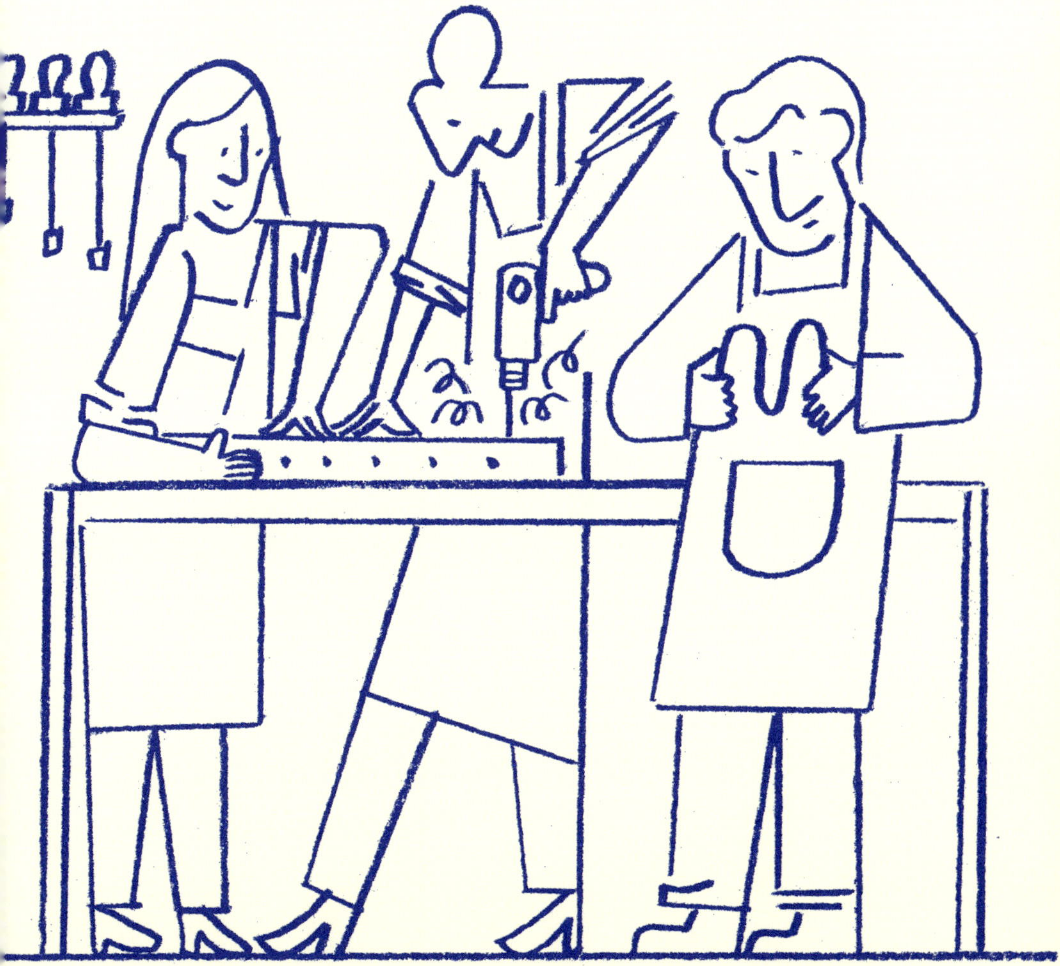

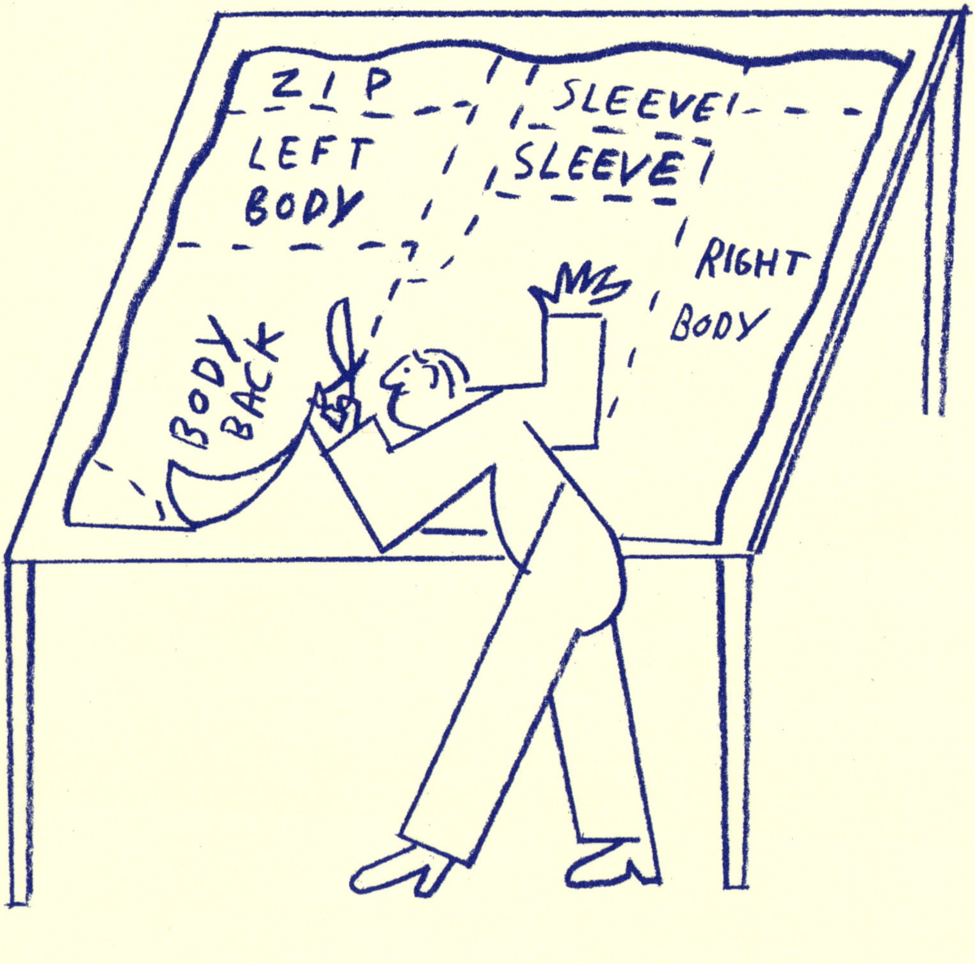

Coming out of the Textiles Environment Design research group (part of the exciting Textile Futures Research Centre, or TFRC, based at University of the Arts London), the VF Project required participants to produce exhibits showcasing new approaches to sustainable, resilient design. Brands under the umbrella of the US-based VF Corporation include Timberland, Vans, Wrangler and The North Face; at a conference and exhibition in 2012, in the TED-curated 'Responsible Living' section, representatives of these brands were presented with innovative prototypes. These included a denim double cloth, made in collaboration with Philippa Brock of Central Saint Martins, UAL, and woven in response to research on pressure points on jeans; a beautiful second layer of cloth was revealed in response to friction and wear. Other innovative and practical solutions included a no-waste jacket pattern, with minimal seaming (design by David Telfer) and a no-launder textile prototype.

AMBIGUITY

Lucy Orta

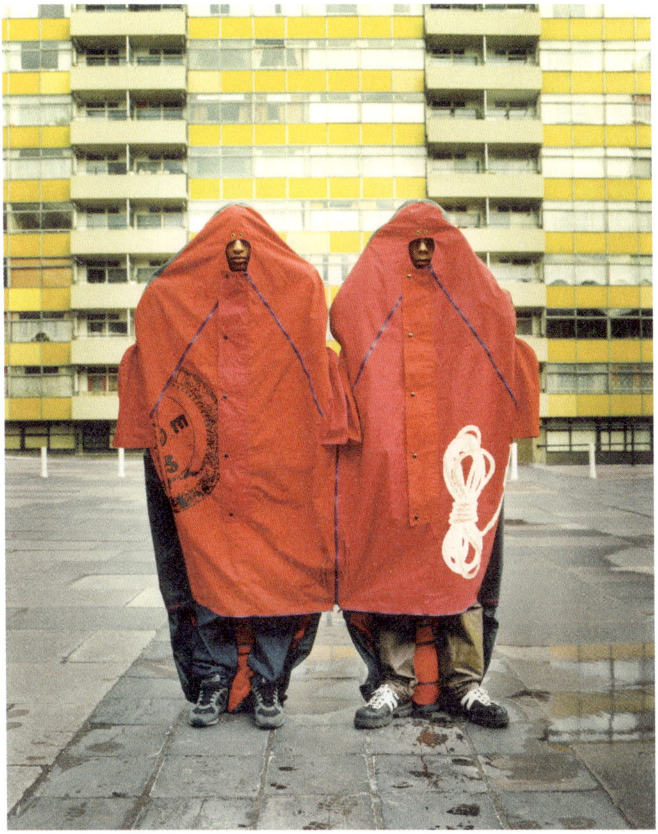

Lucy + Jorge Orta, *Refuge Wear Intervention*, 1998.

By definition, *ambiguity* itself is ambiguous. It is up to us to make a judgement – nothing is dictated, nothing is sure. Ambiguity can either imply 'uncertainty', in the sense of 'open to multiple interpretations'; or it could mean 'uncertain' in the sense that something or someone is 'dubious', or even 'dodgy'. The latter meaning is somewhat pejorative, so for the sake of this reflection I will make reference to the word's Latin root, *ambi-*, meaning 'both', or, as I interpret it, 'not having one obvious meaning'.

Actually living or being in a state of ambiguity is a very demanding idea to entertain – it is a state of limbo, a frightening space of uncertainty, like that of a tightrope walker who is constantly unstable. Ambiguity requires us to adapt to the surroundings, like a chameleon, which transforms seamlessly from one colour to the other. But isn't this exactly what makes ambiguity so intriguing? Being ambiguous is always on the cusp – neither-nor, casting doubt. Where there is doubt, there is space for great imagination.

As an artist, ambiguity is something I grapple with every day, on different levels. During the process of creation, as an idea evolves from the doodle, to the sketch, to the synthesis drawing – a two-dimensional drawing that synthesises all the preceding doodles into a form that can be clearly materialised in three dimensions – I am constantly questioning that idea's level of ambiguity, i.e., whether it has the capacity to evoke or stimulate ambiguous responses. I judge the potential success of the final idea when I think I have left enough space for the observer to question, to wonder and to be bemused by what they see, so that they are not sure if it's one thing or the other. If the hypothesis proves successful, then it's more than likely that the observer will engage more carefully with the work – their immediate, spontaneous interpretation will be knocked off its rails and will have left an immense, wide-open track for meandering and contemplation. In essence, the work can be said to be successful if it offers multiple deeper meanings that perdure over time.

The eminent neurobiologist Semir Zeki expresses this idea as follows: 'Great art is that which corresponds to as many different concepts in as many different brains over as long a period of time as possible. Ambiguity is such a prized characteristic of all great art because it can correspond to many different concepts.'[1]

Zeki's comment about the 'many different brains' places the role of ambiguity in an even more important position in our societies today. Not only will our work be subjected to the scrutiny of our close peers in our networks, but it now has the ability to traverse continents and cultures, thanks to the reach of social media. I'm not suggesting that when we create work we should be catering for all the world's opinions, but it does strike me that the work of artists who deliberately toy with notions of ambiguity will have a better chance of transcending communication barriers, and offering something of interest to a larger number of people.

According to scientific research in the field of visual perception, there are a number of methods and techniques that artists can use to deploy formal ambiguity. The researcher Pascal Mamassian from the laboratory of the Psychology of Perception, Université Paris Descartes, lists these as: composition, spatial scale, illumination and colour, three-dimensional layout, shape and movement.[2] I would add to this list intentional ambiguity, which is something I try to incorporate in my work, and which operates on the semantic level, i.e., the image or object may be perceptually unambiguous, but the meaning and narrative may be ambiguous. Take, for example, the series of works *Life Line* (2008–ongoing). These resemble a life-saving device (a life jacket), but on closer inspection they're not really; the objects carry multiple meanings and messages associated with survival – the provision of empathy, drinking water, food. Another example would be *Refuge Wear* (1992–8, see p.89), a series of works that resemble, simultaneously, tents and sleeping bags, rucksacks and clothing; the work is intentionally designed to be ambiguous, because it is all of these things at the same time, hence the title.

We must develop new vocabularies for describing the ambiguous methods we employ and the things we create as a result. Mamassian describes this kind of artistic practice as 'violating principles' and 'promoting new styles'.[3] Although he does not intend this as a negative criticism, as an artist it is a scary place to be, because it implies notions of transgression and rubbing up against set conventions. It also suggests, however, that you can be pioneering and innovative, forging a new and exciting path where no one has trodden before.

If what we do as artists is so new that it 'violates principles', it is then impossible to talk about ambiguity without touching upon conformity or stereotype. We live in a system of categorisation and monitored data sets that force us to define our sexuality, race, profession, etc. We are constantly asked to conform to a set of established social norms, to be either one thing or the other, and more often than not we are not allowed to be 'ambi', let alone several things at the same time. I wouldn't be surprised if the number of 'other' survey boxes ticked by creative individuals is significantly higher than for those in more 'conformist' professions.

However, there is still a lot more work to be done to de-categorise our artistic disciplines and allow them to become more ambiguous and mutable, to become *ambi-disciplinary*, or even *trans-disciplinary*. I am constantly being asked if what I do is art, fashion, architecture, design or even social work because, at first glance, it is ambiguous. I think the kinds of question or misunderstanding that ambiguity provokes are down to our immediate unwillingness to accept or process it. Processing ambiguity means we need to step outside our comfort zone of conformity, convention and stereotype – we need to develop patience for reflection and a capacity for deep analysis. And, we need to no longer be afraid of doubt.

We have to learn to balance confidently on the tightrope and develop the reflexes to change colour like the chameleon. Then we can confidently use the characteristics of ambiguity to cast doubt within ourselves and others with intelligence and sincerity. Where there is doubt, there is space for self-innovation and for stimulating the imaginations of others.

Notes

1. Semir Zeki, 'Neural Concept Formation and Art: Dante, Michelangelo, Wagner', *Journal of Consciousness Studies*, no.9, 2002, p.67.
2. Pascal Mamassian, 'Ambiguities and Conventions in Visual Art', *Vision Research*, vol.48, issue 20, 2008, pp.2143–53.
3. Ibid.

In conversation on 'ambiguity'

Sophia Al-Maria

William Raban

Pratap Rughani

Sophia Al-Maria
(SAM)

Artist, writer and film-maker

William Raban
(WR)

Film-maker and Professor of Film at London College of Communication, UAL

Pratap Rughani
(PR)

Film-maker, Reader and Course Director of MA Documentary Film, London College of Communication, UAL

The participants were asked to discuss the topic of creative ambiguity, with particular reference to their respective fields within film-making and writing for film. They begin with their definitions of 'ambiguity' in relation to creativity.

WR:
Ambiguity for me is about non-fixity of meaning. And in my work – certainly the work I was doing in the 1990s, up to 2010 – my films construct meaning by image and sound alone. Without voice or text as the primary agent. *About Now MMX* [2010], my last work produced on 35mm film, is a good example. There is no text at all, except for a few words on advertising hoardings and anti-capitalist slogans that appear within two shots. Working with ambiguity, for me, is less of an aesthetic choice and more of an ethical, perhaps even a philosophical imperative. That's because it's anti-didactic, and empowers the spectator to exercise agency in the construction of meaning. It's about having open texts, as opposed to closed texts. Film communicates through the senses – constructs an embodied experience that is to do with both thinking and feeling.

PR:
Ambiguity, for me, has a very significant function – not just in helping me explore the vector and direction of a film work, but also in informing the way that one conducts oneself throughout that process. What I mean is that film is a kind of dance through which a visual idea comes into focus and then dissolves into, sometimes disparate, associations. The image I have in mind is sort of like an hourglass, with the place where the hourglass goes wide standing for the function and role of ambiguity. Ambiguity can draw me away from fixity, or certainty that I know the way that life plays out for the key ideas or people who are typically the subjects of my documentaries. It can arrest the imposition of my world view on the 'other'. Ambiguity has a very useful strategic role – it can help interrupt, disrupt, some of the meta-narrative that can prevent me from seeing the person I'm working with in something more like their own terms, with their own history, identity and way of seeing the world. At the same time, that function of ambiguity in forcing interruption, and taking apart preconceptions, means that one's practice and the film-making process will have to be more finely attuned to the 'crucial moment' – the point where the hourglass narrows – in order to find coherence and focus. So, for me, there's a dance, if you like, between opening the windows, casting the net of interpretation wide – moving towards the wideness of the hourglass – and then, once that's integrated and understood, moving into a period of disambiguity, or of making clear that which has become apparent. When you're filming, you ask yourself, where are the ruthless edges of my frame, of both the image and narrative? Those are very distinct and clear decisions that one has to make continually. Makers who I admire manage to elucidate a vision embedded in their subjects' experience yet still manage to encode a range of readings in their final film.

SAM:
I'm going to talk more as a screenwriter than anything else, in response to both of your definitions. Because I think that the scriptwriting process is the bedded-down mulch, if you will, of what will eventually become the finished film! I'm at a strange moment, where I've written a dozen scripts. And, as is the case for many screenwriters, nothing has been made yet. So I exist, as a screenwriter, in a very ambiguous place of not having seen the final frame or the embodiment of a character in an actor and their performance. It's almost like being in the amniotic fluid of one's creative process. I find it a bit terrifying sometimes, handing over my work to the director.

WR:
Is that to do with relinquishing control?

SAM:
It is. To relinquish control is obviously a liberating thing in itself, but I find that the power dynamic is very tricky. I frequently end up in very long midwifing relationships with directors.

PR:
I used to work as a script editor for BBC1, particularly with new or young writers navigating that path. So I appreciate what you mean about that process, and it reveals the double-edged nature of ambiguity. The beauty of ambiguity is to hold us open to different kinds of reading, to suggest that life is different from how we might imagine it. The more treacherous side, or the side that can threaten an integrity of practice, is where ambiguity becomes a kind of excuse *not* to know more deeply, an excuse not to come to make a difficult decision or commitment to pursue a central meaning as it unfolds in relation to the other.

A phrase resonates here in relation to my recent film *Justine* [2013; see opposite] – a phrase that I was given by Kate Adams and that we used in the book connected to it: 'the art of not knowing'.[1] This film is a portrait of a young woman, a wonderful woman called Justine, with what's called Advanced Neurological Disorder. She barely speaks. And, unlike William, I use words and interview material quite a bit ...

WR:
Well, my three most recent films are wordy. *The Houseless Shadow* [2011; see overleaf] voices the Charles Dickens essay 'Night Walks' [1861] on the soundtrack, though it was my intention that the images would have the primary function of revealing that, in terms of homelessness, nothing has fundamentally changed in London over the last 150 years. But for sure, I do strive for verbal economy.

PR:
Yes, and my recent films have used far fewer! But, you know, with words, there's the attraction of thinking that one can fix a particular meaning. But that can be a mirage, an illusion – it's not the whole truth. So, coming back to Justine, I'm working with somebody who barely speaks, and many of the ways in which one would usually talk about a subject's consent, even informed consent, in documentary practice are not relevant.

The filming situation completely rested in the potential of ambiguity – the beauty of ambiguity – on being able to step into a space where what I thought I might do could be interrupted by trying to intuit how it might have been experienced by another. In this case, it was about exploring the language of gesture, of intuition, of inference and feeling. And ultimately, it's beyond text and it's beyond words.

I have found it important to develop a methodology in film practice that can acknowledge this realm of 'not knowing' – a place of doubt. But I also see a potential danger in ambiguity, where it becomes a get-out from making the most difficult artistic decisions, about how a work finds form.

SAM:
It's also dangerous in terms of that ambiguous space that you're talking about – getting to it with your subjects. Are you ever, in your work, concerned about that final 'ruthless' frame being a projection of your own concerns?

PR:
Yes, and I think that if you're not open to that possibility, then that's more

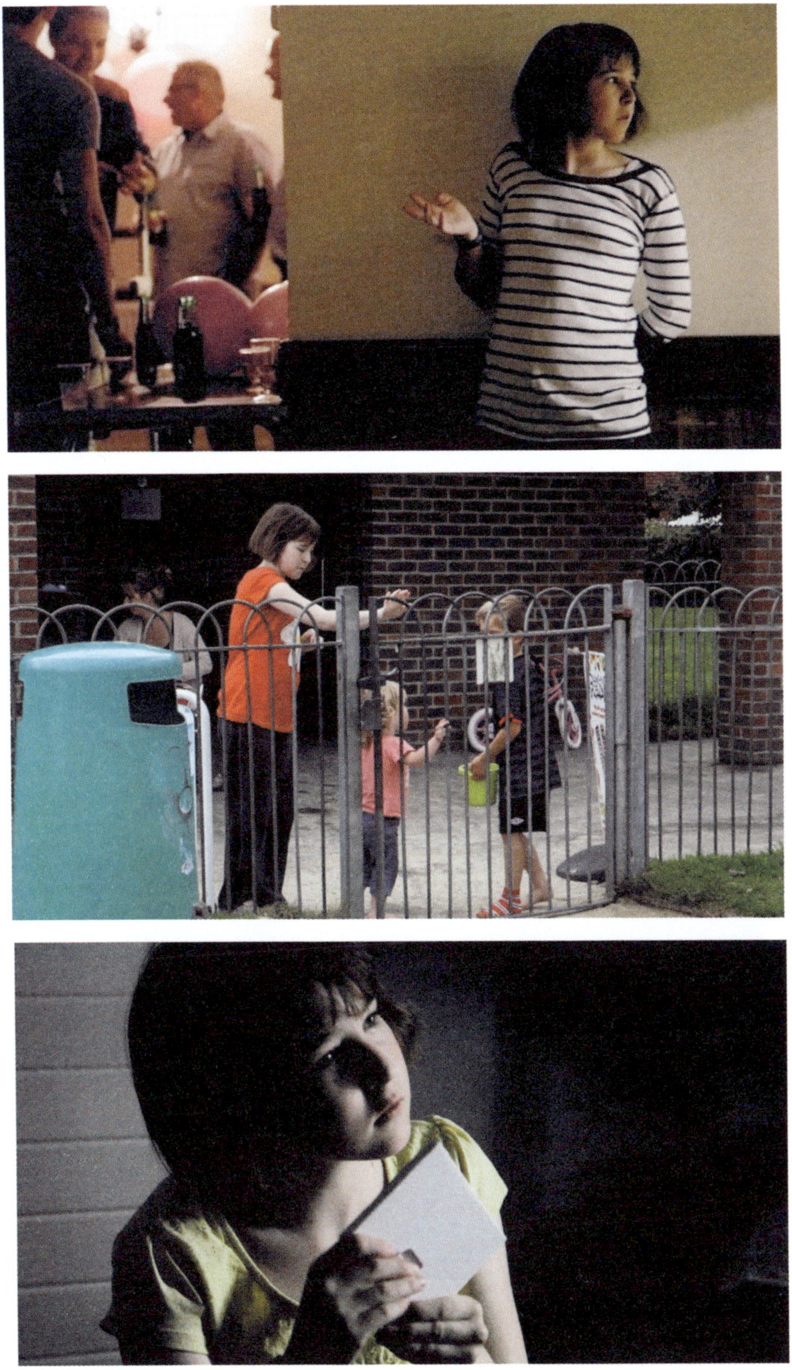

Pratap Rughani, *Justine* (stills), 2013.

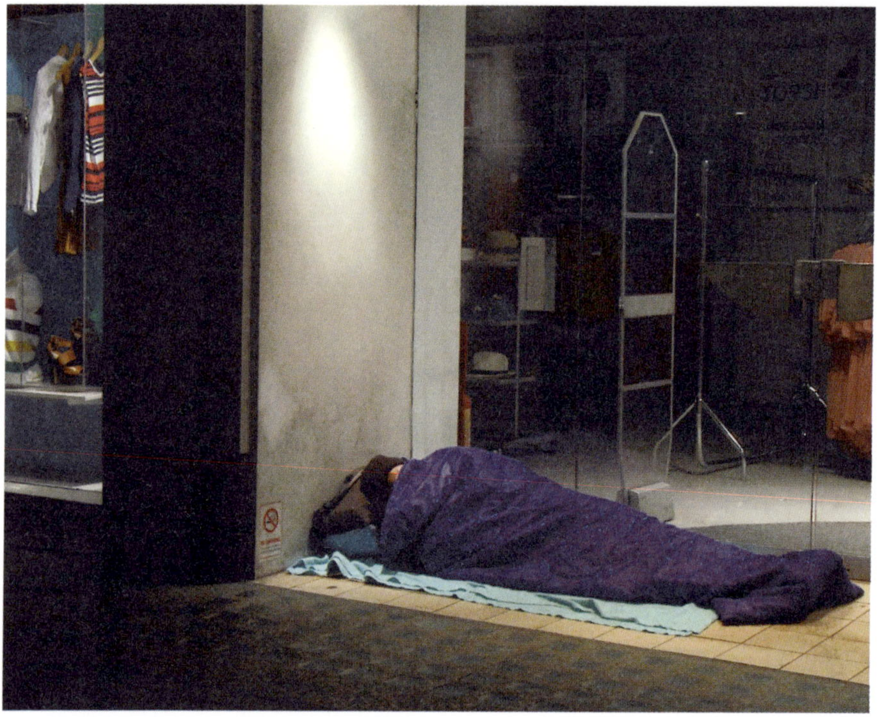

William Raban, *The Houseless Shadow* (still), 2011.

dangerous than if you're not worried! But I think a conversation like this, if it comes from a place of honesty, can help. And I should say, I don't mean 'ruthless' in the sense of imposing a director's or camera-person's view of things over the sensibility of another. I mean ruthless in recognising that edges of a frame mark borders of exclusion; choices that are at the heart of directing.

WR:
I want to open this up and pick up on an earlier point that Pratap made, which is to do with the slipperiness of words. There's a wonderful quote from Hermann Hesse, the German writer, which articulates this very well:

> Words do not express thought very well. They always become a little different immediately they are expressed, a little distorted, a little foolish. And yet it also pleases me and seems right that what is of value and wisdom to one man seems nonsense to another.[2]

And I think in that last point, that what is of value and wisdom to one mind may seem nonsense to another, is a terrific comment on the ambiguity of text, and of language. I am interested in how ambiguity informs my process, and I think it's very much at the level of process that it does so, and certainly with no deliberate intention to obfuscate meaning.

PR:
Is there a sense in which ambiguity serves the bigger exploration going on in your writing or film?

WR:
I think there's a lovely contrast between what I think I might be doing, and what I find that I have done when I look at the shot in the edit. And I may have gone out with a very specific intention – to get a particular shot, with its own dynamics, and conveying one particular meaning. And then I look at it in the edit, and actually, it's telling something quite other than intended.

SAM:
I wonder if the process is any different ... You were saying you shoot on film?

WR:
I used to shoot on film.

SAM:
No longer?

WR:
Up until six years ago.

SAM:
That immediacy of seeing something on a monitor or on a little LCD screen, in digital film-making, is very different from only seeing what you've got post-development. So I'm curious for both of your takes on that moment: the alchemy that happens inside the camera and the alchemy that happens in the edit being very different things.

WR:
[Soviet director and film theorist] Dziga Vertov writes about this brilliantly. He talks about the different levels of editing; there're six different stages of editing he identifies: from the first observation of something, to the editing in the camera – the shooting of it – and then, of course, the extended levels of editing during post-production.

SAM:
Of course, that's forgetting the series of drafts and edits that began even before filming, too.

PR:
There is definitely something about digital technology that's affected how I work. In the first six years I was typically shooting on 16mm film – or sometimes Super 16 – and you wouldn't fully know what you'd got ...

WR:
That was the beauty of analogue film – the latency of the image.

PR:
Yes. You might be a month on location, maybe somewhere a very long way away; you might get reports or occasionally see some rush prints, but that was more to do with technical considerations – just checking that things were at the correct exposure, etc. Whereas now, if you're really not sure about things, in a break or if you feel it necessary at the time, you can go back and check and re-listen. You can even, if appropriate, involve your contributors in that process. That is tricky and interesting territory ... I think it just shifts the ambiguity to somewhere else, though. I don't feel that it's heralded 'the arrival of certainty'.

WR:
That touches on what you were saying about research ethics. Being able to show your participants the shots you've just taken gives them some agency in or control over how they're being represented on film.

SAM:
Or how to represent themselves in the next take?

PR:
Yes, it may do that. For some people it can make them seize up with self-consciousness; for others, it can build their confidence. But I think there's an important editorial step between sharing what you've shot, as distinct from allowing the other a chance to say, actually, no, I don't like that – can I say something different instead? Or, can you get my good side?

There was a particular stage in making *Justine* that threw this up for me. We had made a rough cut of the film – edited by a very talented young film-maker, Esperanza Jimenez – and took it to show Justine and her family. We had a wonderful interaction with the family, which we recorded as well. At the end of it, the family said, yes, that's good, but *we* want to say something now. And I'd thought of this as a nearly wordless film – Justine's film. The one thing I didn't want was people speaking on her behalf! And then I thought more about it and realised, well, it's their film, too, and if they're saying that they need to express things in order to help people understand their experience of being Justine's family – and they had their own agenda of agitating, quite rightly, for more support – I thought, well, who am I to stand in the way of that? Yes, it's completely different to what I'd imagined, but let's do that. It's a strange film, in a sense, because there's no one talking about Justine in interview through the main body of the narrative. However, you hear the ambient, synchronous sound, so the audience has an immersive experience of being in Justine's world, where at times people do talk *about* her, without necessarily speaking directly to her. Then, in the final sequence, we have a moment in which a series of hard-cut interviews offer insights into how her family experiences life with her, which repositions the whole thing.

SAM:
I have two questions for you. Firstly, I find it quite, perhaps disturbing isn't the right slippery word …

PR:
Troubling?

SAM:
Troubling. Mother-daughter relationships are eternally ambiguous, so a situation where the mother takes agency to speak for her daughter is, I guess, troubling? But then, my question to you is, where does your responsibility lie? Towards the subject, or towards the work?

PR:
Yes, that's a great question. I've tried in the past to write about this question of which gods we're following: the god of artistic expression? The god of the relationship between ethics and aesthetics?[3] It's hard to weigh competing responsibilities, and I'm not sure how fruitful it would be to try and answer in the abstract, but it makes sense in specific filming conditions. I was making some documentary work in the aftermath of an atrocity, a series of murders designed to spread terror, and I ended up writing about it in a chapter called 'Are You a Vulture?', which was asking documentary practitioners what on earth we think we're doing – making our work, our practice, from the suffering of others.[4] And it wasn't an argument that we shouldn't make work that responds to suffering, but that we should be 'decently troubled' by the attempt: that our practice should live in the tension between the two positions that you're

rightly pushing me to show how I make decisions about. Yes, one's artistic practice has to be alive, in order for it to have a chance of communicating something of value, but, at the same time, no film is created, made or exhibited outside an historical or political context. And these decisions are resolved, if resolved is the right word, in the truthful, inventive process of discovering what unfolds in the cutting room. Just to go back to the discussion of editing: there's a wonderful moment – a crucial moment, anyway, for me – when I hand over the rushes to an editor and sometimes I don't really say much. Obviously, you pick who you work with very carefully, and I might even invite the editor to location or to meet some of the people in the film, but I'm interested in how an editor – someone with perhaps a different gradient of looking, or sensibility to mine – might see the rushes that I bring back, so I try not to *tell* them how I want it to be in any really specific way, at least initially. It's another moment in which you can cast the net wide and see what can emerge.

SAM:
Collaboration, in terms of what I do, is often very painful, though. The number of voices one has in one's own head while writing something can be very dangerous for the final product. It's certainly the case with things like workshops. I went to the Sundance Screenwriting Lab last year, for example, with a screenplay of my own to direct – we'd already shot a load of documentary footage of the Eid el-Adha slaughter in Cairo. And in the end, having ten extra voices, after having years of too many finance and producer voices (it was my rookie error), I feel I didn't perform my responsibility to the work by protecting it from this cacophony. Film, essentially, is at a certain scale, and the scale at which I wanted to achieve that project was necessarily going to have to be collaborative, so I falsely believed that to allow more voices would only make it better. It was an important lesson to learn.

WR:
I feel that there's a kind of balance to be struck. A lot of my work is, of its very nature, documentary, in that I don't go into studios to create my shots. There's definitely a documentary aspect to what I'm doing – I am more interested in what is happening out there on the street. And I try and do as much as I can by myself, because that's the way I've always worked; for me, it's very important that I shoot the images and, as far as possible, edit the images myself as well. I'm not sure it would be productive to hand over the picture to an editor. I do rely on David Cunningham to process all the sound and produce the soundtrack – I have done, for the last twenty years or so. The luxury that I demand when I'm making something is time. Particularly in the edit. The twelve-minute film *A 13* that I made in 1994 took me fifteen months to make, and that was all time in the edit, figuring it out. And it went through many different transitions and changes over the course of shooting, and editing on a Steenbeck [flatbed film-editing table].

SAM:
How delicious.

WR:
Well, it's delicious up to a certain point, but it does make radical changes quite difficult. You've got to have a system. You've got to be very well-organised and know where all your shots are, to start with. Then, if you're going to break it up – what you've edited, what you've spent two weeks working on – you've got to put

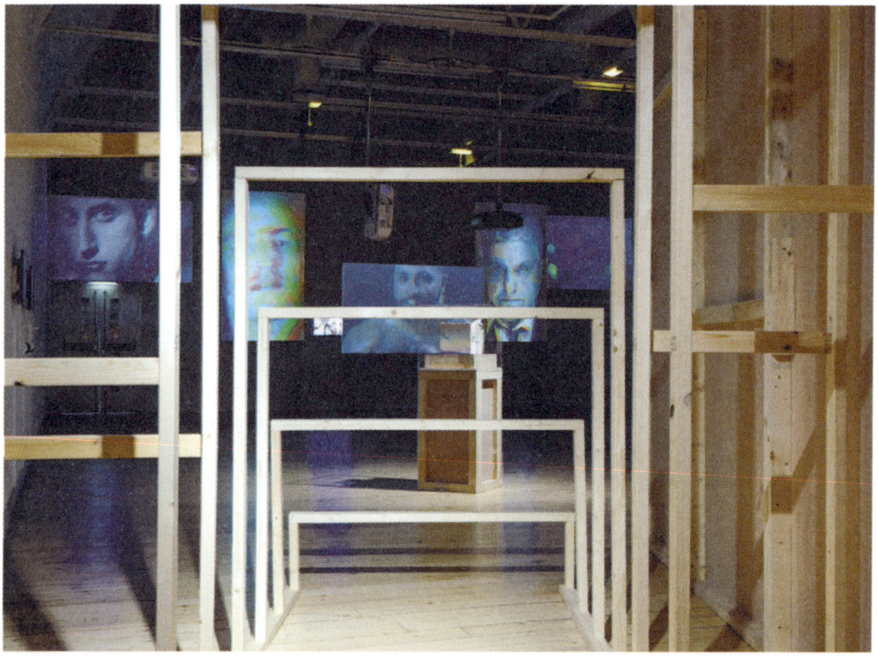

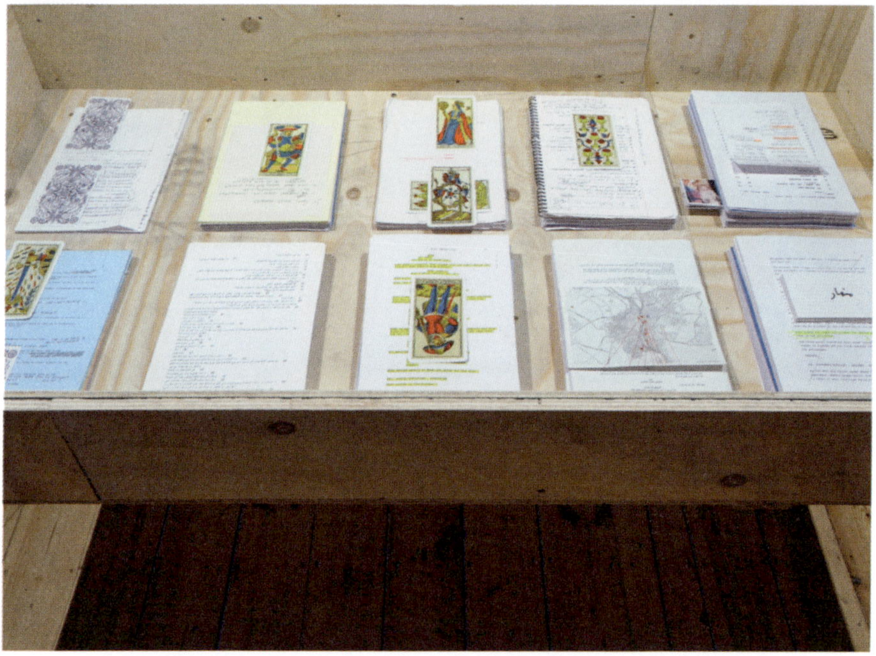

Sophia Al-Maria, material for unmade film *Beretta*, including draft scripts installed with 'a Tarot reading my friend Fatima did for me which gave me the clarity to stop', *Sophia Al-Maria: Virgin with a Memory*, Home Gallery, Manchester, 6 September – 2 November 2014.

everything back in the place that you found it before you can start again.

PR:
That is one of the gifts of the digital revolution – to have a number of edits and be able to check and change things.

WR:
Well, you can have thirty simultaneous cuts going on at the same time if you choose to. And then, ultimately, choose between them. For me, that limitless choice is actually a problem with digital, though, and I loved working with film because I found it a much more committed materiality. You only had one rush print; I could only afford one rush print! And that comes back to a principle of economy of means where choices are necessarily limited and that limitation becomes an overarching ethical choice.

PR:
I haven't been on a Steenbeck for some years, but there is something different about the experience of being in that cutting room, and not being on a [computer] screen, where you do loads of other stuff. You're in a space that's dedicated to film in a different way. And it makes me wonder whether we can protect that materiality somehow.

SAM:
It's funny that you mention that, because this has been something playing very strongly on my mind. It reminds me, actually, of something that one of the advisors at Sundance, Walter Mosley, told me about. He writes novels, he's a film-maker, he's also an artist, and he told me that his workspace configuration has to be very specific. So, on one computer he does this, on another he does that. He even has a different chair for different roles. It's all in one room. I do all of my work – I write my screenplays, I make my video art – on the same device. And that can actually be claustrophobic. The fact that there is constant background radiation and noise, more than anything is very detrimental to the creative process.

WR:
Yes, I agree totally with that.

SAM:
That might seem very old-fashioned of me, but I do feel that way.

PR:
I think it's increasingly becoming an issue. Because at the moment there are lots of people who were trained and developed a kind of, I'm going to say depth, though that's not to say that others lack depth. In the analogue world, though, we weren't dealing with that same level of distraction, and the requirement to respond to things, which certainly has a tendency, for me at least, to bring me more to the surface, rather than back to where the practice might be. To go back to the opportunity and the danger of ambiguity; for me, lately, if something is uncomfortable in my perception or for my particular value system, then that opens a door in my practice.

WR:
Yes, it's also about sharing that not-knowingness with your audience, with the spectator who watches that film. I'm far more interested in trying to solicit an engaged audience as opposed to offering that audience entertainment. I'm not interested at all in making work that's entertaining.

PR:
But your work is entertaining. I don't think it would reach people if it didn't have that aspect?

WR:
Oh dear! I would hope it's engaging rather than entertaining, as such. I think you can, in the way you frame a shot, for example, you can put something visually interesting on the screen. And you can do things with sound that are engaging. I try never to work with sync sound, for example. I find that sync sound kills the screen experience dead for me, and I always like to have a pull-push relationship between what the image is doing and what the sound is doing. It opens the possibility of a new, more total, space.

SAM:
It's very generous, because it gives the audience space to fill that gap, between sound and image. At least, that's my experience of seeing things that are unsynced.

PR:
That's interesting, because I always shoot sync sound. I might not use the sound synchronously, or at all, in the final edit, but it's very important to me that the sound world has a relationship to location and the filming moment and that I have that option to work in sync with every frame. I agree with William, that being able to think about the sound world in a way that's not literal is important. But for me, the answer isn't to walk away from synchronicity; I want diegetic sound to remain a tool in the toolbox?

WR:
I would distinguish between literalism and illustration. So, if the soundtrack's telling me what I can see in a picture, I become instantly bored. The counter to illustration is evocation, and that's what I want a film to do – I want the screen experience to evoke something for me through the sum of its elements.

PR:
That is very beautifully put. I mean, even worse than what you describe is the soundtrack telling you what is happening in the shot. There's quite a lot of film practice where, in addition to the location sound, and what you're seeing there, you've then got someone telling you what to think. It's the kind of 'voice of God' that became identified, slightly unfairly, with the work of [early Scottish documentary maker] John Grierson. The Grierson stable was much broader than that.

WR:
It's a discussion rehearsed in film theory and criticism. [American film critic] Bill Nichols is more of the opinion, I think, that documentary is there to inform. Whereas, I think that [ethnographic film-maker] Toni de Bromhead argues that it's more about giving visual pleasure.

PR:
Exploring the source and definition of aesthetics leads back to the realisation, from my perspective at least, that the integration of ethics and aesthetics is primary. If ethics are stripped away from aesthetics, then aesthetics becomes merely a conversation that hovers somewhere 'above' history and cultural politics – a parlour game about naming, say, the fifty great painters back to the Renaissance. This effacement of context tries to situate the artwork as though it somehow doesn't have a relationship to politics, society and the relationships out of which the work emerged and is made and seen. There was a big movement in cultural history – post-[literary and cultural theorist] Edward Said, particularly – which insists on this reconnection. Ambiguity can then be a strategic way to insist on a broader range of connections, which can be

read out from the artwork and which reveal context. A way of saying, no, the work – the film, the script, the sculpture, whatever it is we're doing – exists and intervenes in culture and history. It's not just superficial or a kind of wallpaper or a parade of celebrity artists primarily to be read in relation to each other.

WR:
I've always taken great exception to close textual analysis because it mitigates against ambiguity. And it's something that has informed a certain approach to film theory. Because, whatever the discipline, close textual analysis is based on the notion that a text cannot speak for itself, that its meaning is not self-evident on its face. It runs quite opposite to the view I've always taken, which is that an artwork can never be fully interpreted but can only be experienced. Close textual analysis, for me, tends to eliminate ambiguities of meaning. William Empson does say in his book of litererary criticism, *Seven Types of Ambiguity* [1930], that ambiguity is used by writers as a means of engaging the readership. There's enjoyment to be derived from ambiguity in writing.

PR:
But I think close textual analysis is very important if it's done well, because it insists on the individual's experience of that work. When it's working well, I don't think that narrows down the work, but shines a different light on it. For example, for centuries, literary critics only really talked about Shakespeare's *Othello*, say, in terms of personal jealousy – the green-eyed monster – or about *The Tempest* in terms of the magic and release towards the end of Shakespeare's life. But look closely at those works and encoded in the language of *Othello*, for example, are the specific racial dynamics of what was happening in Venice in that period. *The Tempest*, likewise, encodes the dynamics of imperialism in a particular historical, colonial moment. I'm talking in very broad brushstrokes, but those debates were suppressed or not visible to the literary establishment for most of the history of these plays, even though Shakespeare's language insists on their centrality. Close reading attends to Caliban's desperate calls for restitution. So I think close reading can release all of this and more, as long as it doesn't think that somehow the critic is bigger than the work or that he or she is able to nail it down or reduce the slippages of meaning into one sole reading.

WR:
Just linking this back to ambiguity, it seems to me that ambiguity acknowledges the fact that we all see the world differently. I think, in terms of art education, those differences in ways of seeing have to be nurtured in our students. This becomes more of an imperative given the increasing cultural diversity among them.

PR:
Yes, and the potential value of close reading is that it insists on returning the individual to their experience of the artwork. That has to be central – it can't just be our preconceived or favourite ideas just rehearsed on a new artwork. The artwork is a place where our preferred views may actually be loosened.

WR:
Do you mean, in other words, that there's often a position that needs to be challenged?

PR:
Well, it's been played out in Oxford. The Cecil Rhodes statue [at Oriel College, Oxford] is a focus for competing

versions of how to respond to Rhodes's record. One version lauds him as a pioneer, entrepreneur and benefactor, not to be judged by changing mores. There's another view, which is that the wealth he bequeathed to Oxford should not be celebrated, because it was won by ruthless exploitation, supported by an explicit ideology of racism and white supremacism.

SAM:
They've just removed that statue at the University of Cape Town [UCT] in South Africa. I was having a conversation with some students at UCT who were involved in the protests going on there, and they certainly saw it as a great triumph, that it had been taken down. But I found that erasure - although it's an important symbolic act - it's also a certain erasure of history that can be extremely dangerous. One of the arguments that was posed by one of the individuals I was talking to was that not being shackled to history was the only way to forge ahead into their future. And this is very young people speaking.

PR:
But I think, whatever position one takes on this, one of the useful things about ambiguity is that it helps us juxtapose these competing readings.

We need a conversation that is mature enough to hold different aspects of a work or an individual or an historical moment in consideration. That's central to pedagogy, as well - after this, I'm going to a class and there'll be people from all over the planet there, who've got very different takes on what happens, and we need to be able to be in relation to each other - to learn from each other - as we seek to surface a range of views that an artwork can stimulate, through its ability to embody multiple readings. Being alive to ambiguity is a conceptual key to help us embrace pluralism and encourage it to crystallise.

Notes

1. Pratap Rughani, 'The Art of Not Knowing', in Kate Adams and Phyllida Shaw (eds.), *Anthology: Project Art Works 1997-2012*, Hastings 2012, pp.204-7.
2. Hermann Hesse, *Siddhartha, Demian, and Other Writings*, ed. by Egon Schwarz, in collaboration with Ingrid Fry, New York 2001, p.98.
3. Pratap Rughani, 'The Dance of Documentary Ethics', in Brian Winston (ed.), *The Documentary Film Book*, London 2013, pp.98-109.
4. Pratap Rughani, 'Are You a Vulture? Reflecting on the Ethics and Aesthetics of Atrocity Coverage and its Aftermath', in Richard Keeble, John Tulloch and Florian Zollmann (eds.), *Peace Journalism, War and Conflict Resolution*, Oxford 2010, pp.157-71.

HIDDEN

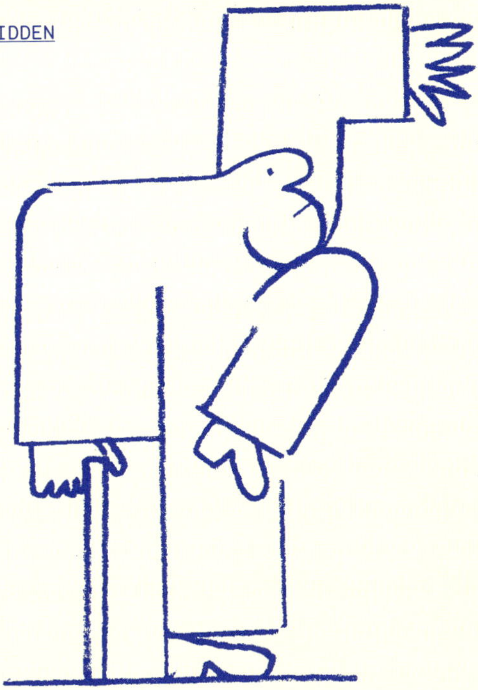

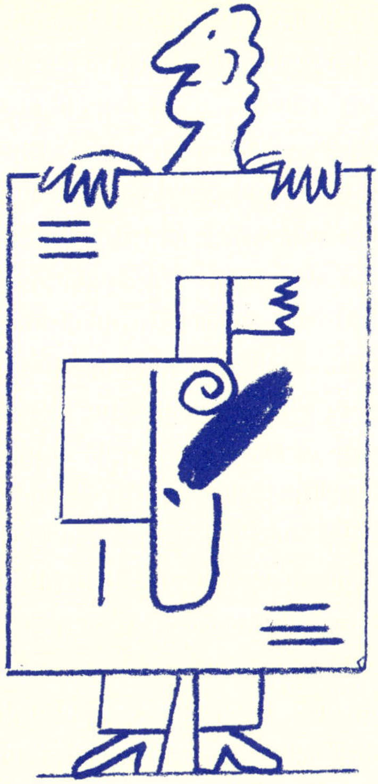

How often do you step outside your routine, your area of expertise? Do you collaborate with people in other disciplines? Michael Spencer, course director for BA Performance Design at Central Saint Martins, UAL, believes that to do so as a designer is to exercise your most important skill: 'the ability to negotiate an external agenda, someone else's ideas.' Or, as dance educator Julia Gleich puts it: 'Nobody has the right to have the answer to every question in the room, artistically.' The two threw their students together – young choreographers and young designers – to create original works, for 'Dance Lab', part of a series of collaborations spanning London's creative institutions. 'Hidden' (2013) was another of these collaborations, bringing members of the London Sinfonietta together with design students, many of whom had little experience of contemporary classical music.

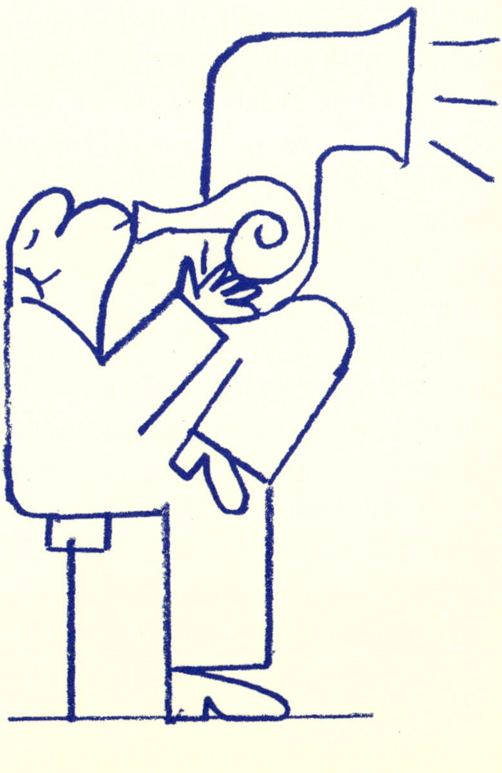

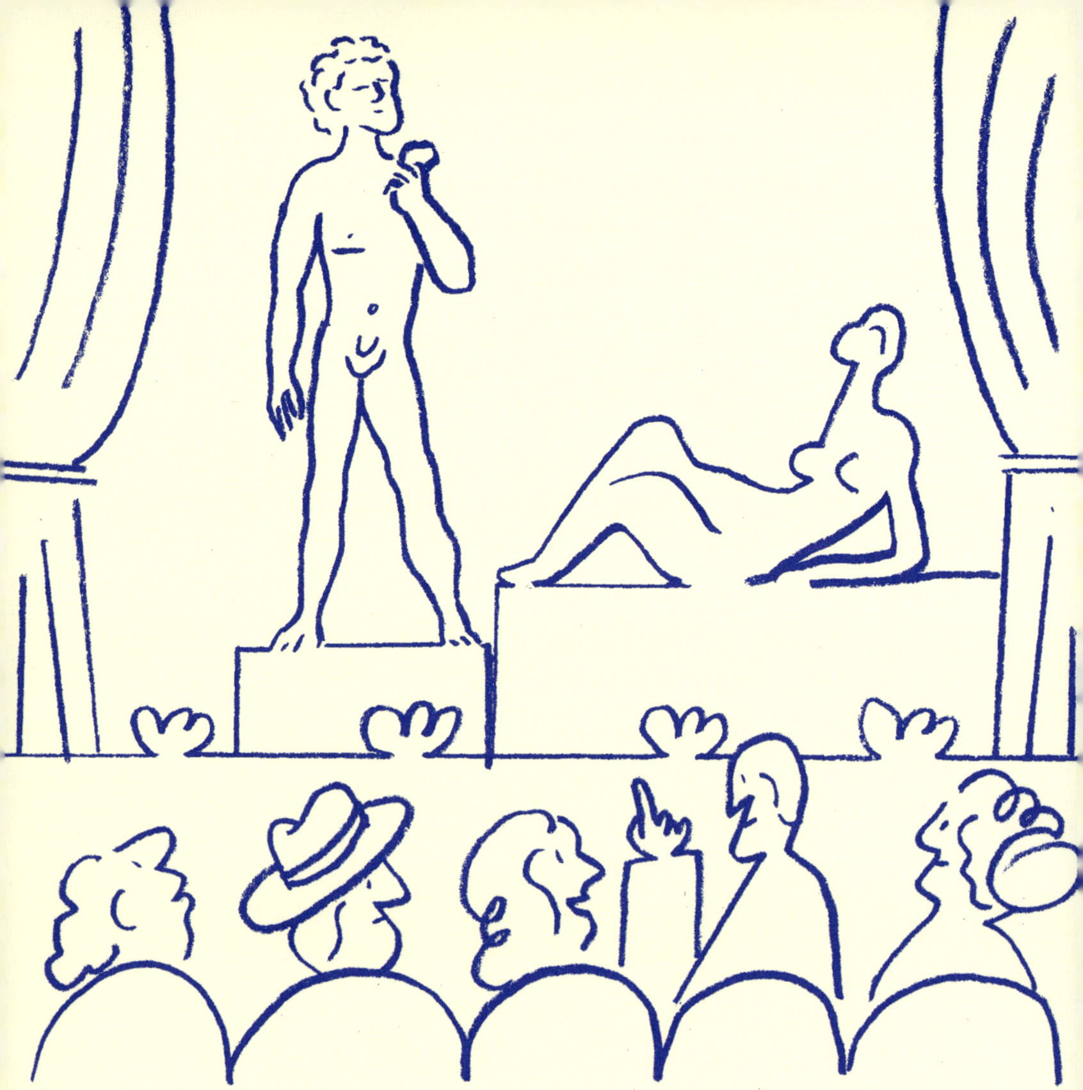

ACTS RE-ACTS

The art critic and historian Michael Fried, in his 1967 essay 'Art and Objecthood', declared that 'Art degenerates as it approaches the condition of theatre.' The month-long 'Acts Re-acts' programme, hosted by Wimbledon College of Arts, UAL, challenges this rigid distinction between fine art and performance or theatre, inviting practitioners and critics to explore the ambiguous and 'dangerous border zone' between the two fields. Talks, seminars, workshops, performances and screenings take place, with the programme imagined as a kind of 'lab' in which experimental work can be tested. Marvin Gaye Chetwynd – Wimbledon's Practitioner in Residence – led a day-long masterclass on invention through performance in the 2016 iteration, taking in urban sites as well as the college.

AGENCY

Sonya Dyakova

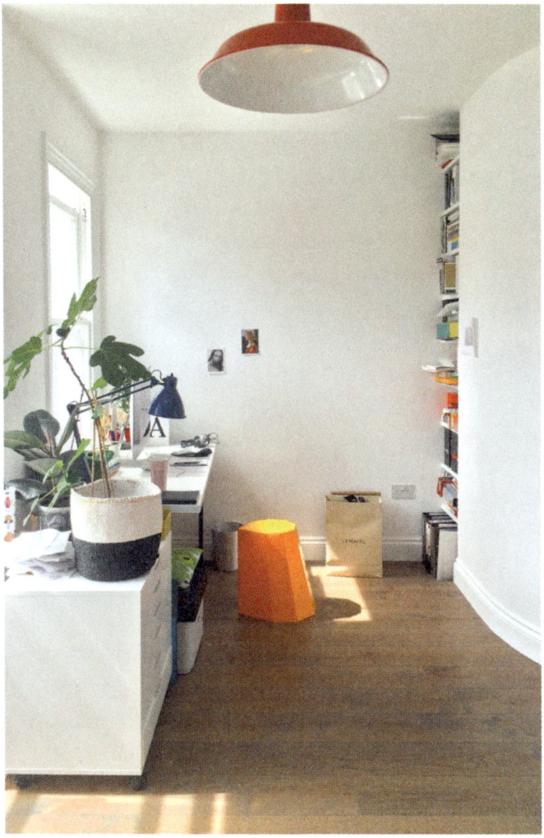

The designer's workspace, London, 2016.

It is admirable to stand up tall and independent; to be able to achieve a lot with very little; to be able to negotiate your *own terms*. Agency, for me, is very much about the self, and, in terms of creativity, about how one positions oneself in relation to work.

Where does one begin the journey towards self-definition? Arguably, the first steps are taken at art and design school. My family left Siberia in 1989 and emigrated to San Francisco in 1990; I was a teenager when we left Russia. I attended a Jewish high school, followed by a Catholic university and, simultaneously, art college – this has exposed me to an array of characters and ideas. I enrolled as a student at the University of San Francisco to gain a Bachelor of Arts degree – to get a well-rounded education, as they offered great humanities courses, as well as an affiliation with the same city's Academy of Art. My teachers included a graphic designer, Paul Tsang, who eventually became a friend; he gave me confidence, and made me feel intelligent and funny, and this alone goes a long way. His presence was empowering and inspiring. I enjoyed publication design classes with Cheri Gray, and learned the very foundations of typography from a calligrapher, Claude Dietrich, who had his students ink letterforms with a tiny brush for hours on end! I remember having to justify my work in front of fellow students; doing so must have helped to develop my presentation skills, so vital to my practice. As Alan Fletcher used to say, it's all in the presentation.

During my studies I also came up against conventions I didn't agree with. This is part of education too – learning how to deal with obstacles and swim against the current. Aside from the nostalgia and intense longing for home I experienced at this time, I have often wondered what my career would have been like if I had studied in Europe – at the Royal College of Art, London, for example, or Ècole cantonale d'art de Lausanne (ECAL). I was taught very little graphic design history as an undergraduate in California and never once visited a printer. I felt the void when, later, I started working in London and had to catch up; I learned these aspects of my trade on the job.

Indeed, art school formed only a slim portion of my creative education: a much bigger, more influential part were my first two jobs in London. In my last semester at the Academy of Art, my friend and fellow student Precious Bugarin called me and said, 'Let's go to London. I have a friend there, we can sleep on her sofa.' We came and I fell in love with the city. Despite the miserable weather, London was full of energy and gave me a real buzz. I was attracted by the level of talent, not only in the graphic design field, but in every strand of life. Working, I found, was the best way of learning – dealing with design challenges, conceptual as well as practical, in the real world. My homesickness also abated when I came to London and made a new home for myself.

After contacting numerous design studios in the city (it's safe to say I had at least one interview a day for a month, sometimes two), I had landed an internship with Vince Frost at Frost Design. I worked there as a designer for two years, followed by two years at Kerr Noble. At each stage I gained more and more confidence. In 2005, I was recommended for a position as a design manager at publishing house Phaidon, where I eventually became an associate design director. Working alongside Alan Fletcher, the creative director, I presented design concepts that were entirely my own for the first time. This period was also an education: Alan would mention names of great figures in graphic design and I wouldn't know who he was talking about – I was deeply embarrassed. Kindly, he then started giving me a new name to look up each week, offering a small history lesson, a story, a joke.

Turning points, after which I produced work with more power of self-determination, occurred each time I attempted to jump above the standard approach, challenging my own expectations. In my very first week at Phaidon, the publisher, Richard Schlagman, asked me which designer would be best suited to designing an 800-page monograph on renowned Japanese photographer Nobuyoshi Araki (see overleaf). My jaw dropped and, before I could catch my own words, I blurted out: 'Me, I would like to design it!' To my astonishment, I was given the go-ahead. This was a turning point for me: there was no one else to rely on. Sink or swim. So, I started paddling with all my might. I was passionate about Araki's work and, reading his quite personal texts, was inspired to make the best book I could make. My original proposal was so extravagant in terms of production that it couldn't be printed and sold for the intended price. Alan cleverly suggested simultaneously printing a simplified edition, alongside a numbered special edition with dozens of pre-dyed paper inserts and hand-glued chapter dividers, making the whole project financially viable. This was a key experience of reconciling personal agency and design conviction with commercial considerations. It was a very difficult book to produce, and the production department did an amazing job. I am so grateful for their excellence and patience – during my time at Phaidon I endlessly made their life difficult, coming up with intricate book structures and processes!

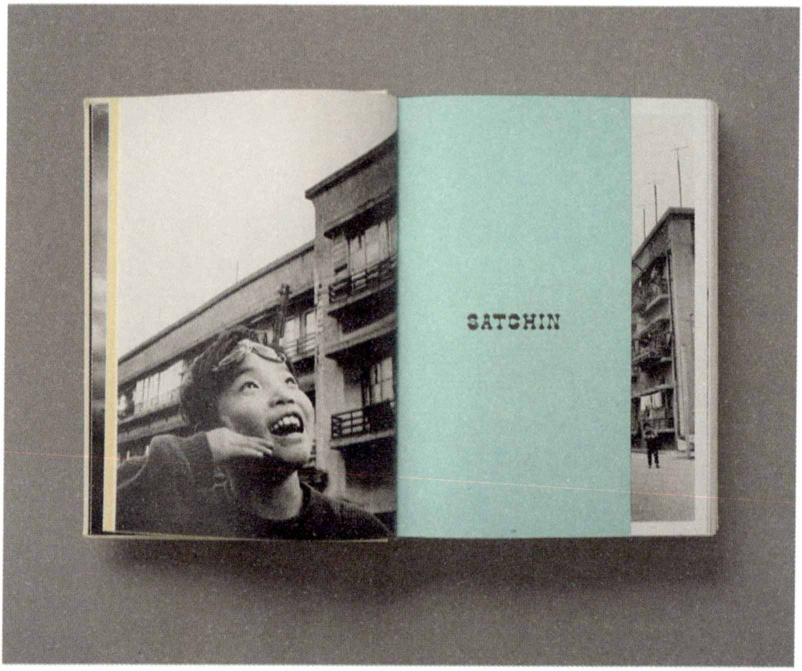

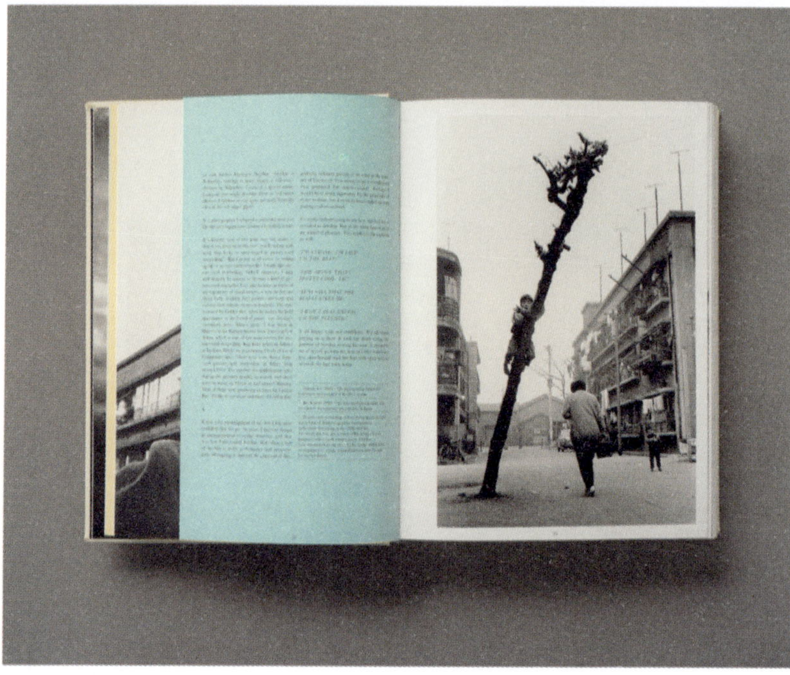

Nobuyoshi Araki: Self, Life, Death, Akiko Miki et al. (eds.), Phaidon, London 2005.

Another major turning point was my decision to leave Phaidon in 2011, and work independently – it was the true beginning of my own agency. During my time at university, there was a general assumption that one would start working at a (design) agency immediately after graduating, and there were very few people from my year who started to work for themselves straight away. I always considered it incredibly brave, and didn't see it done so widely and freely until I came to Europe. Perhaps my attitude to self-employment – I was attracted to, yet also wary of, it – were inflected by having grown up in a country governed by a system of beastly organisations and institutions, where everyone (and yet no one!) is responsible for their actions. Growing up in the Soviet Union in the 1980s, you would never hear anyone say they ran their own business, although this has obviously changed since.

In some respects, I wish I had become self-employed earlier, but working in other environments taught me a great deal and, at the time, my route felt more secure: I worked for and learned from others before standing on my own two feet. It sounds like a cliché, but when things are tough, or I'm not certain, and I need a push, I read advertising guru Paul Arden's *It's Not How Good You Are, It's How Good You Want To Be* (2003). It helps me to get over fear and make the leap.

I love the flexibility and independence that comes with running my own agency – you can't beat it! I feel that I am taking care of my own creative priorities, rather than anyone else's, and, aside from the freedom to use my time as I wish and divide my hours between work and family, I appreciate the much more focused mode of working that self-employment brings. Working in an office or organisation invariably involves meetings, phone calls and admin, and, while the independent designer has their share of these, they are much more concise, and you are able to concentrate on the thing that most artists and designers love doing: creating. Having a small team means that you design every day. With just one or two people to work with, instead of ten or twenty, you remain very much in control of even the smallest details. Perhaps that is not the most efficient or traditional way to run a business, caring about every single line-ending and production specification, but detail, I believe, is what makes for good-quality work. Personally, I find that not investing 100 per cent of my energy into everything I do does eventually show and therefore, in the long run, is not a good strategy. It's much better for every project to be something to be proud of – and, at the end of the day, if you're not enjoying what you do, then there seems hardly any point.

The presence of independent and freelance designers is undoubtedly a strength of my industry: they bring a fresh approach, because they are not part of an institution. They offer solutions that are not influenced by ulterior, or interior, concerns or conventions. (Although publishers can tend to forget the reason for hiring an independent designer and, little by little, manipulate and force the work into their standard mould. This is an unpleasant experience, to say the least.)

There is a popular notion that collaboration is always positive, and working alone negative. Collaboration is accompanied by ideas of openness, sharing and community – all lovely and jolly concepts – and, by contrast, working alone or in small groups may appear selfish, self-focused and needlessly competitive. I would like to challenge this assumption. I like sharing and discussing ideas and truly believe that it is a productive process. More broadly, I do feel part of a European and London-based design community: in 2013, I became a member of Alliance Graphique Internationale (AGI), a group of talented graphic designers working worldwide, and am thrilled to be part of this organisation. However, equally, I enjoy time spent wrestling with a design challenge, working things out alone, and I believe there is a place for both. For me, it's just a question of scale and, for now, I like to keep things small – I do not actively seek collaboration. I like individuality and single vision – there is strength in that.

In fact, this would be my advice to aspiring designers and creative professionals – trust yourself and follow your intuition. Don't be afraid of solutions that may seem strange or unusual. Aren't those the best ones? Try to find clarity in what you are trying to say – don't hide behind stylistic or decorative noise. Fight against design by committee. Start here and don't stop. It's hard work, but the rewards are sweet.

That's what I've been after, all this time.

In conversation on 'agency'

Phil Baines

Teal Triggs

Lawrence Zeegen

Phil Baines
(PB)

Professor of Typography, Central Saint Martins, UAL

Teal Triggs
(TT)

Professor of Graphic Design and Associate Dean of the School of Communication, Royal College of Art, London

Lawrence Zeegen
(LZ)

Professor of Illustration and Dean of the School of Design, Ravensbourne, London

The participants were asked to discuss the topic of creative agency, with particular reference to their respective fields within graphic design and its history. The work of Tom Eckersley at the London College of Printing (LCP), now London College of Communication (LCC), UAL, was a jumping-off point for the discussion – Eckersley worked in design education at LCP throughout the 1950s. He was instrumental, along with a small group of colleagues, in conceptualising modern graphic design as a professional practice of communication distinct from commercial art. The participants used this moment as a lens through which to discuss the topic of 'agency'.

TT:
'Agency' to me, in the context of what Eckersley was doing, actually connotes the advertising 'agency' – an organisational aspect of the creative industries whereby artists and designers, marketing and business people, and others, came together to deal with or problematise what was being asked by a client. I wonder if there are other ways of talking about the designer's role, such as the designer in terms of their own self-interest and how that's been manifested through client work, and also how, historically, the particular notion of authorship has completely shifted from the early days of graphic arts practice, where graphic authorship was very much about the self and 'agency' in terms of almost political acts, to something that is nowadays fully embedded in the design process.

LZ:
I agree – there is an understanding of 'agency' that is about the relationship that practitioners, educators, students and graduates have with the creative industries. But I think the role of designers in the process of making creative work, that's where there're interesting stories to be had. I think about Eckersley at London College of Printing (LCP), a college that was extremely linked to creative practice and creative industry, and his role was an important one because he both pushed what happened in the industry through his own work and, at the same time, brought industry into education. It was an important point in LCP's development, for the college to have someone heading up graphic design who was so recognised, so able to push the agenda in terms of what graphic design could be and who it could be for. For me, that's a kind of agency of change, of social change ...

TT:
Yes, I think it's important to acknowledge the importance of the period of time that we're talking about as well, because Eckersley joined LCP in 1954 as a tutor and then, in 1957, became Head of Department of Graphic Design, a post he held until 1976. He's operating in a particular kind of post-war context, within which LCP was not necessarily so unique – other educational institutions were bringing in graphic design practitioners: for example, Professor Richard Guyatt joined the Royal College of Art [RCA] in 1948 from industry.

LZ:
And the idea then that you didn't have someone absolutely engaged in practice running a school of graphic design would have been completely out of sorts; it would have been very odd to have a pure academic running a design school.

TT:
Yes, and the same was true at Central Saint Martins [CSM], wasn't it?

PB:
Well, yes, because at CSM, you've got [founder of Central School of Arts and Crafts] William Lethaby insisting that all his teachers are practitioners right from the beginning in 1896. Then you get [British graphic designer and Pentagram co-founder] Colin Forbes setting up graphic design in the early 1960s at the Central School of Art and Design, and he's one of that whole group who go on to form [professional association] D&AD in 1962.

So I think they all know of each other and they all have different takes on the same approach, really – somehow embedding their knowledge of practice, their contact with industry, in their teaching. And that's really important; it's crucial to the schools.

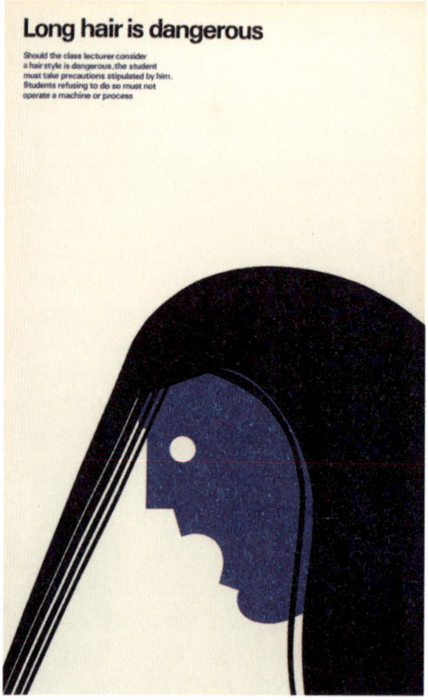

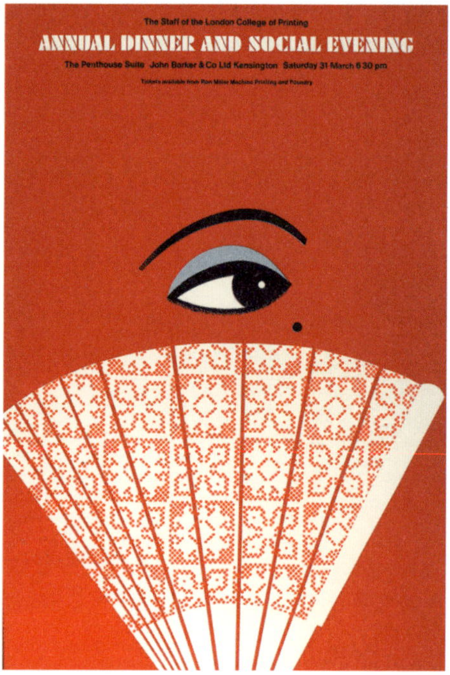

Left: Tom Eckersley, 'Long Hair is Dangerous' (health and safety poster for London College of Printing), 1976.
Right: Tom Eckersley, 'Annual Dinner and Social Evening' (poster), c.1980–9.
Overleaf: *Tom Eckersley: Master of the Poster* (installation view), London College of Communication, UAL, 11–29 January 2014.

TT:
I think the interesting thing for many of the British institutions where graphic design is this emerging field of operation, is that they're within an art school context, and that tension that's created between the artistic practice – the artist as 'individual creator' – and the role of the graphic designer as a mediator or facilitator or interpreter of a client-driven message is where it gets really interesting. The role of education is then in helping particular students better understand that process, that tension – working with, not against, the tension that exists between art and design.

PB:
And LCP and the Central School both have trade schools attached to them as well, so even within the institutions you've also got this tension between straight trades like printing and then graphic design, as an activity that's aside from them – there's a bit of tension between the two, quite a bit of fighting ...

LZ:
I think that's key, though, because I think that sometimes the sense of the wider art school gets slightly brushed to one side. That the teaching of graphic design is training for industry – we get that assumption from all quarters. And it's really important that we understand

our responsibility to the vast numbers of graphic design students that we are teaching; we have to bring them to a point where they can enter the creative industries. But if that's our only raison d'être, then we're in trouble.

My view is that we should be creating the kind of graduates that rock boats rather than row boats, and practice will only move forward by creating the kind of graduates that will go and question and push. I think too often the teaching or the understanding of the teaching of graphic design is relegated to the relationship that it has with industry, and I think Central School and LCP, for some, are associated solely with that very technical training.

TT:
I think the context has shifted as well. LCP has its roots in [London's professional association for the print and publishing trades] St Bride Foundation Institute of Printing and was associated with the hardcore printing industry; then the name changed [at LCP] to 'printing and distributive trades', signalling a contextual shift. The word 'vocation' has been thrown around a lot since; 'vocational' used to mean you were doing a trade – you were learning your craft, you could go out and then perform those functions accordingly. And there was a period of time, in the 1980s and 90s especially, when 'vocational' was the dirty word ... Now the government is again promoting a skills-based education; not necessarily recognising that a decade earlier it was about creative leadership and about going into industry being disruptive in your thinking and actually generating innovation out of that. I think LCP, in its very essence, was about providing skills to students, but the nature of those skills has shifted in the present day, from 'here's the grid and here's how you print something and here's what "die-cut" means' into being much more inclusive about creative thinking, design thinking.

LZ:
Yes, and the recognition of our responsibility as educators to ensure that students understand their own responsibilities, not just as designers but as people who have an opportunity to contribute to society. That's a bigger issue than it ever was – students shouldn't leave university without having been challenged, in terms of their part in what they're going out to do. They still go to LCC, for example, for a very pragmatic, hands-on, design-doing aspect to their curriculum. But they also go because there is some deep design-thinking alongside design-doing [Zeegen was previously Professor of Illustration and Dean of the School of Design at LCC].

TT:
I think the 'brief' ... well, the relationship between the client and the designer, and that's the context in which the brief is positioned, I do think that has shifted. Though, in my historical understanding of designers' processes, there has always been an imperative to look at a brief and question the brief.

PB:
Yes, I think that's been taught and knocked into students for a long time, really. The first step is, question the brief – is it right?

TT:
There can always, potentially, be tension between the individual's political beliefs versus what it is that the client's asking him or her to do. So how do we help students better understand that space and how to work within that space? I remember, when I was taught at university in America, that it was very

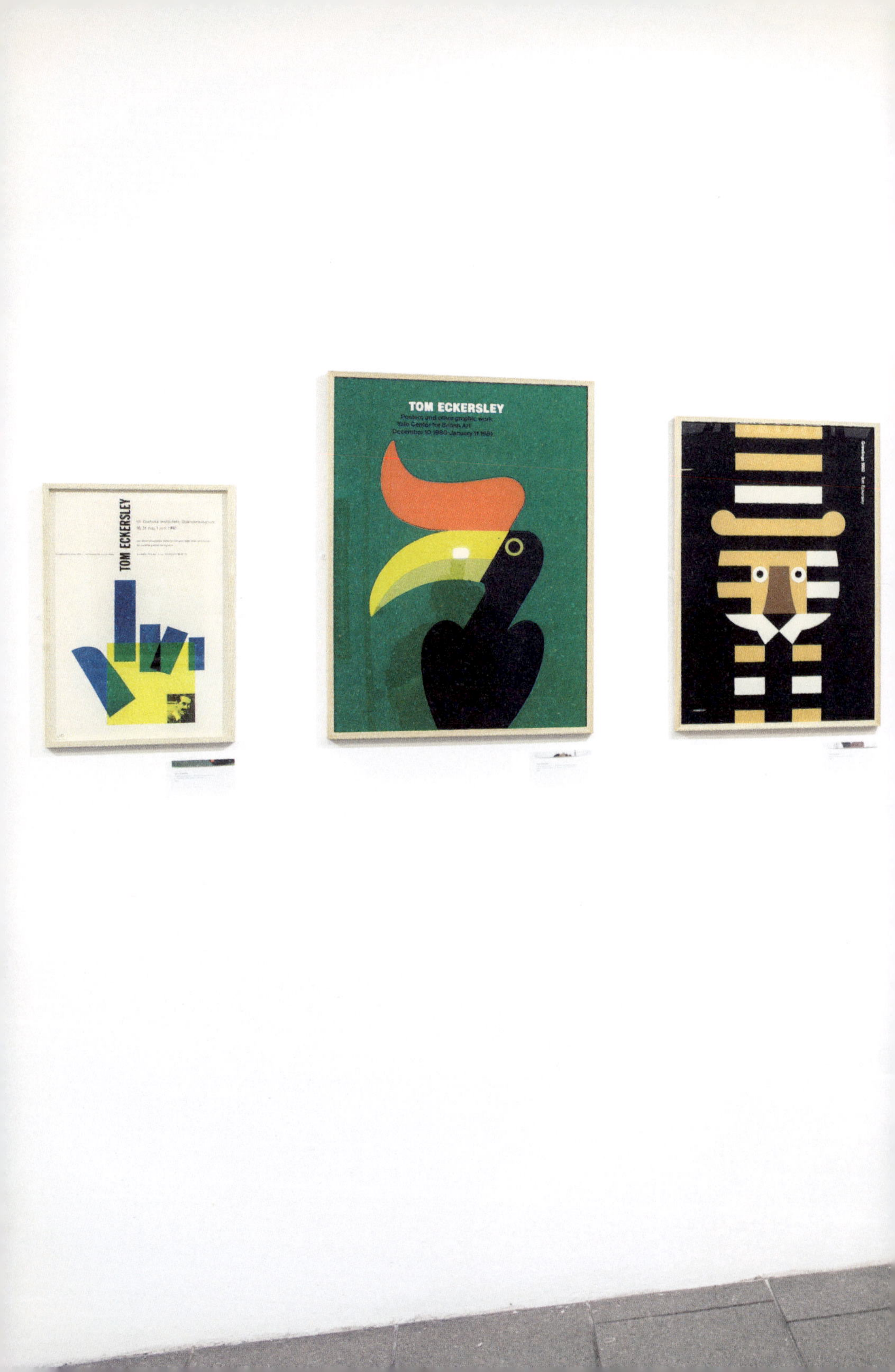
TOM ECKERSLEY
TOM ECKERSLEY
Posters and other graphic work
Yale Center for British Art
December 10 1980-January 11 1981

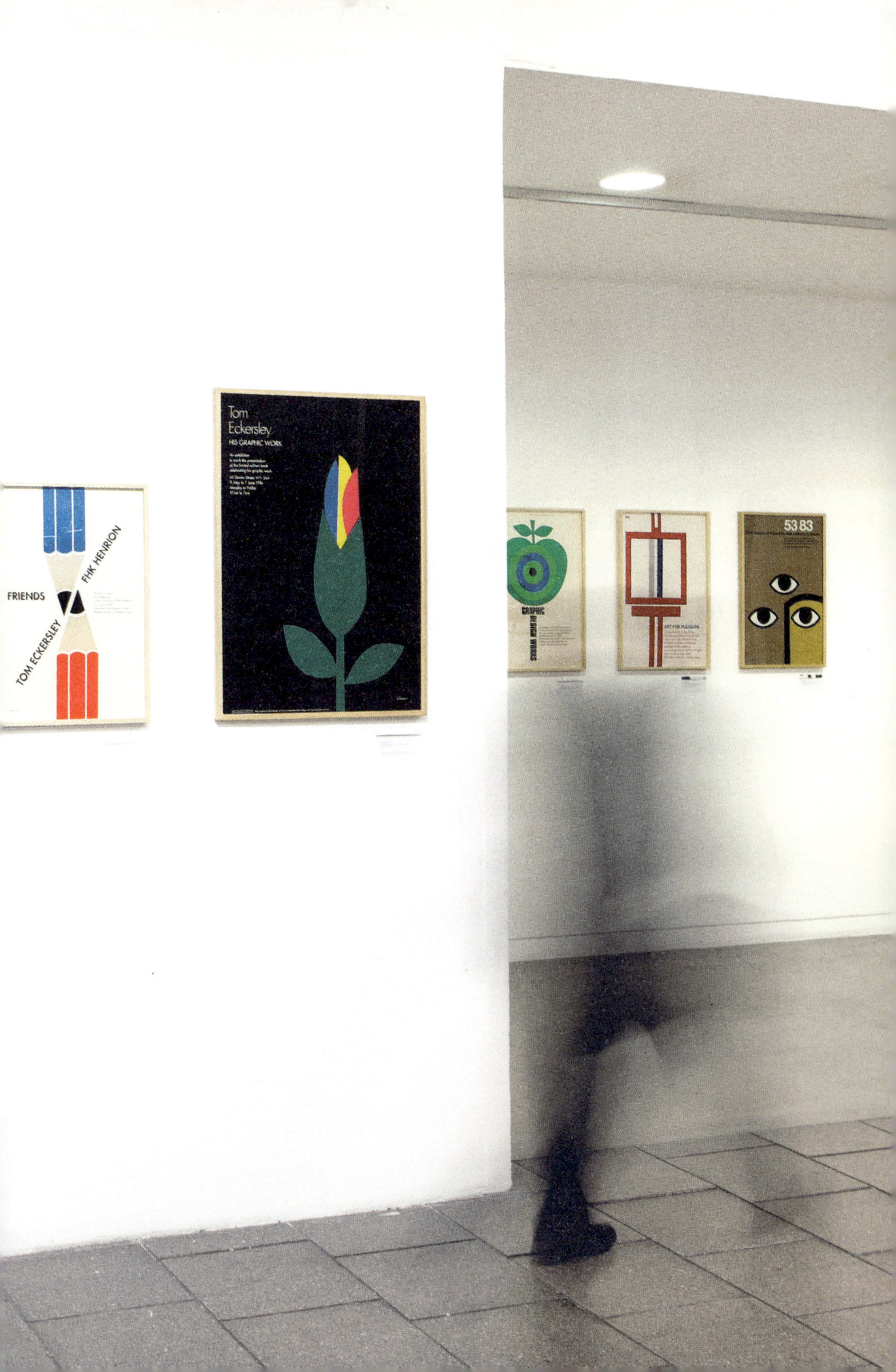
FRIENDS
FHK HENRION
TOM ECKERSLEY
Tom Eckersley
HIS GRAPHIC WORK
GRAPHIC
DESIGN WORKS
ART FOR PLEASURE
53 83

much about questioning the brief, but also helping the client better understand what it is that they wanted to get out of that brief.

LZ:
Sometimes the worst person to write a brief is the client.

TT:
Absolutely.

LZ:
I recently attended an event at Pentagram – a lecture by Sophie Thomas. Now, Sophie's a CSM graduate and a Royal College of Art graduate; one of the projects she still talks about is writing her own brief while she was a student at the RCA – it was about demonstrating the environmental impact that the canteen had by not using, at that point, recycled paper cups. She and her then-partner washed and cleaned every single poly-styrene cup that was taken out of the bins over the course of a week [see opposite]. And I can't remember the figures – it's about 3,500 cups or something very dramatic; so sometimes it is about creating the brief.

And Sophie can still talk about that with great effect, because all of the work that she's done in running her design studio, Thomas.Matthews, goes back to the designer taking responsibility for their actions. And you know, many designers now will refuse to work with clients if they don't adhere to their approach to design and communication and production methods. I think that, twenty years ago, that was very difficult for people to take on board. That, I think, has changed dramatically, and it's changed because graphic design has, in some ways, fallen out of favour; more people can do it. And because more people can do it, because there's wider access to software, those who really want to do it well are doing it much more according to their own sets of principles; and I think that's to be applauded.

I can remember Dan Fern, as a course leader at the RCA when I was a student there, standing up and making a presentation about why he wouldn't work for Saab. He was invited to do an ad campaign for Saab cars in the mid-1980s, and wouldn't do it because Saab also made fighter planes. Suddenly, as a student, hearing that in the mid-80s, there was this sense of, okay, yes, I do have to take responsibility for who I'm working for.

TT:
There is this bigger context where, increasingly, education is being squeezed out. We're having to be quite creative in finding new ways of being funded, new kinds of opportunity, and we are finding that there are certain kinds of student who want to engage with corporations, in that they feel they can change the mindset of that corporation by working with them. So rather than refusing, and taking a political stance that cuts off certain kinds of opportunity and opens up others, they're actually embracing that and beginning to work with them.

PB:
You get the reverse as well; you also get organisations going to [art] colleges because they want to be shaken up; they want to be scared a little bit.

LZ:
Once you've got that relationship working well, that's fantastic, and I think you're right, Teal, that rather than just flatly refuse, you can guide people, clients, agencies, through a process that will help them understand what they need to do to change and improve.

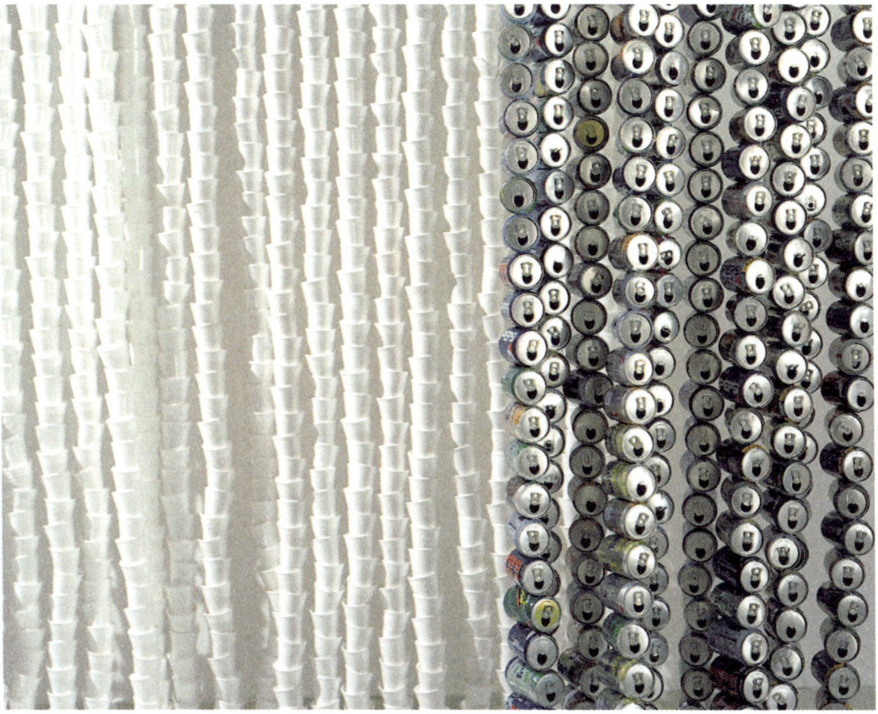

Sophie Thomas and Kristine Matthews (Thomas.Matthews), *What Comes Around Goes Around* (installation of one week of canteen waste, detail), Royal College of Art, London, 1997.

TT:
As educators, this is a really key point for us, because what we don't want to be is in service of industry. I think Phil is quite right, that when an organisation comes into an art school, to a design programme, and wants to work with students, our role as educators is to be negotiators and mediators and interface between the student and the client to ensure that learning is still at the forefront of that process; it's not about capitalising on ideas.

This is why I think the educator's role is so important – it's always about that negotiated space and what value is there, not just for the corporation. It may be that they want some disruptive thinking, so we can be disruptive, that's no problem; but what is the value then to the individual student in their own learning process about disruptive ideas?

LZ:
I think we will always drive students towards understanding not only their own responsibility, but how they develop their own design personality, their tone of voice, and how they're individual in a very crowded marketplace. And I think that a myriad of platforms, including social media, might be making that a more complex mission for them than it was ten, fifteen years ago, but then these are students who, if they're looking at studying communication design, have

a strong understanding of how those platforms can be utilised.

You know, if you think back to a world prior to the digital, where showing your work to people meant ringing up, making appointments, trudging around with a portfolio – it could take six months to show thirty people your work, and in an instant nowadays you can show 30,000 people your work. And I think there's a lot to be learned about how important it is for students to understand how they work within the context of social media and just how much they give out, if you like.

TT:
Going back to talking about basic skills in any student's education, I think 'editing' is one that's absolutely key at this particular point in time. I've just gone on to Instagram, and I'm finding it fascinating, but difficult at the same time; and I think this is where a lot of our students are editing what it is they want to convey visually to the world. Students are kind of working out in public their ideas of what the visual is and what it means to them. And I think for visual communicators, for graphic designers, this is an interesting platform that perhaps we're not utilising as much as we could be within our teaching.

LZ:
You are writing your own brief. At the same time, though, as we know, there's been a huge shift towards the tangible, and the interest in print, the interest in …

PB:
The designer as maker again. Making physical things, there's been such a sort of return to that, particularly in the last ten years, perhaps as a reaction to the digital. But then students have actually been very savvy at harnessing both.

The designer as maker – that's something you could take back to Eckersley as well, because there's a craft aspect to it.

LZ:
LCC is teaching typography through letterpress [see opposite] and the teaching of … yes, design through making.

PB:
Learning through doing.

LZ:
Ten years ago, when we taught 'new technology' to students, that term meant 'digital'. New technology, now, means letterpress, it means etching, it means getting your hands dirty, because these are students to whom, as a result of art education in Britain being stripped back to being almost non-existent, this is new technology. They've had a computer, an iPad, a smartphone in their bedroom, their playroom, their classroom since the age zero, and actually new technology is about: okay, what can I do when I'm thinking and I'm making?

TT:
I think it's important to note that – and Phil, you will remember this – there was a period of time at LCC for instance, when the technicians, having engaged with the printing industry as compositors, retrained to be technicians for digital technologies. I was fascinated by that: they weren't supposed to be teaching, but demonstrating, but the way they were talking with the students sitting there looking at a screen, trying to figure out what kerning was – the technician could actually talk about what things looked like in print. An invaluable learning experience. What's great about it now is that it is student-driven. It's not so much about what our generation feels that students need to know, it's about students wanting to know.

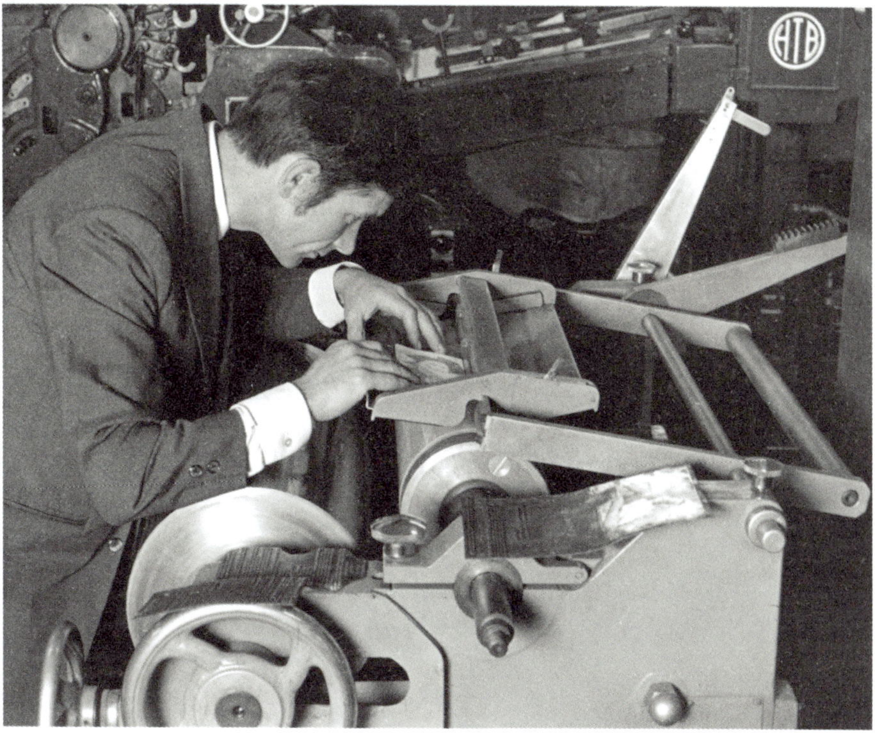

Student using a rubber plate mounting (letterpress), London College of Printing, c.1964.

PB:
I started letterpress, not because of any notions of proper type or any of that stuff, it was because I could control everything, because I didn't need to mark up a typescript to give to a technician and wait twenty-four hours for this bit of bromide to come back. I could just get on and do something and make it, and when he knew I was interested he taught me how to do it properly, so I didn't need to bother him in letterpress. So it's control, I think.

LZ:
And it's immediacy as well. Whether it's letterpress or whether it's screenprint, there is something tangible about it happening before your very eyes; there is the fact that you're committing to something through print, through the process that isn't instantly changed, that isn't instantly shared. So maybe that sense of alone-ness, or 'I'm in the moment creating this work' ...

TT:
Yes, but it's also about the exotic. To see the printmaking or working a letterpress is so different, it's an oddity, and there's a curiosity as a maker about a new medium to be operating in. The notion of the lone creator – I just don't think exists any more.

LZ:
Because if you're not sharing it once

you've created it, it's just going to sit around.

TT:
Exactly. And I think, you know, we're seeing in social media ... as you were saying before, Lawrence, it's really facilitated that networking aspect and that desire to put material out into the world.

PB:
I think freelancing is easier now, as well. Digital tools have made that easier; although there's a cost implication with computers, actually every student has one. It's just much easier than I think it was when I started out.

LZ:
What I think it's meant is that – certainly in my subject area, more so I think in graphic design – there isn't that need for the illustration community to be within a courier's distance of every client.

I think this goes back to our earlier conversation about people wanting to take responsibility for their own direction, and take control over their place in the greater industries and in the world. Rather than commit to working for a design agency or a design studio and realising that the first six months will be on absolutely no pay, I think people will choose independence.

TT:
Yes, but I think we also need to understand that if you're talking about the fashion industry, for example, there's a whole kind of mechanism that operates, whereby one thing needs to happen before another, and then you've got the garment that comes off the manufacturing line. With graphic design, it's not dissimilar, in that the freelancer is still not a lone individual, because they're working with people, whether it's the client or the printer or a distributor ...

LZ:
It's collaborative by nature ...

PB:
So you might be a lone person working in a room, but you're part of a network.

TT:
Yes, and that's where that difference crops up, between being in artistic practice, versus being an illustrator working for the *Guardian* newspaper. You can still be the lone individual, but it's that intent and that distribution that define your output, to an extent.

PB:
I think, in terms of teaching, that having students seeing what you're doing is also really interesting. You know, it gives them some sort of framework to help them think about what they're going to do, even if they don't like what you're doing. That's almost as useful, because it gives them something to fight against.

LZ:
Eckersley was absolutely motivated to ensure that all teaching staff continued to engage in their practice as they taught; so much so that if they didn't have commercial projects on, he would set them projects for the College, because he thought it was absolutely imperative that they'd be working on these at the same time as teaching.

TT:
I think he was able to bridge both the kind of professional activity he was engaged with but also the academic, the educational context, and pull those ideas and those principles of practice together to create something quite special. I'd like to think that all three of us are engaging with that in very particular kinds of ways.

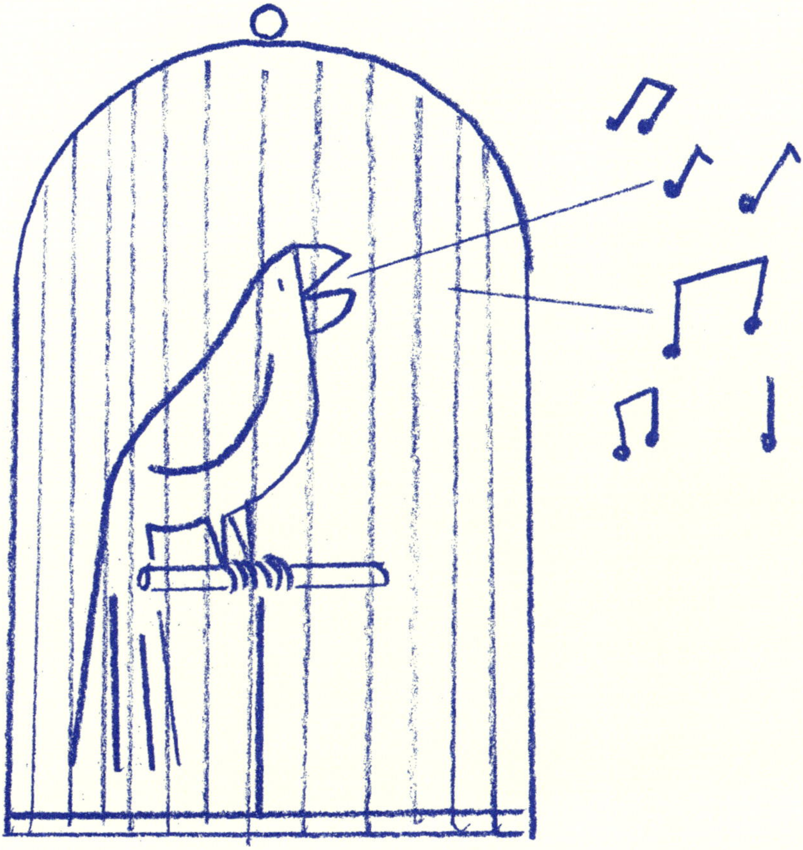

Fashion is about engaging with change, but it's also, as Julia Robson, editor of this magazine's third issue, put it, 'a great vehicle for self-change'. 'The Beauty's Inside' engaged serving women offenders at HMP Send in the creative work of writing, editing, modelling for and styling a glossy magazine. Between 2009 and 2016, four issues were produced, in collaboration with industry professionals and students from the School of Media and Communication at London College of Fashion, UAL – each different and each increasingly shaped by inmates acting under their own agency, with features on topics ranging from androgyny on the catwalk to gay marriage. Winning the Times Higher Education Award (2013), Big Society Award (2014) and Green Gown award (2011, for an upcycling feature), the project also impacted on both inmate and student participants, who testified to their increased confidence and changed perceptions as the project closed.

101 THINGS TO DO IN AN EMPTY SWIMMING POOL

'101 Things' was a collaborative project that breathed life back into an abandoned pool in Maribor, Slovenia. Through workshops, live artworks and surveys, more than a hundred local people were invited to contribute their ideas for the future of the pool. These ideas, expressed as drawings, photographs, collages and photomontages, were published in a book to be presented to the Mayor of Maribor. Alenka Banic, the project leader, describes how 'some suggestions are playful, some abstract and dreamy, and some very realistic, but they all reflect the visions, needs and desires of the citizens.' Experiments included running a painting workshop in the pool, filling it with fairy sculptures and having breakfast in the space. The project was about giving people the opportunity to express their agency – allowing them 'more say in what their city could become'.

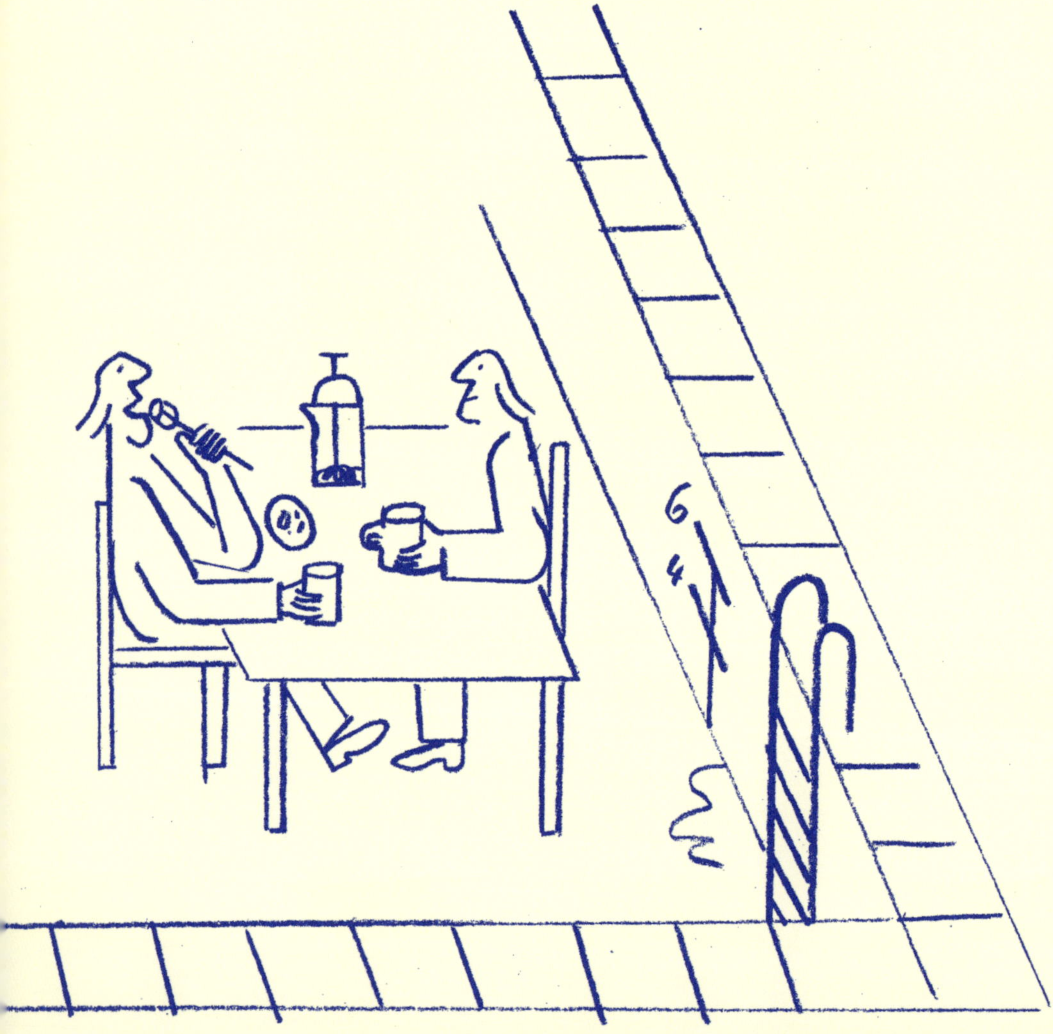

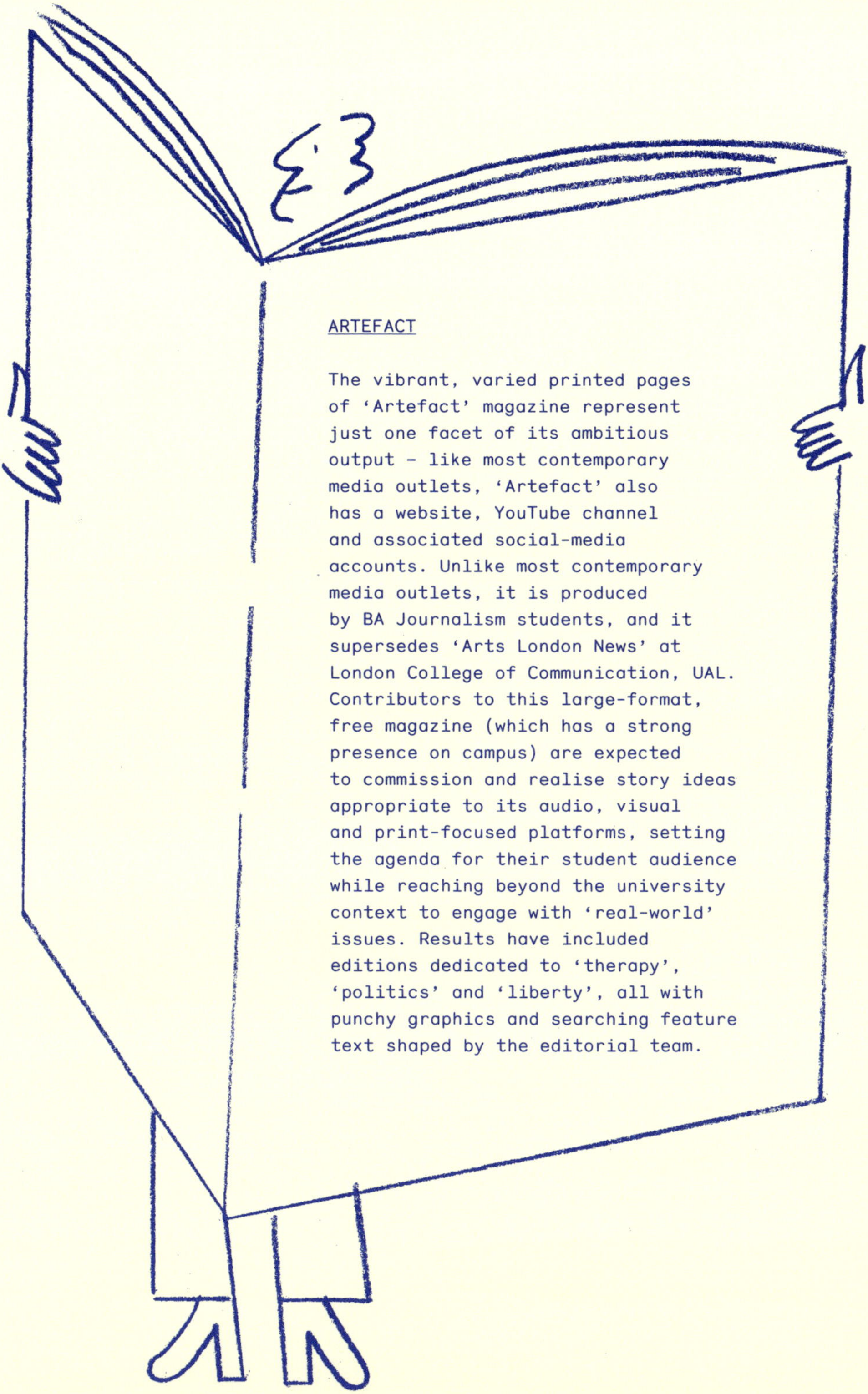

ARTEFACT

The vibrant, varied printed pages of 'Artefact' magazine represent just one facet of its ambitious output – like most contemporary media outlets, 'Artefact' also has a website, YouTube channel and associated social-media accounts. Unlike most contemporary media outlets, it is produced by BA Journalism students, and it supersedes 'Arts London News' at London College of Communication, UAL. Contributors to this large-format, free magazine (which has a strong presence on campus) are expected to commission and realise story ideas appropriate to its audio, visual and print-focused platforms, setting the agenda for their student audience while reaching beyond the university context to engage with 'real-world' issues. Results have included editions dedicated to 'therapy', 'politics' and 'liberty', all with punchy graphics and searching feature text shaped by the editorial team.

DRAWING THE WORLD

Public, participatory events – such as this one-day celebration of drawing, organised by academics and students at UAL, alongside independent arts practitioners – enable professionals to reflect on their practice in the context of performances and workshops that also invite non-professional audiences to expand their visual literacy and creative agency. As part of the world's largest international drawing festival ('The Big Draw', organised by The Campaign for Drawing), and in partnership with House of Illustration, London, and Central Saint Martins, UAL, visitors of all ages were invited to sketch urban scenes, follow drawing trails, and explore henna design with local artists and community groups.

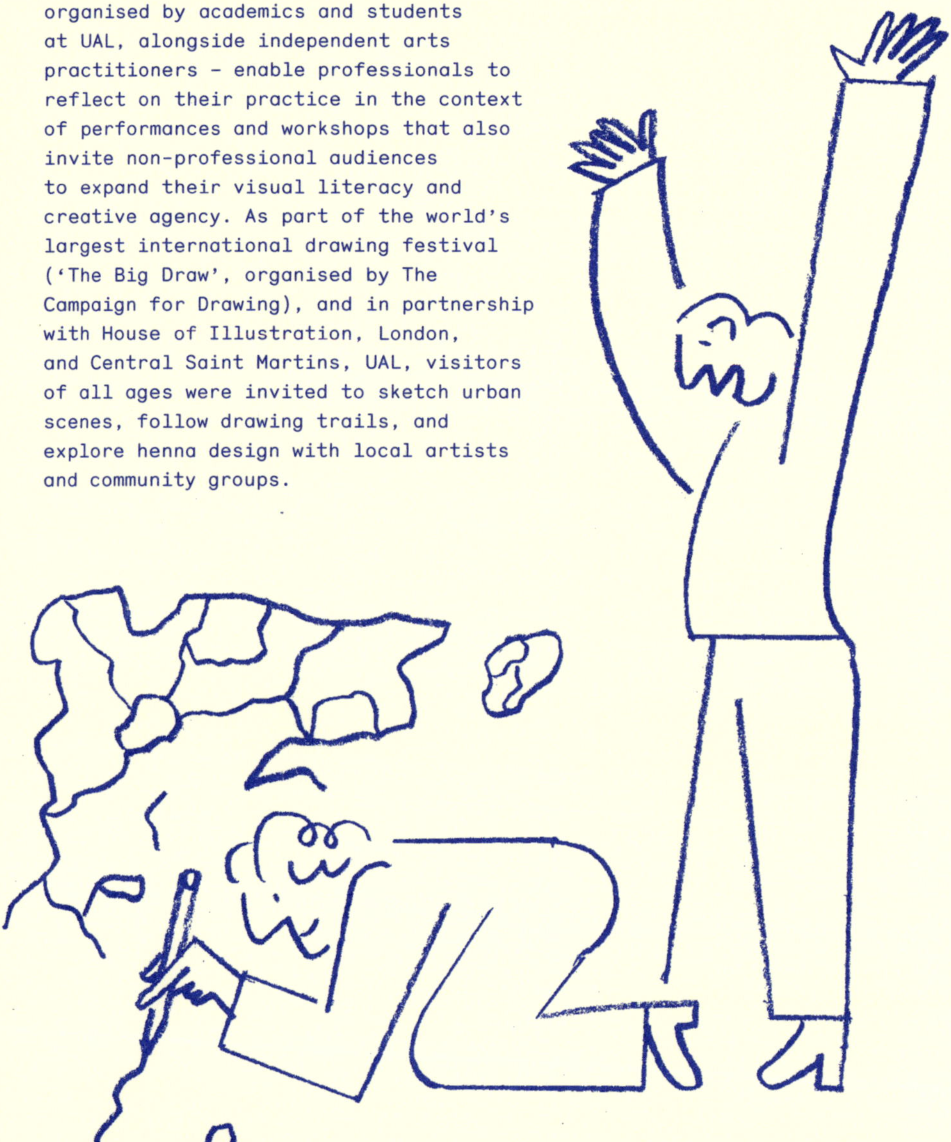

Meanwhile, Professor Stephen Farthing encouraged a group of thirty graduate students to reflect on the politically-charged theme of cartography, creating a giant world-map drawing using chalk, drones (as 'eyes-in-the-sky') and mobile phones.

IMAGINATION

Bob and Roberta Smith

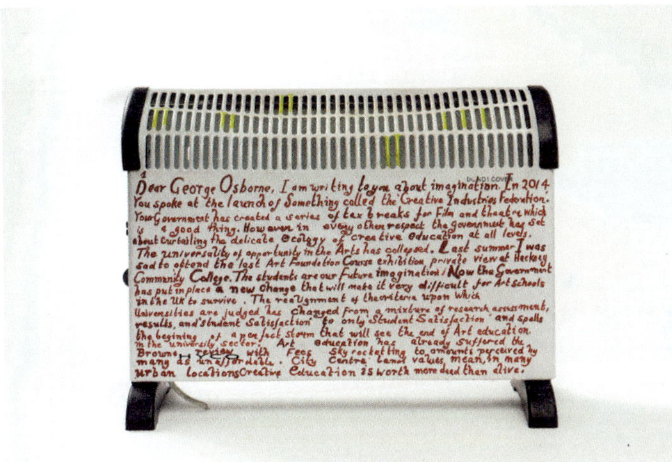

Bob and Roberta Smith, *Letter to George Osborne*, 2015
William Morris Gallery, London.

The text overleaf appeared in its original form in the work above. This *Letter* was painted before George Osborne lost his position as Chancellor of the Exchequer in 2016, but, in the words of the artist, 'applies equally to his successor, Phillip Hammond, or, indeed, anybody who holds the governmental purse strings.'

Dear George Osborne,

I am writing to you about imagination. In 2014, you spoke at the launch of something called the Creative Industries Federation at the new site of Central Saint Martins art college – the Granary Building in Kings Cross, London. I am not sure what the Creative Industries Federation is, but I understand it does good work, presenting to Government arguments in favour of a whole range of creative and commercial activities, which contribute in excess of £70 billion to your exchequer.

Your government has created a series of tax breaks for film and theatre production companies, which is a good thing. However, in every other respect, the government has set about curtailing the delicate ecology of creative education at all levels. The universality of opportunity in the arts has collapsed.

If a kid has a great voice, musical or visual talent, but attends a free school or academy that does not offer arts subjects at GCSE, how can they overcome your educational system? The current system discriminates against artistic promise and is socially engineering a cultural world that is more about privilege than talent – less about something to say and intent on limiting access to the media.

Last summer I was sad to attend the private view for the last exhibition of the Foundation Diploma course at Hackney Community College. These students were from the local area and were a diverse bunch. Their show was full of talent and exuberance. These young people are our future imagination. I have spent the last four years campaigning, with others, for a more serious assessment of the benefits of art teaching in school. This effort has been largely fruitless but, as a visual artist, I cannot stand by and see the art education from which I have benefited being diminished.

Now the government has put in place a new change, which will make it very difficult for art schools in the UK to survive. The alignment of the criteria upon which universities are judged has changed: from a mixture of research, assessment, results and 'student satisfaction' to 'student satisfaction' only. And it spells the beginning of a perfect storm that will see the end of art education in the university sector. Art education has already suffered the Browne Review, with fees skyrocketing, in response, to amounts perceived as unaffordable by many. City-centre land values mean, in many urban locations, creative education is worth more dead, in the form of empty property, than alive. Now we are subjecting students who study on arts courses (being taught to 'think outside the box') to a box-ticking exercise whereby, if they don't tick the *right* box, their course may be closed.

Art students are notoriously critical beings. Art students look at the world as outsiders and demand change. Artists and designers do not celebrate the status quo but ask questions demanding new creative ways of thinking. Art is about rebellion. If I had been presented with a 'student satisfaction' survey while studying at Goldsmiths in the 1990s, or at The Cooper Union in New York or Reading University in the 1980s, I would have said that all the tutors were middle-aged, out of touch, white and mostly male. Their ideas were rooted in fashionable ideas of the 1960s and their teaching methods were obsolete. However, now I think of my days at art school, being grilled by art lecturers, as the best days of my life. Formative criticism from tutors I had reservations about at the time resonates daily as I make my art. I recognise now that art school changed my life. No art student worth his or her salt would ever write: 'Wow everything is great!' Because everything being 'great' is not what art is about.

The university where I teach [London Metropolitan University] is closing twenty of its creative industry courses and closing its Aldgate site [The Sir John Cass Faculty of Art, known as 'The Cass'], largely on the basis of 'student satisfaction' and the cost of moving workshops. Destroying what I have called the 'Aldgate Bauhaus' is a mistake. The original Bauhaus, based in Weimar, Germany, developed a new model of teaching art and design, which was inspired by the technological innovations of the early twentieth century. The 'Aldgate Bauhaus' offers a similar prospect. We introduce students to an interdisciplinary menu of twenty-first century digital and design skills. The closure of our school will crush and thwart innovative thinking. Interdisciplinary activity is the magic from which all great design comes. William Morris, England's great visionary designer, knew this. Morris mixed things up! If Morris were alive today he would passionately campaign to save and develop art education.

I fear that the Cass closure is just the beginning. Art schools are expensive to run, with complex workshops teaching valuable practical skills like ceramics, mould-making, woodwork and metalworking. At the 'Aldgate Bauhaus' ... we teach people how to build guitars, we have photo labs introducing students to methods of making photographs

– the paper and processes of photography are important. Your plans will destroy the base upon which the creative industries thrive.

Now, not only is art in schools in decline, but a concerted attack is being made on further and higher education. One visitor to the Cass called it a building full of promise. I implore you to cherish our art schools – not put in place the mechanisms of their destruction.

Looking at university provision through just one metric must be misleading. We should acknowledge the complexity, nuance and need for the still-rich variety of courses we teach. The perversity of this move is that it will make universities unfit for purpose in the twenty-first century. As all knowledge is increasingly available at one's fingertips, through digital media, the educational premium of practical experience will grow in importance, across disciplines and industry sectors. Engineers want to make and mill objects; surgeons want to get their hands into clay. Musicians love records. The book trade is growing not shrinking. Removing the playground, the laboratory, the workshop, the physical world, from education is the wrong thing to do.

George, I have tired of presenting endless evidence for you to ignore. If you cannot understand that, without art and design education, our creative wealth will collapse – then more fool you. But understand this: the arts around the world are under threat. Whip the blogger, blow up the ancient city, shoot kids at a rock concert, lock up the artist and kill the poet – that is how dictators frighten the people.

In this country we are in danger of telling kids their voice is not worth hearing. If you don't teach a child to sing, you won't develop their voice and you won't hear from them later. By unpicking the arts, cut by cut, you are guilty of undermining human freedom. I am asking you to honour the imagination and also to have some political imagination. Free societies celebrate the arts.

By protecting and developing arts education we strengthen freedom and deepen democracy. Making art and developing design are fundamental attributes of human beings. We must encourage people to imagine a future where their voice can be heard. Through education, politicians can offer that very rare commodity in an increasingly frightening world: namely, hope. We can talk about the arts as contributing to the creative economy, but I think of the arts as saving humanity.'

In conversation on 'imagination'

Marvin Gaye Chetwynd

Nils Norman

Helen Storey

Marvin Gaye Chetwynd
(MGC)

British artist, working in sculpture, performance, installation, painting and video

Nils Norman
(NN)

Artist and Professor at the School of Walls and Space, Royal Danish Academy of Art and Design, Copenhagen

Helen Storey
(HS)

Professor of Fashion and Science, London College of Fashion, UAL

The participants were asked to discuss the topic of creative imagination, with particular reference to the topic of ‘play’, in their respective fields. They begin with their definition of ‘imagination’ in relation to creativity, and describe the role pure imagination plays in their work.

MGC:
It's interesting to be asked this question, I'd say. I'm not used to being asked this, which is interesting, I think, in itself. I immediately think of a 'SpongeBob Squarepants' episode where Squidward has a really annoyingly posh TV arrive in a box, and then SpongeBob and Patrick go outside and play in the cardboard box and they annoy Squidward by making too much noise! They're using their imagination and they're having much more fun in the cardboard box than Squidward is having watching the TV. So, in some way, I'd say that imagination is ... it's something that you can sort of exploit. It's very cheap and the sky is the limit. It's infinite, isn't it?

HS:
Yes, and for me, I've tried to avoid answering questions like this because they invite you to revisit what you believe to be true continually, and that, for me, changes all the time. The idea of what you might retrospectively imagine your imagination was when you were young is different from what you imagine when you are older. So I think it's, in some sense, an un-nailable thing. But that's also its beauty. The thing that I'm about to do next, it's not the thing that I know right now.

NN:
Yes, I would agree with Helen. I think imagination is specific to a context and is always changing. But I wouldn't want to put my finger on it.

HS:
I've lived a life as a designer, where there is either a self-imposed brief or a brief that's given to you, and that's often quite useful, because your imagination is then called upon to respond to something quite specific. Whereas I expect, in both of your worlds, imagination is far less often bound by that, and so it's a very different experience.

NN:
I recently finished the first stage of a collaborative project with the artist Gareth Jones for the new Milton Keynes Gallery. It was a public-realm design project inspired by Gareth's knowledge of the city - he grew up there - and research that we made together. This first phase was purely hypothetical so we didn't have to make anything and we didn't have any real restrictions. I found that, because of working within the urban realm, I was continually being restricted by my own ideas about health and safety, what engineers might think, or how people might use things. Meanwhile, Gareth, who had no experience in that realm, was completely free in his ideas of what we could do.

We made two different models [see overleaf]: I made a scale model, and he made an abstract model out of stuff he found in his studio. That was interesting for me in terms of how imagination works and how you control it, or how you're taught or learn to control it.

HS:
I see a great difference between imagination used in design and imagination used more broadly in the arts. I think they're very, very distinct from each other: one responds to the discipline of having been asked to do something, and the other is the one where the mind can't help but ask.

MGC:
I was thinking of this annoying phrase my mum always uses, which is 'you can't turn the tap on.' With creativity and imagination and exciting ideas, you can't necessarily just turn it on like a tap. But you can, as a professional, sort of know your machine and line yourself up in the

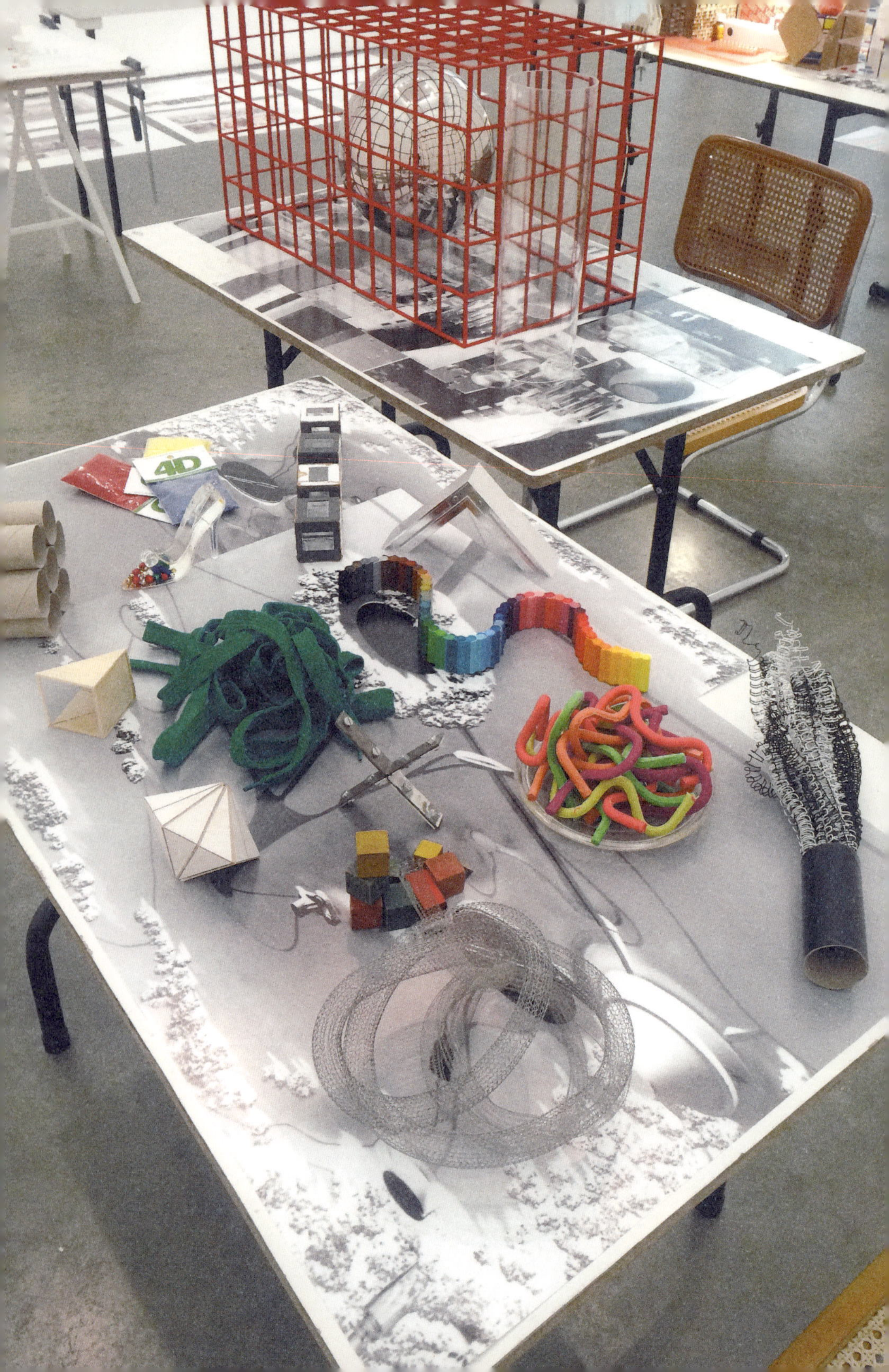
4D

right space to produce. I'm one of those people who lives with really strict routines: I have porridge every morning, I have a banana at 11.00. I'm quite reined in, on a timetable. And everyone finds that really bizarre but, actually, it makes so much sense to me because I feel as if I'm all over the place in the way that I think or process information. So the structure seems crucial.

NN:
It's a bit like improvisation – there has to be some kind of structured space from which you work. Or like playing; when children play, there's a space that's defined and certain things are acknowledged and discussed, like the play area, or what's going to be played. Maybe that's the same for imagination. A scene has to be set or, as Marvin was saying, a kind of routine has to be set up in which imagination can start to work. But from there, rules can be bent and things can be renegotiated.

HS:
I'm still connected to highly creative people who are now in their eighties and nineties, and I'm really interested in the evolution of the human mind and what it's capable of from a psychological perspective, or even from a neurological perspective. You have to have a mind of a certain quality to be able to have imagination, so some of the elderly people that I know who have had creative lives, their capacity to do things is becoming more and more diminished. Conversely, two of them have got Parkinson's disease, and one of them has never been creative in their life but has, out of nowhere, learned to play the piano, aged eighty. So we talk about creativity as if it's something that there's some certainty about, in some sense – that we're all capable of it. But you just need one tiny little thing to go wrong in this thing called the brain, and everything is utterly changed, for better or for worse. It's definitely not straightforward ...

NN:
It's something that should be left undefined, as things become more quantified and evaluated, particularly within teaching and also within play – it gets coupled to economic criteria. Maybe certain things should be left undefined, or strange.

HS:
One of the questions I often think about is what motivates someone to be creative in the first place. What drives them to want to produce something that is of them, but can be independent of them, because it turns into something else. And I've often wondered about whether the first, our very first experiences of love – and I mean in really early life – whether they are positive or negative, have an effect on the urge to use creativity at all. You often see extraordinary types of human imagination precisely because someone is suppressed or there's a deficit in their life, either emotional or practical – sometimes their lives are saved by their capacity to turn that awfulness into something better. I'd almost say it's a precondition for creativity, that there is something that needs transforming. Which is why imagination can never only be about delight. It's very, very often informed by something that other people may perceive as a negative – something that needs fixing, or transforming in some way, usually of an internal currency.

Gareth Jones and Nils Norman, working models for the 'City Club' project, Milton Keynes, 2015.

NN:
I just finished a book called *The Other Paris* [2015] by Luc Sante. It's about what you're describing, but in terms of the city of Paris and its history; how oppressed, working people – the poor, communards, bohemians, ragpickers, clochards – had their own creative methods of transforming their neighbourhoods or the quarters in which they lived. There's a connection between quotidian creativity and urbanism, and the building of cities.

MGC:
It seems rather gloomy, though! All this is very interesting, but if we're saying that imagination is only linked to something that's bad ... I would say no, not from my heart and soul. That's not what I think.

NN:
What we're touching upon is the impulse in Romanticism, in which creativity comes out of some kind of suffering or an obstacle or some kind of oppression.

MGC:
When I think of imagination and creativity, I feel as if it's like blind visionary flashes. I don't feel as if it's necessarily coming from a reaction to something ... When I was first asked about imagination, the first thing that hit me was that it feels as if it can't be contained and analysed. It is something that will endlessly escape analysis. It is not containable and you can't package it or make money out of it. I really enjoy exhibitions about art made under oppressive regimes, and there are artists using extremely minimal and extremely low-economy ways of being expressive. And yes, that definitely comes from a reaction to negativity, I can see that. But I'm more excited by the idea of doing something, as Nils said, that isn't defined and package-able and isn't worked out.

NN:
When I facilitate workshops for children who are users of a playground or will be, we use a lot of different scrap, economical materials that are then synthesised into a design. I create workshops where children are clients rather than designers themselves. Asking kids to design a playground from scratch rarely works, unless it's an adventure playground.

MGC:
But you allow children to do that. You allow children to be spontaneous.

NN:
Well, I don't allow them, it's just that that's how they work. I'm interested in making as informal, creative and spontaneous a space as possible in which ideas can be discussed, and a scrap workshop can really facilitate more intimate discussions around desires and needs. That's why I mentioned this project with Gareth Jones, because he was very spontaneous. Though he still had his own language and his own set of materials collected since childhood: he had a big box of materials that he liked and he used, so even within that spontaneity, there were restrictions and things he was familiar with. And maybe it's more to do with one's familiarity with things – as you get older you become less willing to move out of that box, or less able.

HS:
I think I have trouble, strangely, talking about materials, even though materials are what I'm involved in most often – I'm interested in the ones that you can't see or touch. Working with scientists, it's very much about working in that nano-space, and the bit that I'm interested in is the magic of what can't actually be defined by the eye as we see it. For me, materials cease to be things that we can give

a name, and are more what scientists can offer that we haven't previously imagined or been able to understand. It goes back to the discussion about use. Is an idea supposed to have a use? Or is it okay for it to exist just because you've discovered it? I think scientists do both.

MGC:
I think it's important to have a good portion of irreverence and disregard for what's gone before you, too. Although I'm entirely respectful of the authority of information, weirdly, because I studied history – at that point it was really ingrained in me to respect that – at the same time, I would say, I have a really strong portion of disregard. And that allows me not to question whether or not I should tread in an area that's perhaps very precious or respected. If you have that kind of irreverence, it allows you to reinvent the wheel. Everyone will point at you and say, what the hell are you doing that for? It's been made, it's been made better! What are you doing? But, because you choose to set aside your appreciation of everything that has happened, within that moment it's very loose and you are able to experiment and be creative.

I don't mean to sound like a complete twit when I say that it's like blind visionary flashes, but I literally will wake up and do it. I don't think before.

NN:
I do that when I walk through cities – I do get some kind of flash of an idea. But I know that it comes from other things, it comes out of context.

MGC:
And lots of research. I agree with you, but the wiring, the connection between the research and my receptiveness and observational skills – because I'm constantly questioning and I'm constantly researching – that is not directly why I create. I have to let go entirely. I always talk about that film *Stalker* [1969], the [Andrei] Tarkovsky film, when they're in 'the zone' and they throw a rock in one direction and then walk in the other. The wiring isn't there between the research and the processing and the actual moment of motivation, I'd say. I don't hold on to any of the information.

NN:
One of the things I've found in the discipline that I'm slowly moving towards – in terms of urban planning and architecture and design – is that you're constantly up against a lot of compromises, which you're not taught about at art school as part of an individual's creative process. Within the Romantic tradition, a compromise is frowned upon, but within urban planning – when you're talking to engineers, landscape architects and the people who have to live with the things people are building – through a complex social creative process, there are unavoidably compromises, contradictions and renegotiations. So you come with these ideas that you've had, and they're slowly chipped away at and they slowly get remodelled back into what, basically, you'd find on the street anyway. It's a kind of process of normalisation. How can you change that? How can you shift that so that what you create is not necessarily defined by economics, or by health and safety regulations, or by social norms defined by engineers and landscape architects?

MGC:
You sound as if you're some – and don't

Overleaf: Marvin Gaye Chetwynd, 'Jesus and Barabbas' puppet show, performed as part of *Nic 2 razy / Nothing Twice* project, Cricoteka, Kraków, 2014.

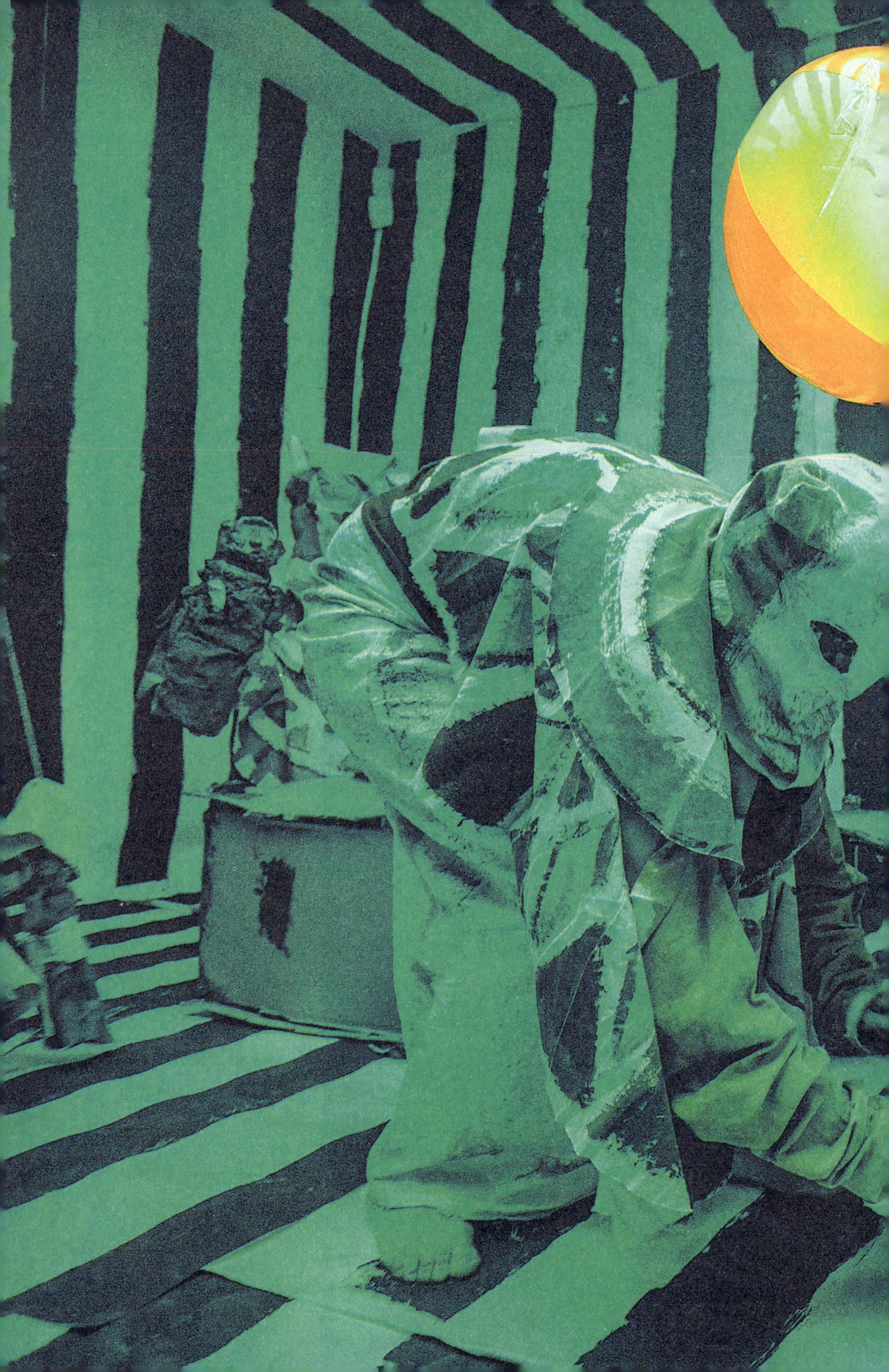

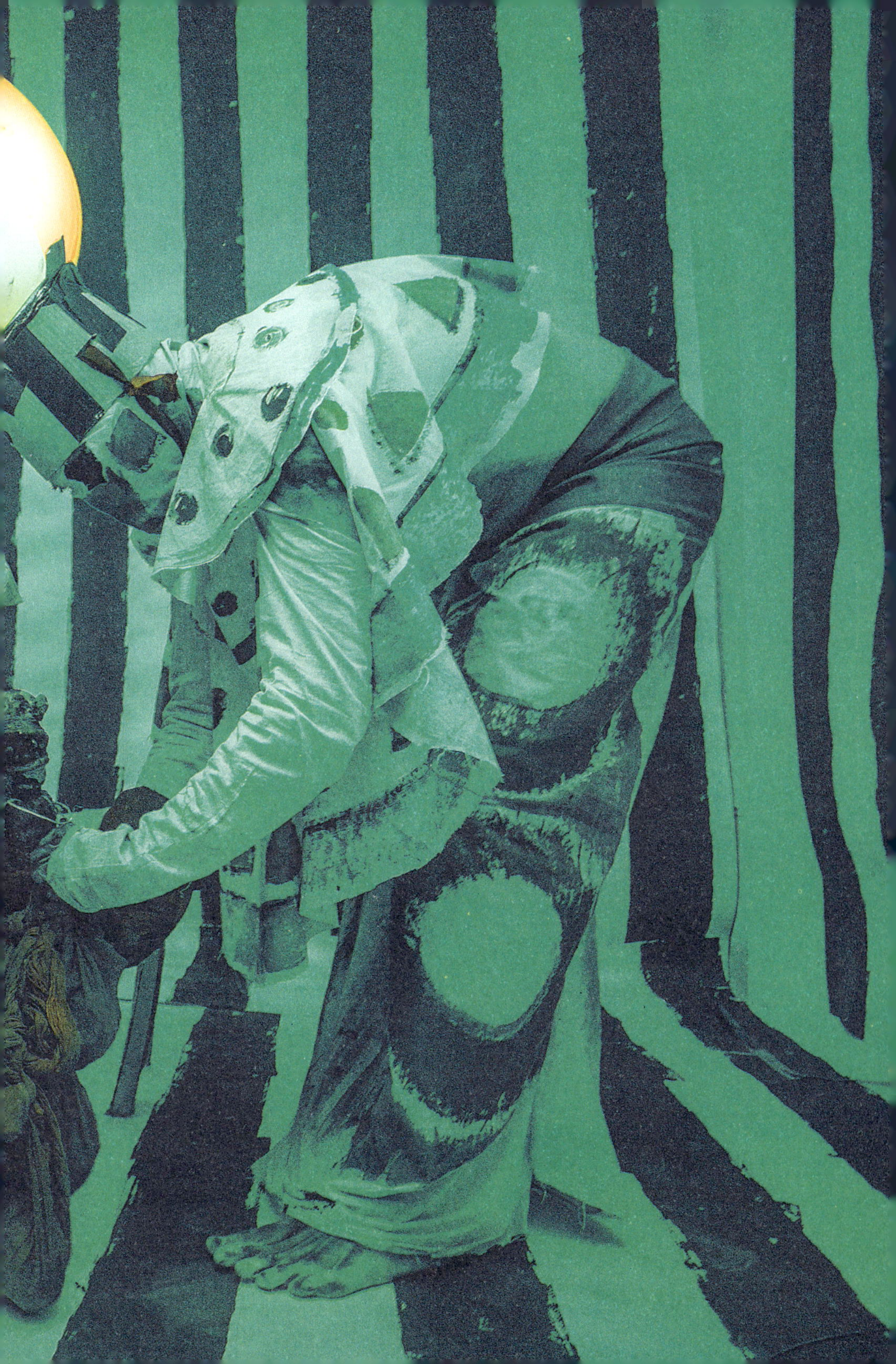

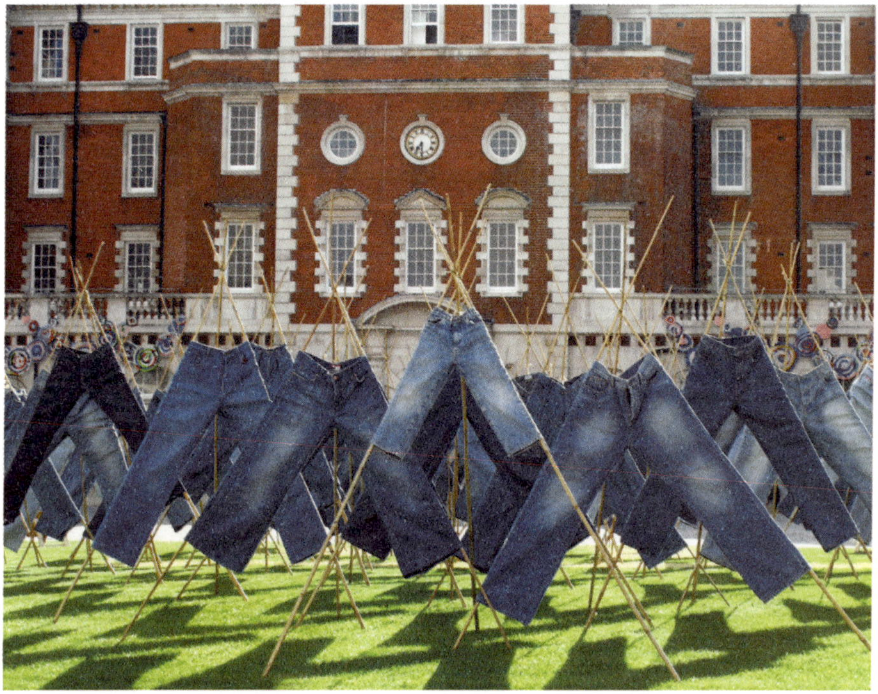

Helen Storey and Prof. Tony Ryan, 'The Field of [air-purifying] Jeans' (part of the *Catalytic Clothing* project), Thomas Tallis School, London, 2013.

laugh and don't feel embarrassed – like some very brave pioneer! And that's why I'm a big fan of yours. You're immersing yourself in another way of working, which is the design world and administration, and you're treading through all of that and being observant, and maybe, hopefully, making room for policies to change and have more space for creativity. But in my opinion, you are really, really in danger of losing touch with your creativity, which I don't mean to sound as a criticism. I'm just trying to explain that what I protect very much, and shield, are the small moments of time when you can make anything happen. All the friends and people I invite to take part in performances, they all have fun and do anything they want within that little moment, that twenty minutes of time when you can volunteer to come and be as random and freaked out as you like. What you're talking about, it frightens me a lot. Because you risk losing your sense of fun, or sense of pleasure in life, or what would you say … gesture? But you don't seem to mind?

NN:
Well, no, because I see teaching as a way of circumventing that.

MGC:
Okay, me too. I understand.

NN:
Working with alternative methodologies with students is really inspiring. And also, like the project that I mentioned, with Gareth Jones – I also collaborate a lot with other artists; these ways of working are liberating, creative and political.

MGC:
So you have protective strategies in your practice, to balance up the practical.

NN:
Yes, and I've tried to make my practice as wide as possible for that reason. If I was only working with urban planning and engineers, I probably would just be …

MGC:
… an engineer, yourself.

NN:
Yes. Or a landscape architect or something, which is not something I'm interested in. I'm interested in a trans-disciplinary practice that's linked to the history of Bohemia.

MGC:
In relation to teaching, I had a really classic experience of working with children, as part of my work on The Idol [soft play centre] in Dagenham. I worked with children at Gascoigne School, and the kids came up with such cool ideas: one of them was to make a giant indoor play area designed to look like a man being bitten by a snake, and the snake could be the slide; another one was a swimming pool shaped like a pizza – all these fun ideas. They basically didn't have to compromise at all with any of the British Standards or the reality of building. I was left thinking, 'oh God, the kids are so cool – their ideas are brilliant and mine are boring!' But it's because of that journey of having to actually make it really happen.

HS:
I think, though, I have really disliked all the thinking that's gone on about calling what artists and creative practitioners do 'play', or behaving like a child. I don't experience it as play any more, and I think that's to do with how one's creativity changes over a life. But I do recognise that in collaboration, which is now all I do – I never work on my own any more. When you find somebody else who you absolutely trust, who has an intelligence that is utterly opposite to your own and you agree to collide, this thing gets born as if it were a child, if you like, which is something neither of you could have imagined. And that is probably, if I had to drag that word 'play' into my practice now, I'd say that's where I find it.

MGC:
I really love [artist and poet] Edward Lear, and he seemed to understand that, within the world of the child in the Victorian era, there was almost what we'd call an underground – a 'scene' – where you could be more playful and random and fun. And I don't mind at all any of that marginalisation – to be thought of as a child or to be thought of as an idiot. I like nonsense and everything that goes with it. To be honest, you're so used to being marginalised or condescended to as an artist, that it just doesn't affect me.

HS:
I think, then, it probably reflects the fact that I had a design education, and have done a lot of work with big companies. They've tried to hijack the world of imagination; I've been in too many rooms where they've been kind of workshopping to try and get play into the room, and it's been so artificial and devoid of the spirit you're talking about. It might be that I'm coming from a place where play has been ruined, because it has to turn into

money. If you go into these big Google-like companies, they have a room where everyone's allowed to go and play.

MGC:
Wearing romper suits …

HS:
And goodness knows what! But there are cameras on them all and the idea is they come out with an idea that can then be turned into billions of dollars. There are so many companies that – and it's quite perverse, really – set up spaces that look like a nursery school. Suddenly the furniture gets soft; there're lots of crazy colours around. The faux naivety and the cynicism with which these so-called play areas are put into corporate worlds …

MGC:
So, one of the things we're nudging towards is how you maximise on the generative powers of play without castrating it or nullifying it – killing it? And I'd say the most simple thing jumps into my head, which is that you just have to have a little voice inside your head that asks whether you're actually enjoying it yourself. I literally have a voice that asks, am I enjoying this? And if I am not, then it's not right. I'm probably not going to earn a lot of money, so it's not the right voice for those reasons! But if you're trying to preserve creativity in your life, or fun or exploration, you should just ask yourself whether you're enjoying it. I feel like it curves away from some of the professionalisation and some of the boredom and some of the nullifying. And artificiality.

NN:
I think one of the positive things about play as a kind of theme, or trend, is that it's changing some cities for the better. In Copenhagen, for example, playscapes and more playful areas are being designed into the urban fabric – and playgrounds are not fortified or fenced off, they're open and integral to public spaces. So you can walk around Copenhagen and easily stumble upon strange playscapes full of children, and they have ownership of those spaces, spaces that were once car parks or empty plazas. Which is the opposite of London. That's a positive thing about the inevitable instrumentalisation of play – in the right hands, it has huge benefits and potential in the way cities can be designed.

HS:
Yes, that would be good here in Britain, I was working with a student who lives in Brighton and she showed me some photographs of a project she was working on. There was a playground – you know, a properly designed playground – but there were no kids in it. Instead, like rabbits, they'd dug a hole under a piece of railing and the other side was a skate park they made. The space they were allowed to make for themselves had the temperature that they needed to be able to play.

NN:
[British anarchist writer] Colin Ward argued that there shouldn't be any playgrounds at all – children should be able to play wherever they like and it shouldn't be so prescriptive. But today I think this idea is too simplistic. The new redevelopment of Kings Cross has an underlying play theme, which is quite clumsy and corporate in its style, but there's a successful area outside Central Saint Martins with a fountain and steps that go down to the canal, and that space is very heavily used by people locally. The only problem is that it's all private property!

MGC:
You know, the conversation went gloomy again! But we're still talking about risk and enjoyment, I think ... One of the things I've had to understand is that there are lots of different types of artist, and I'm not against any of them, but I am one who makes with my hands. There're other types of artist who work very much like designers or they contract out labour and don't make things from scratch. And this has been something that's been a right old gripe of mine for a long time. People try to take work away from me – they say, we'll do this for you, or let's do that, or work in this way, and I've been pigheadedly consistent in wanting to make things myself. I started analysing it and thinking, maybe it's because I'm feminist and I want to do it the way I can – my relationship with materials is different because I'm not strong enough to work with wood and I can't make a five-metre-high wooden structure, so I work with plastic plumbing pipe, which is lighter. And I like all those small innovations. Also, by making it myself, I hold on to experimentation and the creativity. It makes sense to hold on to the fact that I make something myself. You're in a lawless space – I call it a no-man's-land – when you're in the studio and you don't know what you're doing and why, and then you come across something.

Low cost is in that bundle too. It's impossible to take such risks with a lot of money, but if you're tootling around with a piece of paper, no one's going to criticise you.

NN:
I find that, when I do exhibitions or commissions, I make physical and digital models, drawings and plans, which I see as 'materials'. Then I ask someone else to make the finished thing, because I know there is someone more skilled than me at doing that. But even within that process there's still some risk – that person might make it wrong or at least they'll try and do it in the way they want to, which maybe you don't like. And the institution – the curators and the marketing department – they'll want to change the project or maybe shift it in some way. So there's always a lot of risk in what you do in terms of what the outcome will be, and it's never completely what I imagine it to be.

MGC:
I relate to what you're saying with my performances, because I invite people to contribute when I work and contributions, including contracted work, can be interesting ... I don't mind saying that something that I've got an annoyance with is artists who work in a kind of nine-to-five way, where they are not living experimentally. I really passionately feel that artists should always be a hundred per cent questioning and experimenting. It goes back to that idea of whether you can 'switch on' the playfulness or the experimentation. I think it should be something that's applied to everything and every moment that you're alive – a way of being, I guess. But I totally accept that what you're saying can be creative. I understand.

NN:
I don't think that artists or designers or 'creatives' have direct access to this process, or better access than other people. I think that all people in all walks of life are creative. They're just doing it in different ways. And they don't package it, they don't make it into a product – as artists we're just very good at making it into a product.

HS:
And naming it.

MGC:
That's really positive. I used to hate Joseph Beuys so much when I was at art college but I've totally come round to his 'everyone's an artist' kind of thing ...

NN:
But I'm not saying everyone's an artist.

MGC:
No, what you've said is much clearer and it makes sense. You're saying that other people are doing creative things and it's not labelled as art.

NN:
Yes – they just don't see it as that. They see it as something they just love doing or enjoy doing. Maybe it's artists who are the problem.

HS:
That's another conversation!

MGC:
I don't mind not being called an artist. The thing that I would fight to the death for, it seems, is that I can't not be creative for some reason.

HS:
Yes – all I really want to do in terms of my teaching, for example, is to share an opportunity to create something at the same time as I'm doing it. With students, I very much want them to share the authentic artist and designer experience of not knowing where you're going, rather than giving them the rundown of how it happens. I think for it to mean something, you have to experience it.

CAMBERWELL COLLEGE OF ARTS AND KING'S COLLEGE HOSPITAL

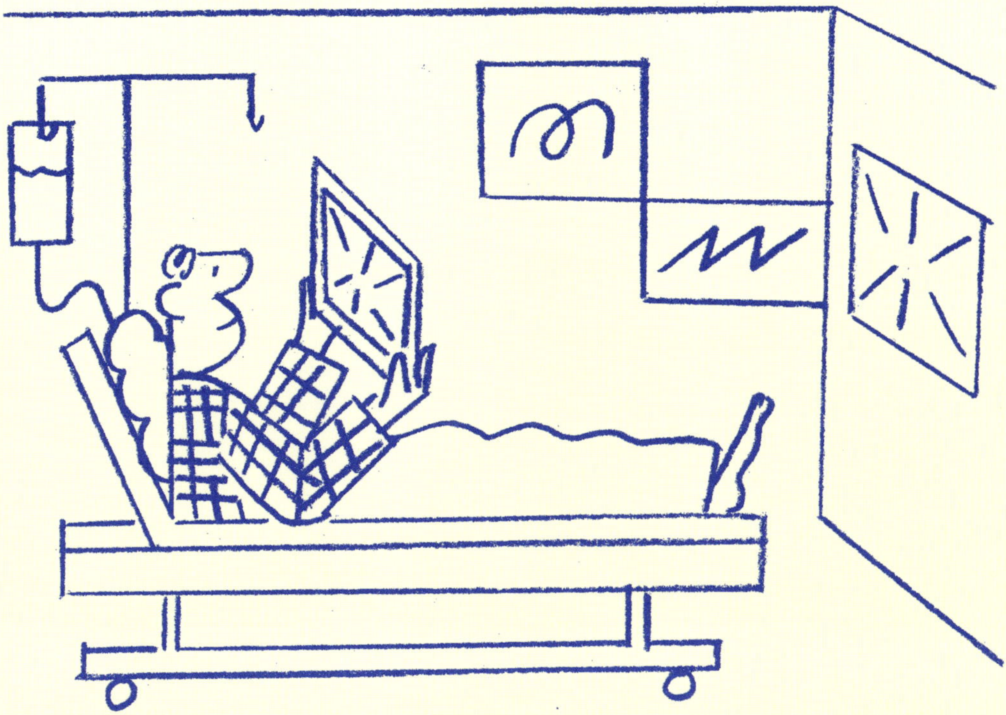

Invited to be imaginative, original and free-thinking, students at Camberwell College of Arts, UAL, were asked to submit designs for the individual patient rooms of King's College Hospital's groundbreaking new Critical Care Unit (in consultation with BMJ architects and Acrylicize art consultancy), and in doing so were obliged to consider a range of context-specific issues, including patient privacy, staff and visitor morale and the effects of sedation on patients' audiovisual perception. The joint winners – Russell Miller and Xavi Solé, and Elizabeth Lowe – sent proposals drawing on natural, positive imagery and, in the case of Miller and Solé, suggesting the use of interactive, app-based technology that would use coloured glass as a trigger for drawing voice, music and video content into the patient experience.

LADYBIRD BOOKS REIMAGINED

Given unrestricted access to the illustration archive of much-loved children's imprint Ladybird Books, participants in the 'Ladybird Books Reimagined' project at London College of Communication, UAL, were challenged to reinvestigate and reimagine the aesthetics and social mores enshrined in a heritage brand. How, they were asked, could illustration, animation and graphic design be deployed to repurpose nostalgia-laden source material, and inform and excite a contemporary audience?

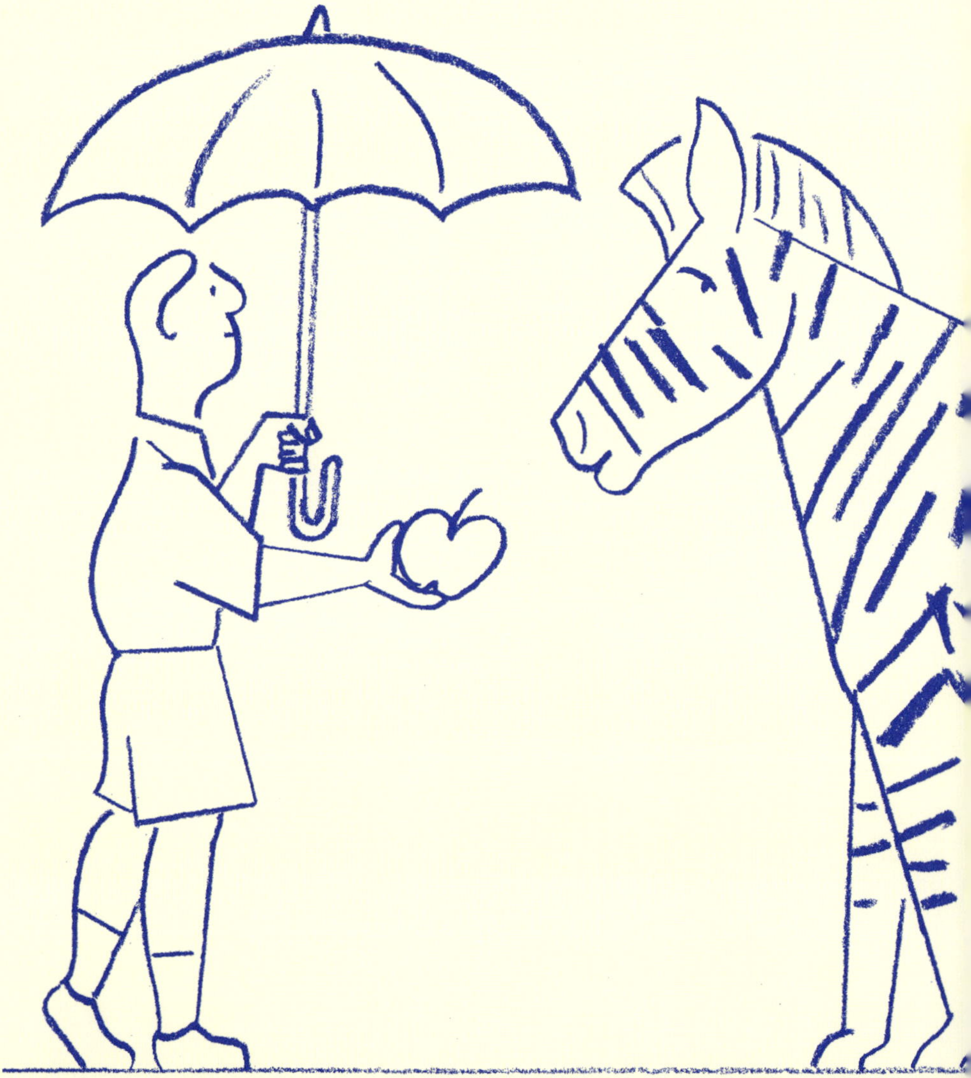

The resulting projects and public exhibition included Rosie Chomet's 'Ladybird Life Hacks' app proposal, which incorporates Ladybird imagery in a punchy new format, illustrating tips and tricks for everyday life; and Luc Bernay's more abstract 'Alphabet' installation, responding to the popular 'Ladybird ABC' (1962) through playful, instinctive animation, photography and sculpture.

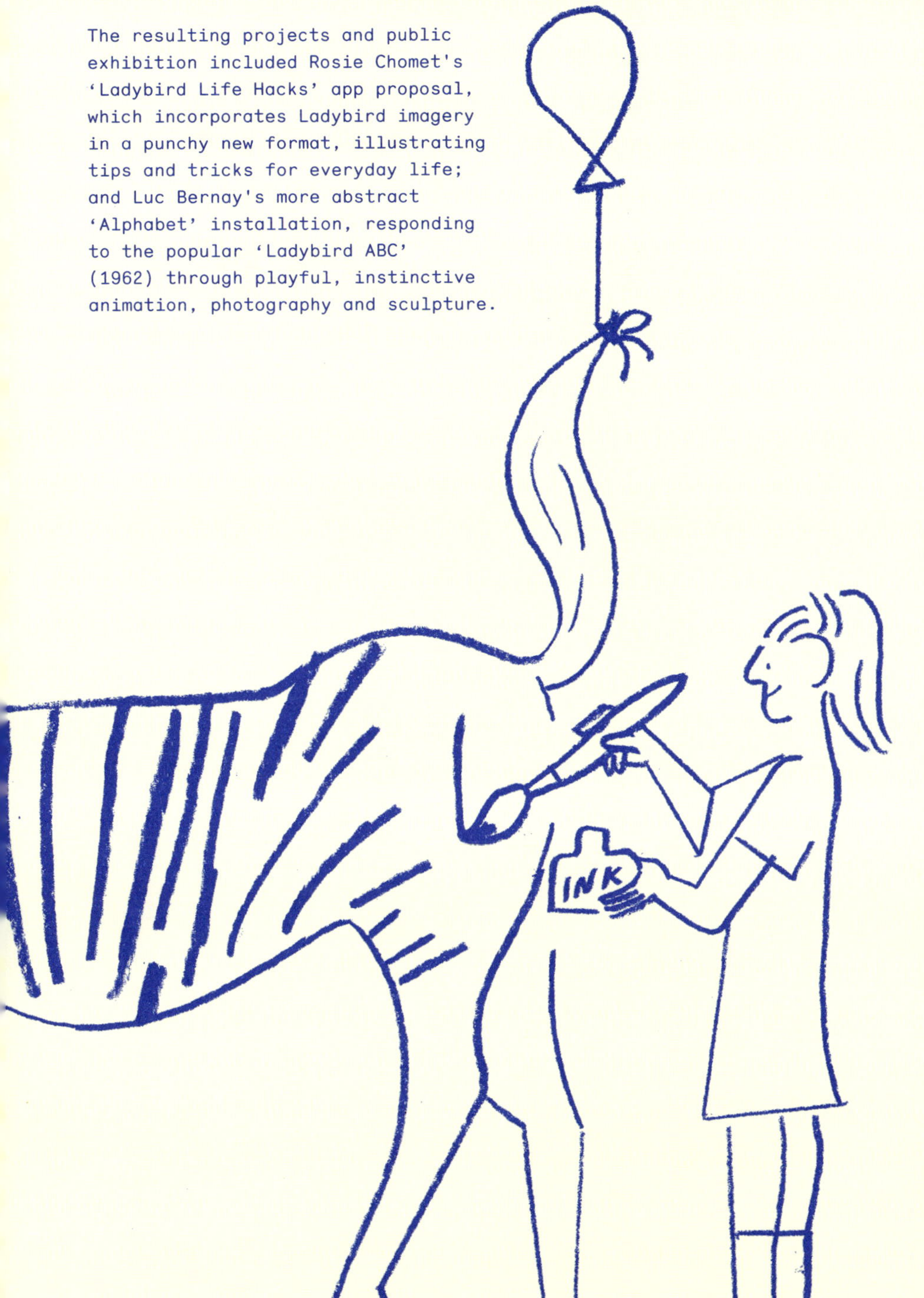

FINDING

This beautiful project – the final result of which was an exhibition at The Foundling Museum, London – took shape in response to the history of the Foundling Hospital (Britain's first children's charity), and its archive, a key part of which is a collection of tokens left by parents in order to identify themselves in the event that they were able to return for their children. The precious items made by students and lecturers on Central Saint Martins' BA Jewellery Design course reflect on love, loss and isolation in imaginative and unexpected ways, with outcomes ranging from jewellery made from offcuts of metal (Fiona Chong's 'Revalued'), to a pin-shaped tattoo, inspired by the pins used to attach identifying scraps of cloth to a mother's record at the Hospital (Lin Cheung's 'Pinpoint').

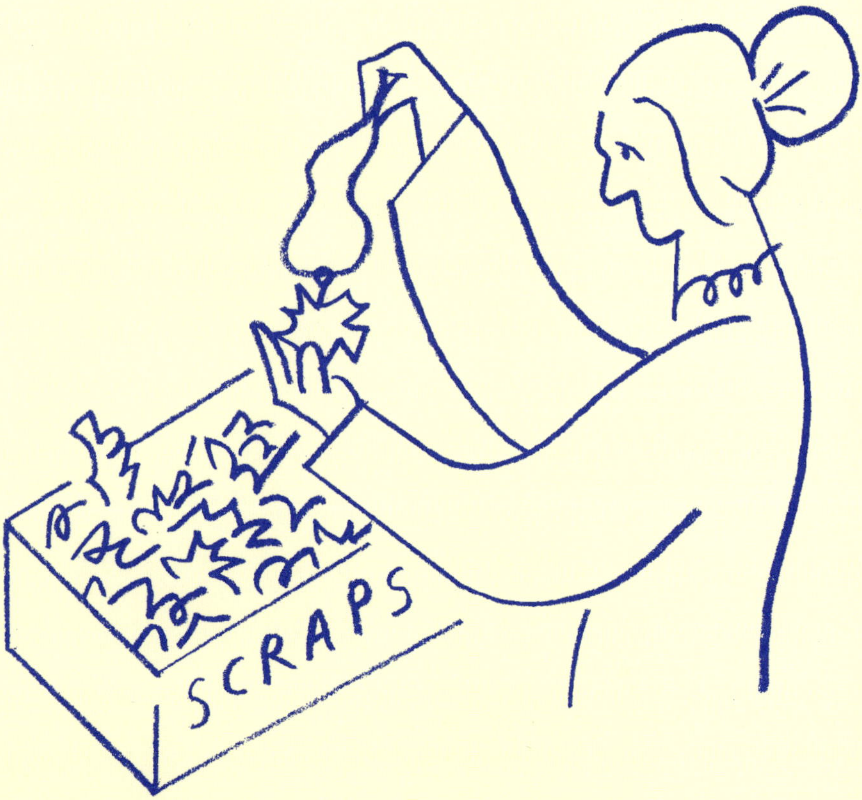

PROVOCATION

Sonia Boyce

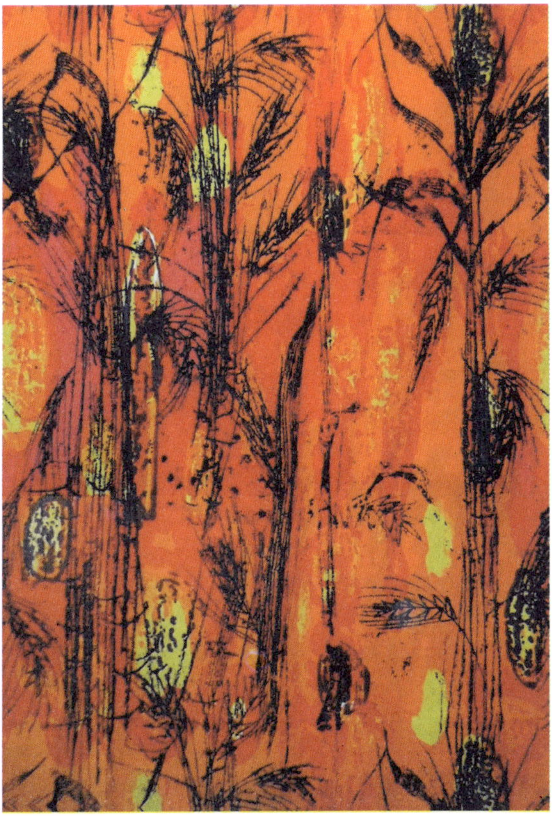

'GOLDEN HARVEST', furnishing textile designed by Althea McNish, 1957.
Printed by Hull Traders, 1959.

These thoughts were dictated by circumstance. Almost everything is, if we ignore those circumstances.

The circumstance was that I was late. Not just late, as I often am, to the room, but four months behind deadline. Lateness is, in itself, provoking. There are manifold reasons for lateness: that little voice inside that is worried about performance anxiety; the attempt to do too much in the allotted time; or the enactment of a small gesture of resistance against obligation. Industrialists invented timeliness as a control on factory workers. We have come to expect something that was not even humanly possible until the latest 'blink' of history. So, while lateness irritates, it also reveals artifice.

What we expect to be taught and who we expect to teach

At one time, I taught BA Fine Art at Central Saint Martins (CSM), UAL, alongside Anne Eggebert (current 'cross-disciplinary' Pathway Tutor on the degree). At the start of each course, I would arrive late, and Anne would start the class without me, standing at the front where teachers always stand. Each time, I would slip in, apologising. The students would shuffle up their chairs for me, taking me for another student. I would go and stand by Anne and see them bewildered. They didn't expect contemporary fine art practice to be taught by a Black woman – certainly not one who did not behave like a teacher.

Without fail, by the next teaching session, many of the students had Googled me. They wanted me to know that they knew who I was. They would recite bits of my CV back to me. This happened every year – the shift from making space for me as a peer to recognising me as experienced enough to be their teacher.

Taking a line for a walk[1]

Those first few months at the beginning of the academic year are the most exciting. They are about challenging and changing perceptions, particularly in relation to art-making. The first project is always a drawing project, but one in which drawing is explored as an expanded practice, not necessarily involving pencil and paper.

Here, the biggest challenge is to encourage students to let go of commonly held beliefs about, firstly, what it is to be an artist, and, secondly, what constitutes drawing. The first few months of the course are spent disentangling, questioning and extending the practice, beyond what constitutes a 'good' drawing, to examine how this practice might be used as a 'thinking' and 'doing' toolkit.

The question of amnesia is perpetual

Many art school tutors will have some recollection of themselves as students, studying alongside a student who was not white and/or not British. Recent research at the Equiano Centre, University College London,[2] and the Royal College of Art has shown the steady stream into British art schools, since at least the 1920s, of generations of artists from the former colonies. Artists from African and Asian backgrounds have been part of the art school experience for a long time. These artists have been central to the development of the British art school system, with many enjoying illustrious careers. This knowledge sits in our collective subconscious. The provocation is here in our midst.

How can the memory of their work be brought back into the curriculum? Thus far, it has not been. These artists have peaked and then, seemingly, disappeared. They are not part of the written record. They and their work are not taught to the next generation. The system momentarily celebrates and, then, dismisses them, neglecting to pass on their story - a fact that rubs against the grain of how making art gets taught (the past is always inflected in the present's challenge).

This provocation, of the forgotten self or the over-determined self (depending on which vantage point one takes), is a problem in the making of art history and therefore in making art itself.

The author's body, the work of art and its reception

Authorship is the primary commodity that is traded in our field - art. It is the basis of cultural capital, and artists are often recognised in ways particular to their social situation.

In her famous 1971 essay, Linda Nochlin eviscerates the question, 'Why have there been no great women artists?'[3] She lays out the partisan nature of the way we read a work and our need to biographise. She asks whose interests this particular question serves and concludes that the total situation of art-making - its production, reception and cultural evaluation - occurs in the context of a social structure. In the midst of this social structure is the spectre of the artist, into whom meanings are relentlessly driven, so as to meet our desire for the legible and explicable framing of artist and work.

Althea McNish came to Britain in the early 1950s. She was championed by Eduardo Paolozzi and became the poster-woman for New Design in post-war Britain. For a long time, she was one of the main designers at Liberty department store in London. She uses strong, bold colours, which critics have welcomed as tropicalising British design. Such language racialised her work.

David Medalla was a central figure in British art practice in the 1960s and 70s. He is best known for his assemblages of bubble machines, called the *Cloud Canyons* series; sculptures that defy the solid state. As a consequence of many conversations, these kinetic sculptures inspired Marcel Duchamp to create a series of works called 'Medallic' sculptures, but Medalla's contribution, if mentioned at all, remains a biographical footnote in most histories of art.

Another artist who studied in London in the 1950s is Frank Bowling, who was a key figure in the emergence of Pop Art while it was fermenting at the Royal College of Art. He quickly moved into abstract expressionism. He was a restless traveller - often corresponding with the art critic and doyen of late modernism, Clement Greenberg. He tried to resist being siphoned off to a place that would instrumentalise his work in a racialised way. His drip paintings challenge the idea of painting as the work of hand-eye coordination, to push our readings into the discursive field of painting-as-process. He used primary colours in colour-field paintings such as *Who's Afraid of Barney Newman?* (1968). Critics again marshal the work into the realm of the tropical. However, he was simply using the building blocks of colour, and clearly in dialogue with one of the foremost practitioners of colour-field painting, Barnett Newman.

When do primary colours become tropical?

The artist and writer David Batchelor, in his book *Chromophobia* (2000), has commented:

> The notion that colour is bound up with the fate of Western culture sounds odd, and not very likely. But this is what I want to argue: that colour has been the object of extreme prejudice in Western culture ... It is, I believe, no exaggeration to say that,

> in the West, since Antiquity, colour has been systematically marginalised, reviled, diminished and degraded …
>
> Chromophobia manifests itself in the many and varied attempts to purge colour from culture, to devalue colour, to diminish its significance, to deny its complexity. More specifically: this purging of colour is usually accomplished in one of two ways. In the first, colour is made out to be the property of some 'foreign' body – usually the feminine, the oriental, the primitive, the infantile, the vulgar, the queer or the pathological. In the second, colour is relegated to the realm of the superficial, the supplementary, the inessential or the cosmetic. In one, colour is regarded as alien and therefore dangerous; in the other, it is perceived merely as a secondary quality of experience, and thus unworthy of serious consideration.[4]

By redirecting the viewer to interpret primary colours as tropical colours, readings of Bowling's abstract paintings indirectly tell us that he is Black. Why is it important that we should know this? The paintings, standing independently, could not tell us such a fact. This particular focus on the artist's cultural background eclipses the work. Bowling's body is used as a framing device for how we interpret the work. Think of Duchamp and try not to see a white urinal and its place in the discourse of art-making. Think of Bowling and we are guided to see a Black man who, although working with abstraction, can yet only speak of his own identity, and not more widely towards the field of contemporary painting.

Comments (McNish, Bowling) and non-comments (Medalla) on artists' production reveal a social bias that constructs a perceived difference – a setting apart. There seems to be an attempt to push the work outside contemporaneous discussions of art's paradigms.

The spectre of the maker

Provocation starts with the meaning projected on to the object, which relates to the many selves that come into contact with it. How do you provoke yourself? Try to understand something outside yourself, not just yourself. Become aware of how the spectre of the artist, of you as a body, is constructed socially. Self is not, however, a cul-de-sac. Self and outside-of-self are interconnected and not easily distinguished – cannot be separated from the wider cultural context for any maker. Many artistic practices are fuelled by the understanding of self as part of wider cultural practice. In fact, without a discussion on race, sex or gender identity, it is not possible to call oneself white, straight or male.

Is the identity of the maker problematic or exciting? Let us start with this essay, which came about through lateness. These thoughts were dictated, according to circumstance. Sonia Boyce is such a circumstance. These words are mine. The co-writer is the man I spoke these words to. He is another circumstance. In some ways it is another provocation to reveal his identity in the writing of this text, which came about through a process of exchange. Who we are is and is not the work.

Who are we before the work and who did the work? We forget. This will be a problem only if we choose to ignore it.

Notes

1. Paul Klee, *Pedagogical Sketchbook*, London 1953.
2. Equiano Research Centre, University College London, *Drawing over the Colour Line: Geographies of Art and Cosmopolitan Politics in London*, 1919–1939, London 2012–14.
3. Linda Nochlin, 'Why Have There Been No Great Women Artists?', in Vivian Gornick and Barbara Moran (eds.), *Woman in Sexist Society: Studies in Power and Powerlessness*, New York 1971.
4. David Batchelor, *Chromophobia*, London 2000, pp.22–3.

In conversation on 'provocation'

Roger Hiorns

Scott King

Tom Morton

Roger Hiorns
(RH)

British sculptor

Scott King
(SK)

Chair of Visual Communication at University of the Arts London

Tom Morton
(TM)

Writer, curator, lecturer and Contributing Editor for *frieze* magazine

The participants were asked to discuss the topic of creative provocation, with particular reference to their respective fields. They begin with their definition of 'provocation' in relation to creativity.

RH:
It's interesting that Tom is here because one of the more provocative works I have made, or the one that seems consistently to provoke, was something I worked on with Tom when he was a curator at Cubitt [an artist-led gallery space in London]. Essentially, it was an adding of semen to the light fittings of the Cubitt gallery space [*Untitled*, 2006; see overleaf]. There were a number of reasons why I thought that this was, maybe not an important, but an interesting thing to do, and a provocative action. It was about economy to a certain degree, and about a biological sort of expression. I also wanted to claim some territory - Cubitt was going through a period of being a really fascinating place to show work, and I suppose I felt a need to find a provocative stance within that space.

TM:
This was in 2006.

RH:
The reason I bring this work up is that I recently talked about it at an event at Tate Modern and there was an uncomfortable response. Someone afterwards commented on it as being a troublesome act - something that they weren't particularly impressed or encouraged by.

TM:
We should perhaps explain that this wasn't really a show, as such - it was a sculpture. That's how Roger usually defines himself, as a sculptor. Semen was introduced on to one of the strip lights at Cubitt between shows - we didn't tell anyone which strip - and remained in place as part of the lighting, so that every subsequent show was bathed in this light - anointed or polluted by this particular filter. If you looked very, very closely at the light you could tell it had been treated, but from ground level not at all. Installing it was quite interesting - nobody wanted to help Roger and me. The gallery manager hid in the office the whole time! There was a wall label near Cubitt's entrance, listing the work's materials and an announcement on the website that the work had manifested in the space, but no explanatory text.

SK:
I was going to ask you that, because it's interesting to me that in many ways the provocation is simply the announcement. The act itself is ignorable or invisible, and quite harmless, ultimately. To me, it's more about an idea as a catalyst for the viewer - that feeling that somehow you've been intruded upon.

RH:
Yes, there was a sense that the light would be contaminated, that everything that was going on, the comings and goings in that space, would be seen through this filter. There was a sort of psychological response that you were to have, because perceptually, as you say, it was pretty nominal, but the psychological response one had depended on your prejudices to the act. I think an interesting thing to talk about in this context is the neutralisation of activities. If there is a provocation, it's like a rusty nail that's sticking out and people want to hammer it back in. These days, protests of all kinds are mostly anticipated, and so provocation can get neutralised pretty quickly and effectively. Maybe the future of the provocative act, if it's going to be used as a tool for change, is the unanticipated or unannounced.

SK:
I think it has to be. I was going to say that provocation or 'being provocative' is something you are labelled with. My work

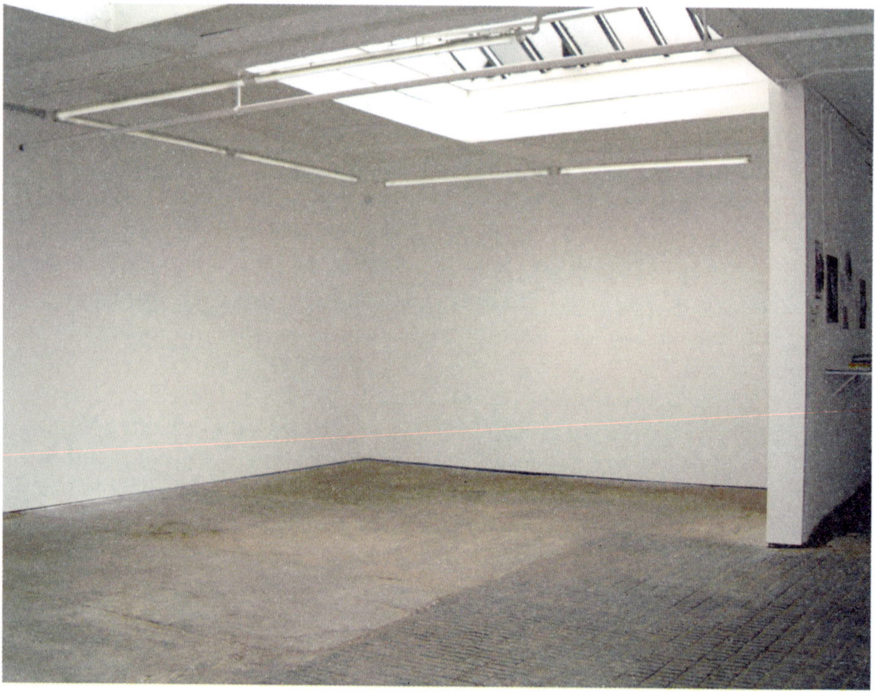

Roger Hiorns, *Untitled* (installation view), Cubitt Gallery, London, 2006.

might be called provocative, or moronic, or whatever, really, but as an artist, you don't necessarily set out to provoke. That's why I asked about the title and announcement of your work.

TM:
We made that work again for the [2007] Athens Biennale, actually. The light was one of the rather grubby lights that sit around the Acropolis and illuminate the Parthenon – one of those was treated. The announcement was in a Greek newspaper, if memory serves, and also in a gallery space with other wall labels. So it partly existed by rumour, I guess, although it was in the catalogue, too.

SK:
Did it cause issues?

TM:
No, not at all. I mean, we didn't take out a full-page ad in the Greek version of *The Sun* …

SK:
That's interesting. It's very obvious, of course, but I keep thinking about Malcolm McLaren and that wilful use of the media. What's famous is the Sex Pistols period, and everything we all know about that, but, before that, McLaren was managing the New York Dolls, at the tail end of their career. It was the mid-1970s and he was having them

dressed in red patent leather - making use of Soviet, Russian-Eastern Bloc symbolism - and touring to places like Miami, Florida, away from New York, where those things were acceptable. That's an outward act of provocation in the most base - to me very exciting, it's really rock and roll - but the most base sense. So it's just interesting to me that you said, no, we didn't take out a full-page ad. The pop thing, the McLaren thing, has the act of provocation really under the trigger.

RH:
Well, we could've gone the other way. We could've said, yes, we will tell everybody. But then it would have been for the sake of the publicity. There are a number of artists who use publicity as a tool as much as any tool in the studio. But it becomes exhausting. You're making a negotiation with the present, I think, when you're dealing with that kind of context. I still think there's something fascinating about the fact that art can be an escape from time - that you can create relevancies that come backwards and forwards in time, in and out of focus. If you create a huge amount of fanfare, or if you stir up provocation within the press in that rather standard way - 'here it is, now be outraged' - then you situate your work in the present and it doesn't become a relevant thing. Provocation feels like an act that is crossing a threshold. It's allowing a 'peak' to happen within a rather stable society, which then allows something to come into focus. It's troublesome to be provocative these days ... Do people want to be provoked at this point? Do people want to find themselves in situations that are uncomfortable?

TM:
I think there's a kind of provoked that people want to be, where they want to experience a tingle - look at that Banksy work, say, where he depicts a line of policemen with smiley, Acid-House faces. We all get the gag: drugs good, cops bad. There's not really a lot of thought beyond that, though; you know, if your grandmother gets burgled, you probably really want the police to respond! That cheap, Banksy-ish type of provocation lacks deep resonance. It just feels like normal cultural business, like Lady Gaga or something.

SK:
It is. That is the legacy of punk - protest as commodity and easily consumed.

RH:
But, in the early days, still very transgressive. You know, they built a commercial model on something that is actually about transgression, about allowing a certain new type of act and new type of music, and also a certain type of behaviour. Punk behaviour was something that really fascinated me, because of the spitting and the pogo-ing and the way they would wear Nazi paraphernalia. All this was about stripping away a space that had been grown up by authority to put people in. It was fascinating to watch a youth group saying, well, we're not becoming part of the establishment.

TM:
Or, crucially, we're not becoming hippies, like the kids five, ten, fifteen years older than us.

SK:
There were lots of things that they weren't becoming and that was ultimately what it was about, wasn't it - 'not becoming'?

TM:
Something that has really interested me

recently is BP's withdrawal of their financial support of Tate, which is presumably at least partially because of the press generated by the Liberate Tate protests. It's notable that no artist above a certain level of recognition within the art world, a certain level of sales, publically nailed their colours to the mast on the issue – even those who are usually comfortable trading on their political affiliations kept very, very quiet. By contrast, actors such as Mark Rylance and Emma Thompson, and writers such as Margaret Atwood and Caryl Churchill, were happy to write a public letter of protest to the British Museum calling for them to drop BP as a sponsor. I find that totally fascinating. It seems to me that Tate's (former) sponsorship by BP, and Tate's having made moves to prevent details of that deal getting into the public realm, is far more provocative than the actions of the Liberate Tate protestors, which, to be fair, Tate were fairly good at accommodating.

RH:
Is this to say, because Tate itself has an overwhelming authority, this means the neutralisation of any dissent from artists, simply because they want to get on within the Tate? That would be one interpretation. Sure, I would say that's plausible, but also we may be giving the Tate too much credit, too much implied power – it has its own internal problems to focus on, I imagine.

SK:
For me, coming from a magazine background, and desperately, I admit, wanting to be an artist – this was the mid-90s, the time of the 'Young British Artists' – I was very aware that there was graphic design, commercial design, and then there was proper fine art. But I remember going to see a show – I think it was called *Bad Girls* – at the ICA, London [7 October – 5 December 1993], and it was very clearly sponsored by an oil company, with a huge fucking logo on the back of the invite. As a twenty-four-year-old, I thought this was a bad joke, because I didn't understand, but then you realise that this stuff just isn't mentioned – people just want to get their work out there. In Britain, at least, this is a fall-out of the commercial success of the YBAs, and it's never been challenged since.

RH:
Just a bit of background – there was attrition behind the scenes. A number of artists and a number of curators *were* consistently debating this issue with Tate, and at a number of levels. And, of course, Liberate Tate was incredibly focused and effective; the publicity war was certainly won with the strongest of messages – a war of attrition that probably made the trustees exhausted. It took too long for Tate to get the point.

SK:
But also, it's everywhere – any artist who's in any art fair and sells their work is in indirect contact with any arms dealer, or whoever, who buys their work.

RH:
The 'clerk-to-the-regime' curator, the corporate raider, the arms dealer or manufacturer – these are interesting figures to bring up. Early on, I had a gallery policy, which was not to sell work to people who were evidently profiting from or had evidently profited from anti-humanitarian acts. I think it's really important to have a sense of your own autonomy, and this perceived autonomy can exist ethically as much as contextually and intellectually. Artists can take a stand. So yes, there are contemporary and historical collections built on grim foundations – on pollution,

on asset-stripping and on other versions of systemic violence that infiltrate the common good of the world. Pharmaceuticals too. The art world accommodates, helping people to cross the border into legacy and acceptability. The funding of education departments, academy schools, tie-ins to public institutions, and the discussion about their legitimacy can quite quickly be settled by the art world PR machine. Students – how do they feel about that? That their college department may be problematically funded? Perhaps they feel their silence is bought early on.

TM:
I guess the point I'm trying to make is that the world itself is provocative, and often a lot more provocative than art. Even the apparatus of the art world is a lot more provocative than art a lot of the time. You know, we have institutions that feel, design-wise, quite free and open and like spaces of dissent, but you find out very, very quickly that they're not and that they reflect vested interests. You have collectors who have very, very difficult associations. So, given how provocative the world is, I wonder if we can move the idea of provocation away from Banksy-type, prodding provocation and towards something else.

RH:
Yes, I think you can talk about certain artists who are provocative without a capital 'P'.

TM:
Less 'noisy' practices, somehow.

RH:
Less noisy, but still trying to redesign the way that we're supposed to behave. Because maybe the future of any creativity is about opening new sites for expression, redesigning behaviour, perhaps, as the tired-out traditions of painting and making objects, and the need to make attractive art, wane. I suppose that when we talk about problematic actors, or when we talk about institutions that aren't playing the ethical game one might hope, people who share the supported conditions where art is being made and selected or nominated can become disheartened. As a young artist it's easy to give up your authority to an arena in which a lot of people are not acting in a way that you find very supportive to a collaborative, progressive future – to a progressive idea of what the new future can be. So what do you do? You have to do two things. You have to make artworks that are provocative and, at the same time, you also have to change the landscape that art exists within. So it's not just a situation where you're a passive artist making objects or artworks for the art world. This is important, and has always been the Herculean task – to reshape the world to contain the artwork you make, to create a new reality – because it's never been enough just to make the art. And change is happening. Whatever the reason, Tate and BP have separated. So you do have this new arena where art can establish itself. I think Tate is reflecting the work that it wants to accommodate in the future. The uptake of the art world is so slow, and there is a lot of art being made now – the institutional juggernaut is taking time to react to the world.

SK:
Can you speak a bit more about the artists that are changing the landscape?

RH:
Well, you have to find activities, actions; you have to find ways of putting a wedge into your reality, into the world, somehow. One of the interesting moments in my

experience as a student at Goldsmiths was another student simply saying 'make yourself aware of every single artwork that's ever been made. Just go into the library and digest.' And I think that students, to this day, do this. You become so familiar with the territory that it becomes possible to actually feel some kind of ownership within the system, and to feel that it can be changed from within or without. To become completely present in the present, to understand the world and its systems, allows you also to understand its fractures and locate its Achilles heels – to apply a perpetual present-ness to art history.

TM:
Historically, something like Land art would be a good example.

RH:
Just on the subject of creating that space – one thing just dawned on me. Sorry to talk about the semen work again, but when I was preparing that Tate talk, I had to remind myself about the origin of the work. There was a certain amount of daydreaming that allowed this work to happen, and the daydreaming happened when I was an adolescent who had to spend most of his time in a religious place. I think there was something interesting about the sacred space claimed by a deity. A reaction to this is that you want to reclaim the area and put the human back at the centre of things. So to think about coating the cathedral lights with semen was a sort of humanist challenge to the sacred architecture. You have an area where a language and a symbol is a compound aggression and doesn't allow you to feel – already, at this early age – that you're having a fulfilling relationship to the world, to language. So you want to create a space in which you feel that you can operate freely. There is a flickering of adolescence in this work.

So, does a provocative act have to be based around attention, do you think? Is it always attractive to play to the reactive senses? In this context, being 'provocative' for its own sake makes me think of a work by Ai Weiwei – lying on the beach, re-enacting that photograph of the Syrian child, Alan Kurdi, who drowned in the Mediterranean Sea.

SK:
You look at that and it's just, it's like a Banksy, isn't it? But Ai's position has changed in the last four or five years to the point where he's become a genuinely international figure. Now, with that, you might expect a more sophisticated international language, but I don't think it's ever developed.

TM:
No. To me, the post-earthquake work he made [*Straight*, 2008–12] seemed to have a lot of value as a project of citizen journalism, in so far as some of the activity around its creation involved researching and publicising the number and names of the people who died in the 2008 Sichuan 'quake due to corner-cutting construction practices. But the actual work itself, the rebars straightened out and presented as sculpture [as they were at the Royal Academy of Arts, London, in 2015], seemed entirely inert. And that's probably his best work.

RH:
People don't have a lot of time for art, so if you have an artist who makes it legible – he has a very legible, international, familiar, ready-made practice, which is incredibly readable to the media – people don't have to investigate too much. The work is made to be a direct image: a package of information, news and commentary with a legible, non-threatening, non-alienating aesthetic.

SK:
It seems like advertising, perhaps.

RH:
There's another character within this game, and that's Anish Kapoor. Both he and Ai seem to capture media attention quite consistently. It's interesting how, when you become known for a certain type of art-making, the limitations of that art-making don't necessarily allow for progress. So, what to do? You can design a new arena, which is based on your persona, perhaps. Does this also fall under 'provocation'? A negative provocation? It's not allowing anything other than the individual to progress and survive. I think the provocation that we are increasingly seeing among students is the opposite – a non-individualistic kind – in which an action takes people with it, or a space is entered into that opens up new possibilities and new activities: generosity, essentially. Art is then more than simply a plaything for the wealthy.

TM:
Are you aware of Scott's book about this?

RH:
Yes I am. We should talk about that.

SK:
Sure. Well, it's called *Anish and Antony Take Afghanistan* [see overleaf], and it's a small graphic novel drawn by a young man called Will Henry, though I wrote the story. Essentially, a few years ago, I became quite obsessed with Anish Kapoor and Antony Gormley, and the deployment of public sculpture in Britain, particularly the way in which these artists were poster-boys for this new kind of gigantism in public sculpture. Gigantic sculptures were being deployed in places like Middlesbrough or Gateshead – communities that we often call post-industrial – and I had a problem with the artists' unquestioning dedication to themselves within this role. The book is about sculpture used as a weapon in order to gain cultural and political power, and I thought an extreme example of it would be for the UN to send Anish and Antony to Afghanistan, and to build huge public sculptures in order to save Afghanistan. It goes horribly wrong for them in the end.

But one thing that I'm always concerned about, and still am, is that they're a soft target. That's why I was asking you, Roger, about open provocation as opposed to the 'slow drip' approach – something that's not 'face-on' about bringing direct attention to what is perhaps a quite temporary public or social situation, which is what I think these gigantic sculptures were, ultimately.

RH:
There are conversations now about how to make an art object that is supposed to survive outside the limitations of public art. How is a work supposed to exist outside the institution, in the real world? It's interesting for me as I bury a number of aircraft ...

SK:
Yes, I read about this.

RH:
I'm supposed to be burying an aircraft in central Birmingham, in a piece of post-industrial land (see pp.176–7); strangely enough, right where I grew up, so it's an area that I'm familiar with. Birmingham is a fascinating place – a patchwork and collage of lots of different styles, different starting points and finishing lines that are in no sense cohesive. Friends who walk around Birmingham find it very difficult to get their bearings – it's almost landmark-free, except for maybe the Rotunda.

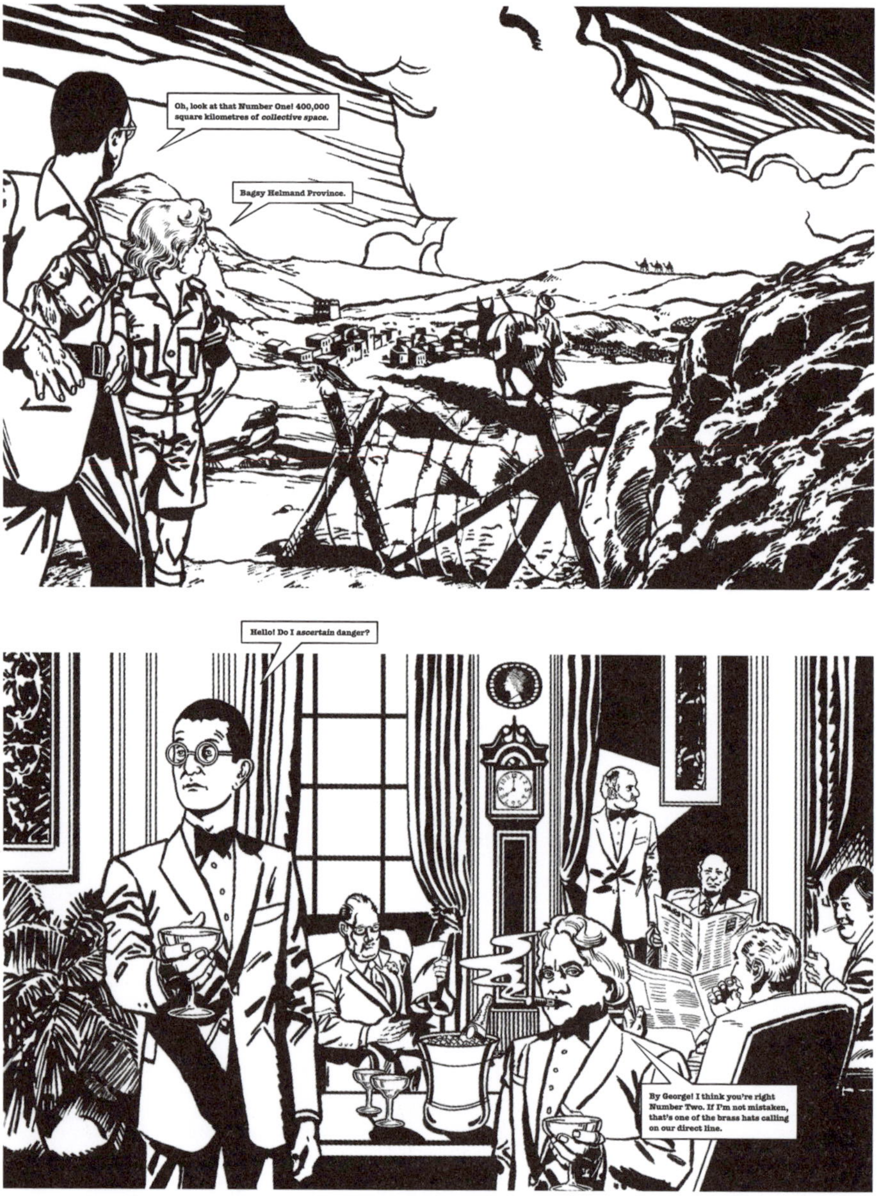

Scott King (words) and Will Henry (illustrations), from *Anish and Antony Take Afghanistan*, 2014.
Overleaf: Roger Hiorns, proposal for *Untitled (Buried Passenger Aircraft)*, 1975–present.

So it's interesting to do this action, potentially an Arts Council of England-funded work, under the socially cohesive stipulations their funding introduces. A self-critical artwork – it's not an artwork that's seen, because it's under the ground.

SK:
But it's accessible, isn't it?

RH:
It's physically accessible. Exactly. It doesn't have that same sense of monumentalism that perhaps the *Angel of the North* [1998] has. This is an age-old work, an idea I've been talking about for a while. It was about taking something that is part of the global world, something that deeply affects our sense of reality – of course, you get on a plane, you land in Rio, Brazil, and you're in a different climate, society, a new reality. The object has a great influence on the present world, so to take this object and somehow insult it is important. There's something I enjoy about taking something that exists in the world and training it against itself: the experience of entering into it, a constant un-ending present.

TM:
Well, if you place an object like an aircraft into this environment, then this thing that you might see as a bounded object now becomes a space to walk through. You can't put a space to walk through on a keyring in quite the same way you could put the *Angel of the North* or the ArcelorMittal Orbit.

SK:
Yes – in your version, people can get inside. I think that's essential to the people who are paying for it. They want the viewer experience, and it will become an essential part of the justification of the work, and also allows for lots of press coverage.

RH:
Yes, it allows for lots of press, and social-media coverage. This is the contemporary media landscape that we have, of allowing people to be their own individuals among the artwork. A work that has not been claimed by myself for a while - funded by the lottery, and local business and enterprise. A circus in a way, the amplified and unlimited image of the self in a place of anxious extremity. Sometimes you want to will an artwork to cross the psychic border into a symptom.

SK:
I was going to ask about this in the context of [London-based architecture, art and design collective] Assemble winning the Turner Prize. Now, how much stock we place in the Turner Prize is for us to decide, but, to me, this decision was an incredibly political act. Not the wet philanthropy that they do, which is political as well, but the fact that they won this thing and what that says about British art and the utility of it. What does it symbolise to you, if anything?

TM:
I think it's a possible misstep by Tate – a dog-whistle signalling something about their intentions: a gesture towards community engagement, perhaps, towards an idea of art having social purpose. It was also a way of injecting life into what had become a slightly moribund apparatus – the Turner Prize. The winners had increasingly become curators' favourites; whether you like, say, Duncan Campbell's films or not, this wasn't the kind of work that was discussed on the top deck of the bus by a vast tranche of the British public. Were you irritated that the winners were people who, however good they may be at what they do, were not artists?

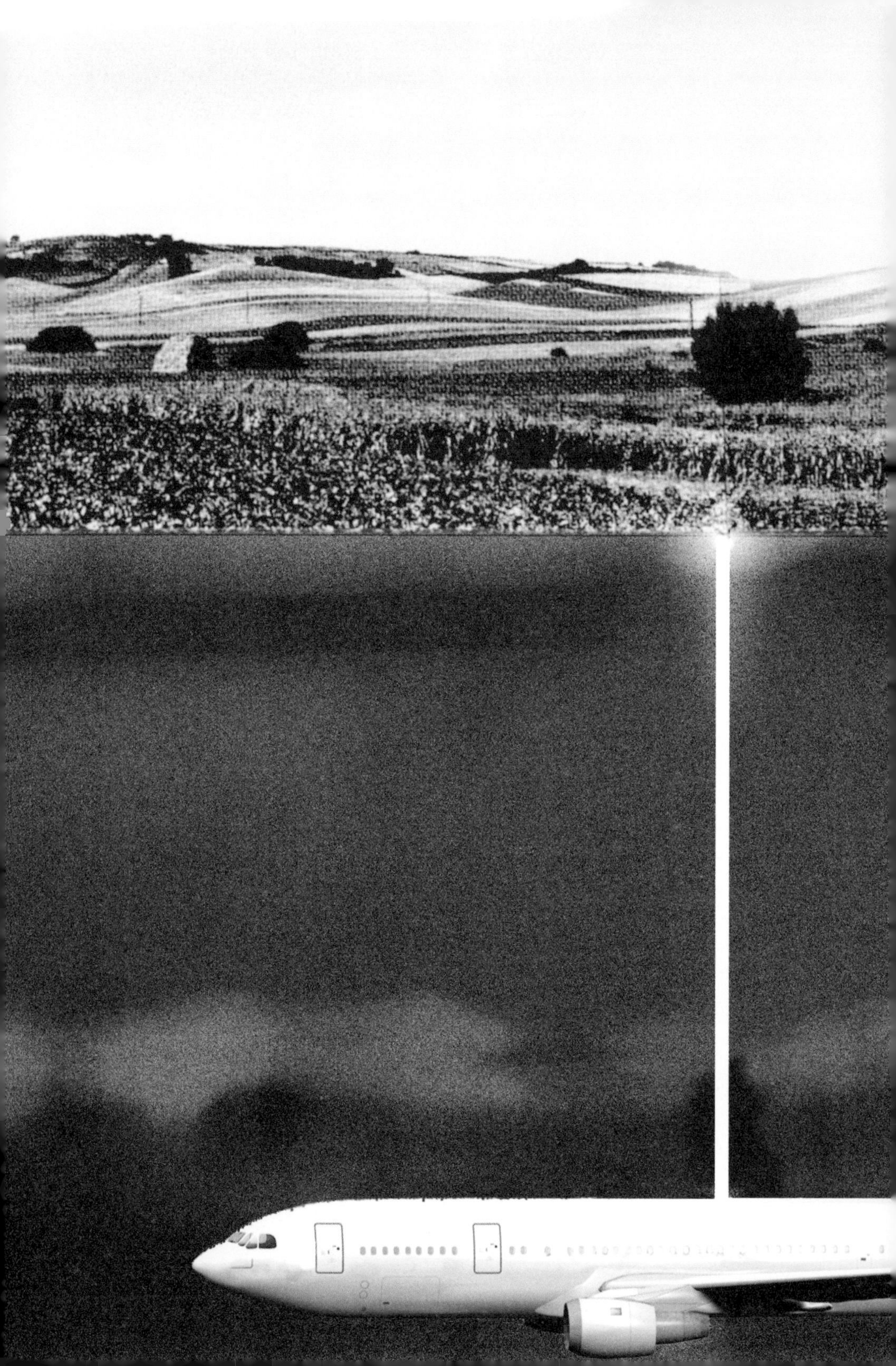

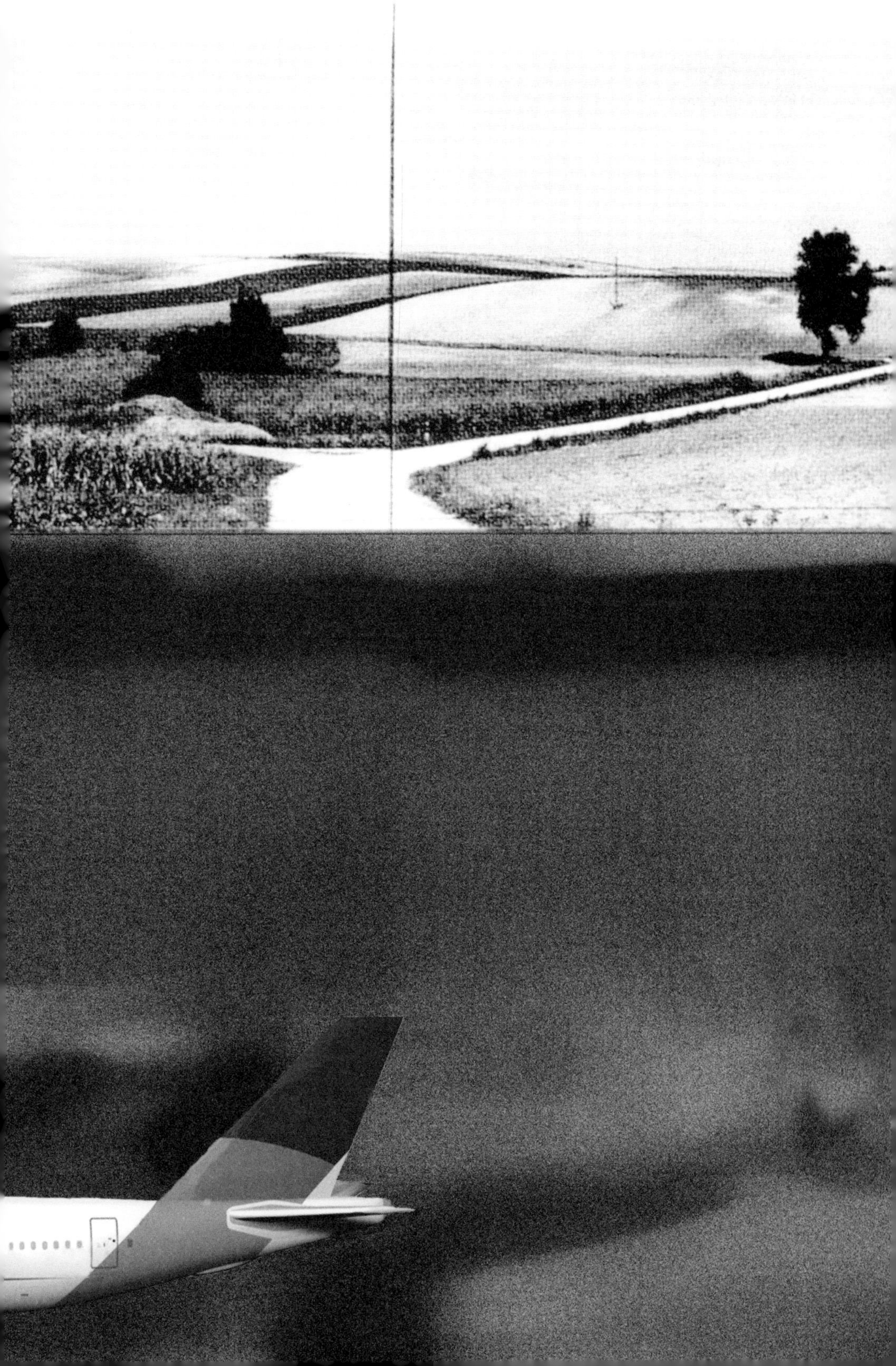

SK:
No, that didn't annoy me. What annoyed me was that it appeared to be a complete negation of the real politics. Assemble are such an easy fit in what Robert Hewison calls the 'age of lead' [Robert Hewison, *Cultural Capital: The Rise and Fall of Creative Britain*, 2014]: this post-funding period that we're now in, this total denial of funding for the arts. Assemble are such an obviously easy solution after the gigantism of Gormley and Kapoor – these lovely, middle-class people bringing tofu and brown rice …

RH:
It's well-meaning and you feel uncomfortable, in that you know you're being manipulated. There's always been that theory within politics, that if a protest group is occupying space, no matter how effective or ineffective their protest is, protest space is at least being occupied and the public perception is that something is 'being done'. But it's a placeholder for effective protest. What happens is that you have this generation who feel that a position of social usefulness – a very legitimate position to take within agitating for social progress or development – has been occupied by unimaginative poseurs.

TM:
The 'provocation' in this is actually not the provocation Tate intended. The real provocation is a message to artists saying, well, you're not as effective social actors as architects. It's saying, we really want people who have a measurable impact. You can't measure the numinous.

SK:
I think you're right and I think it's a huge and public vote for this idea of utility. No criticism intended at all, because I love him, but Jeremy Deller's bouncy castle [*Sacrilege*, 2012] is a great example of that. It was supported by the Arts Council.

RH:
My son adored it, so it worked. He saw it as an art project and he bounced on it – it was working in a very acceptable way. It was also optimistic. It's interesting; I used to use the word 'numinous' all the time and I'm reminded of how my language has changed over the last ten years or so. I would talk about open-ended ideas and metaphysical, numinous ideas. You could make a work by having a mysterious and reflective relationship to the world. Now you have to consider a rogue bunch: the idea of utility, the audience, money, networking, short attention spans, lack of curiosity on the part of the authorities, short-termism. These ideas are everywhere now – dripping out of every institution and every piece of text you read.

SK:
And it's being bred in art schools, I think – the idea of units or the points you need in order to progress.

RH:
Well, use has a value. Students are going to be leaving college with a certain amount of debt and they're going to have to find out what their value is.

SK:
That's where it begins, isn't it? The debt is where the idea of usefulness begins.

RH:
An alien thing. I graduated and then I was a postman. I was a postman in Peckham for five years, and it was a time, in my early twenties, to reflect. It was a time of not doing anything. It wasn't a time of debt, it was a time of being very poor and not having much. A lack of options is important, and idleness allows

a natural thought-process to establish itself. When I talk to students, I relay this. I say, I can only tell you from my own experience – just give yourself a job where you don't have to think too much, pay the bills and just get on with it – start thinking.

TM:
I think, whether we're talking about fiction or pop music or art, the challenge seems to be, perhaps always is, how do we dodge the position of the acceptable provocateur? How do we negotiate dealing with power? What constitutes a genuine provocation? I mean, if one were to invent an analogue of punk now, it would sit alongside a bunch of other options, rather than turning things upside down. This is a product of what I suppose we might call postmodernity, or certainly late post-modernity. So those kinds of formal option are now probably more about changing your own head. Provocation seems to be more localised now.

SK:
It's a difficult one because I don't think you really go around thinking you want to provoke people. You just want to tell the truth to yourself. It's a very difficult question, provocation, because once you've made any kind of gesture, it's almost out of your hands, whether it's out of your hands with immediate effect, in the case of making the four-page announcement, or whether it's the slow drip of the sperm on the light fixture. One utterly ridiculous instance was that of Chris Ofili and the elephant dung thing in New York [*The Holy Virgin Mary*, 1996, was exhibited in the touring exhibition *Sensation* at the Brooklyn Museum of Art, New York, causing then-mayor Rudolph Giuliani to label the work 'sick']. It's not even vaguely, remotely provocative to any right-thinking person.

TM:
It was post-Andres Serrano – that kind of reading of the work was a huge deal in America. The National Endowments of the Arts was attacked as a result of the furore over Andres Serrano [Serrano's *Piss Christ*, 1987 – a photograph of a plastic crucifix submerged, allegedly, in the artist's urine – had been the centre of the so-called 'Culture Wars', whereby the use of taxpayers' money to fund such controversial works was vocally criticized].

RH:
Yes, there is a legacy to provocation. If you're going to talk about provocation, as we've discussed, you're talking about the present. You're talking about that moment when the present is understood in a very specific way, in order then to be prodded, pushed, pulled and coerced – and then people respond publicly. I suppose that's the mechanism of provocation. You've got to question how useful that is nowadays. On the other hand, it's also something for each artist to hang something on ... I'm thinking of someone like [nineteenth-century French poet] Arthur Rimbaud. I suppose that, in 1870s Paris, people were perhaps putting their sexual motivations on show, through the indirect medium of poetry. Then Rimbaud arrives on the scene and writes about cum and the receptive anus. You have that moment within poetry when one might understand the zeitgeist, and how to push at its limits at that exact moment in history, and understand how the authorities push back. I find it fascinating, for example, that the elasticity of the anus was tested using a device by those charged to investigate. We have to look at society as a whole and see where the same illiberal attention is present – a place where we have to push against authorities.

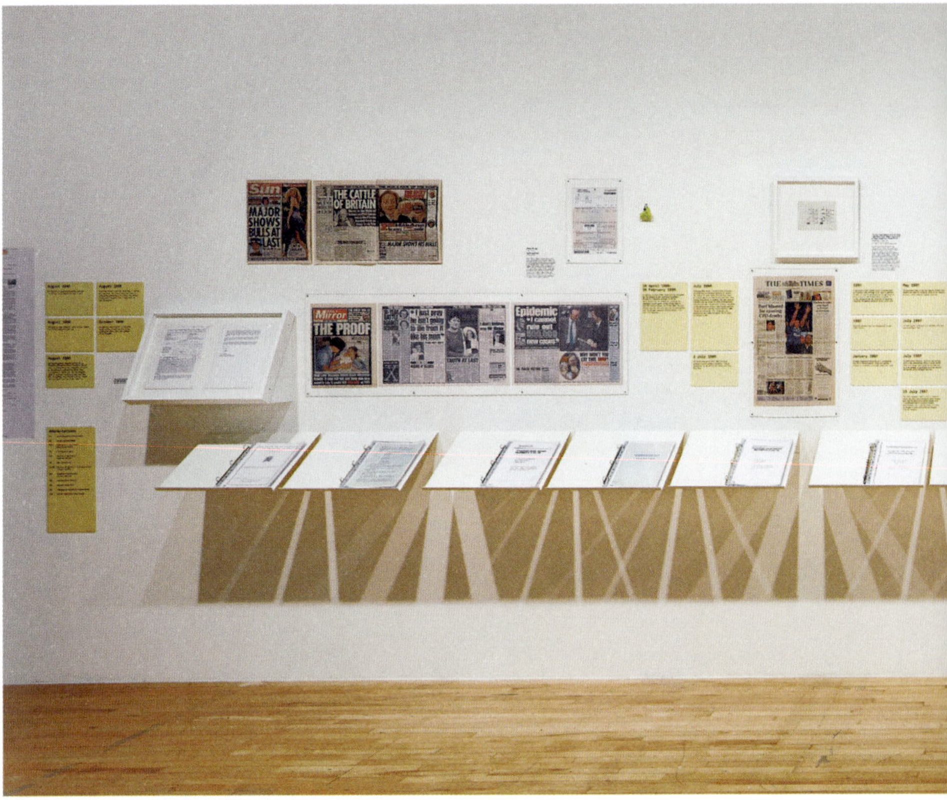

Of course, the problem is that authority now has very effective shape-shifting abilities and it remains difficult to pin-point the actual area where authority should be challenged. The art world might be such a place. When I did a work about the human disease variant CJD [part of Hayward Gallery exhibition *History is Now: 7 Artists Take on Britain*; see above], it was really important to prise open the archives and understand how authority worked at a recent moment in time. At one point during the construction of the work, I wanted to borrow a piece of film from the BBC – a famous moment of John Selwyn Gummer attempting to feed a beef-burger to his daughter, Cordelia, and Cordelia refusing and saying, no daddy. I received a letter from the head of BBC News, explaining that it was politically challenging for the BBC to lend the film. To this day this film still holds political influence, and so it is to take on an archive, which is essentially 'power left lying in the street'.

TM:
I always wonder when you use that phrase, because you use it often. It's Lenin's and Lenin is not a neutral figure!

RH:
Hannah Arendt used it too, though. And I find it useful as a tool – yes, power is left lying in the street by authorities and you

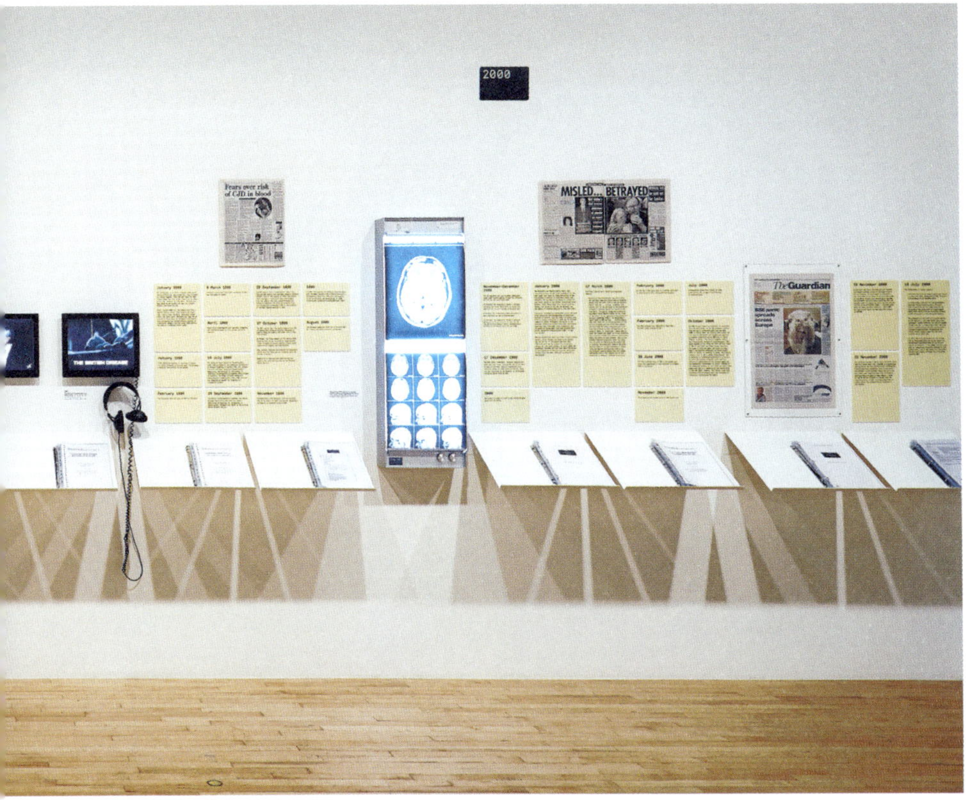

just have to identify it, pick it up and reuse that power. You can open up the archive and re-present the information, which no one is aware of any longer, and, once light is shed upon the materials, you will care about it once again because it is genuine and shocking, and symptomatic of why we are where we are now.

SK:
We all do different things in a different way. For me, the best advice I can give to design students, and I know it's corny, is actually to be yourself. That's something that's lost within professional graphic design, because people are so desperate to make the generic and the contemporary. That's a completely different perspective, of course.

RH:
It's important, because it's not obvious to be yourself. I think the thing that squashes most people is homogeneity. You can look at your phone and you can understand what is being made on the other side of the world within seconds. How are you supposed to make a new

Roger Hiorns, vCJD work (installation view), *History is Now: 7 Artists Take On Britain*
Hayward Gallery, London, 10 February – 26 April 2015.

work in this environment of effective communication – to establish a style of substance, when you're surrounded by the globalised manufacture and promotion of art? How are you supposed to find your stream?

TM:
There's also a difference between self-expression and the cultivation of the self, and I think this is an important thing. We live in a culture in which the self is very central and, supposedly, being able to have one's say, to express oneself, to be creative, is also central. It ends up in an awful lot of bullshit being generated, and we now have the Internet in which that can land. Self-cultivation seems to be something different. [Mid-twentieth-century poet] René Char has this line:

> Companions in pathos, who barely murmur, go with your lamp spent and return the jewels. A new mystery sings in your bones. Cultivate your legitimate strangeness.

That seems to me an interesting way to think about this rather than looking at the untrammelled self, which is interesting if you're living in Freud's Vienna – you know, sort of sticking a spike in your head and seeing what comes out – but doing that in the age of Twitter is something very different, I think.

SK:
That's a good point. Having been on Instagram and feeling less every time I look on it, less of myself, I feel that it's so easy to be distracted from the pursuit of self-education, pursuit of what you *actually* might want. It's so easy to become lost, I think. I think what Tom just said is very true – the importance of perhaps, rather than trying to provoke, trying to alienate yourself to some degree and then, you know, seeing what happens.

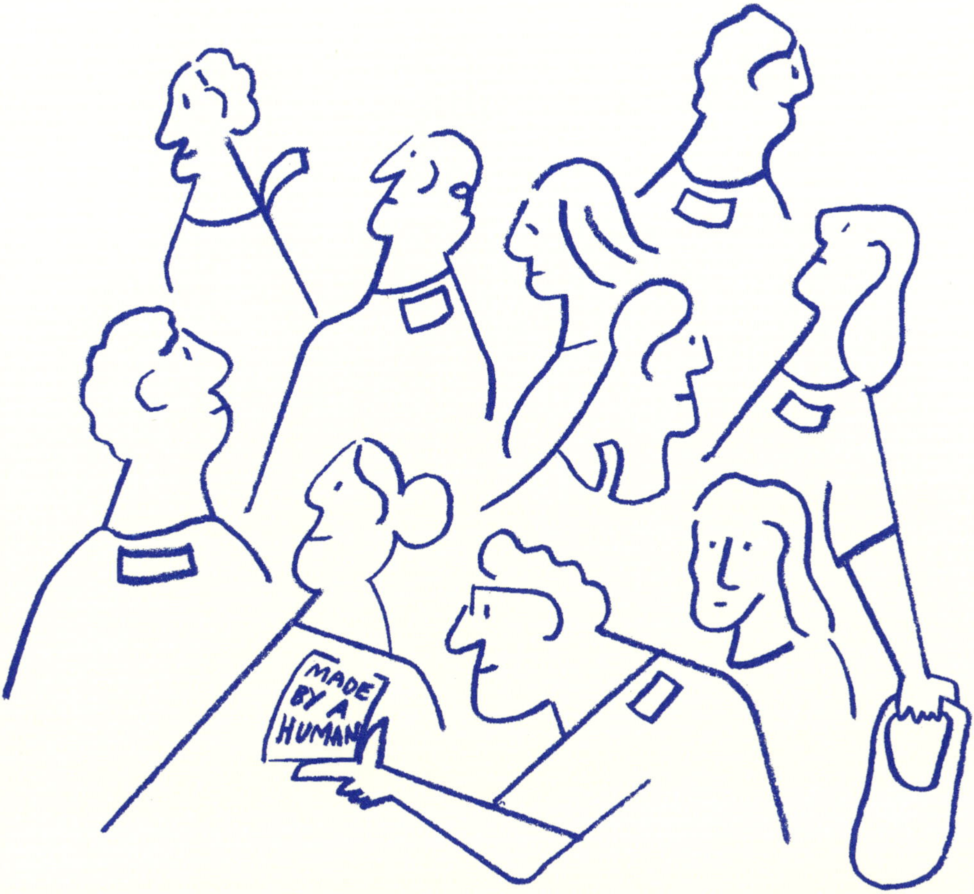

What does it take to achieve a 'Critical Mass' – to provoke real social, political and environmental change? The designers involved in this Conscientious Communicators project (see p.186) employed critical thinking, co-design and creative activism, along with the considerable digital and print skills at their disposal, to mobilise the public on issues including the proliferation of 3D-printed guns, the stigma attached to mental illness and the conditions associated with sweatshop labour in the production of high-street clothing. This last – the 'Inside Out' campaign – culminated in a public 'happening' (or 'FashMob'), on the one-year anniversary of the Rana Plaza factory collapse in Bangladesh (Fashion Revolution Day), encouraging shoppers on Oxford Street to turn their clothes label-side out and question the circumstances of their making.

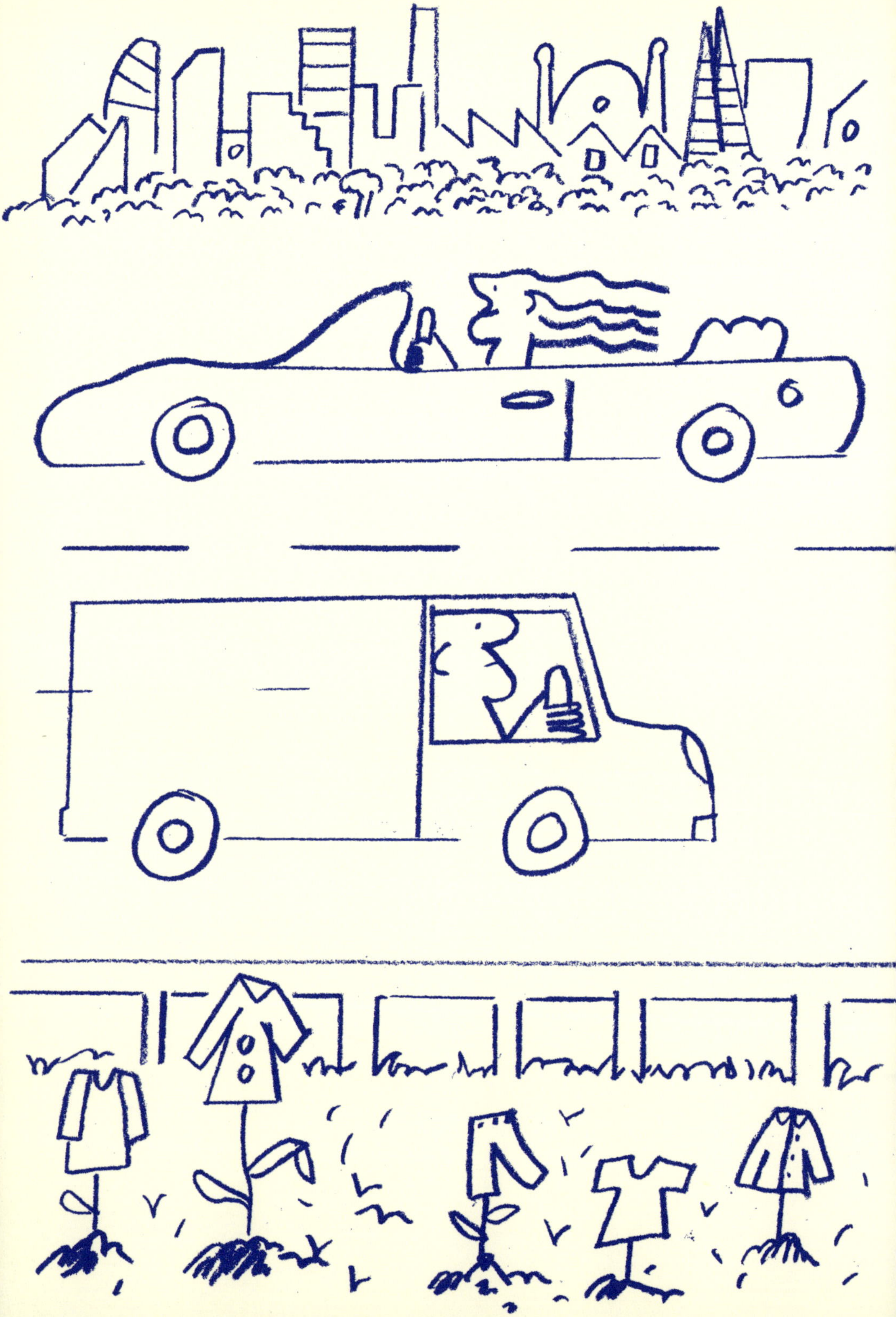

GROW A GARMENT

'Grow a Garment' is a collaboration involving over five hundred people, led by artist Zoë Burt, to grow and manufacture an item of clothing entirely within the M25. Students and staff at London College of Fashion, UAL, community groups, growers and craftspeople collaborated to grow, harvest, dry, ripple, ret, heckle, spin and knit flax into a garment. Groups and individuals across London used spare growing spaces, from large communal plots such as Cordwainers Community Garden (a key partner for the project) to small balcony pots, to sow flax – the plant from which linen is made. 'The project was conceived as a way to highlight the environmental and labour costs of growing fibre, inspire people to connect creatively with their surroundings and demonstrate the power of collaboration' – it stands as a provocation to those who think home-grown fashion is an impossibility.

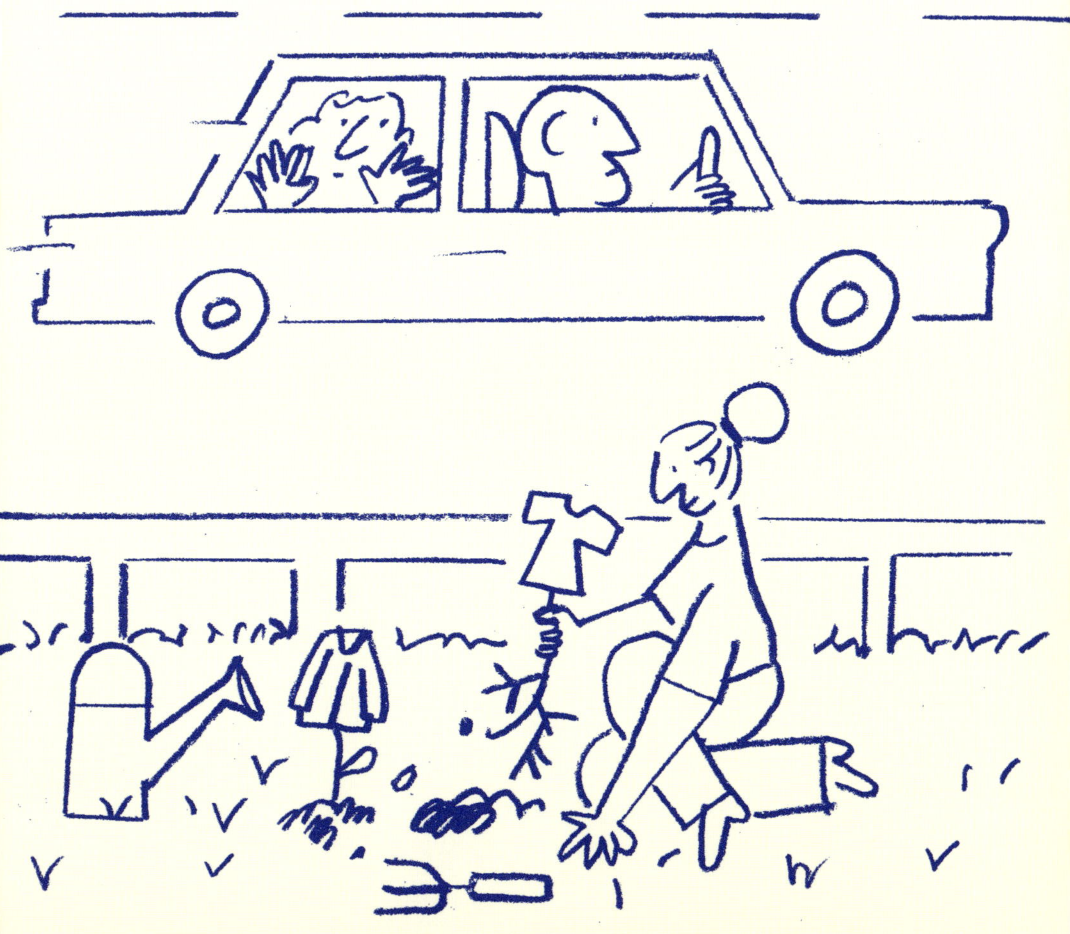

WASTE-OFF

'Designers and makers have a responsibility to consider the substrates they use and ensure that they do not contribute to the 434 million tonnes of waste produced annually in the UK.' This was the provocative principle at the heart of 'Waste-Off', a challenge conceived by the 'Conscientious Communicators Research Hub' at London College of Communication (LCC), UAL, in which participants across the university transformed discarded materials into a variety of purposeful, and oddly beautiful, inventions. These included a swatch-book of vegetable dyes, a giant, triple-height recreational swing, a canal refuse-collection net and a collection of clothes tailored for hospice patients.
A designated free-cycle space is now under construction at LCC as a long-term legacy of the project.

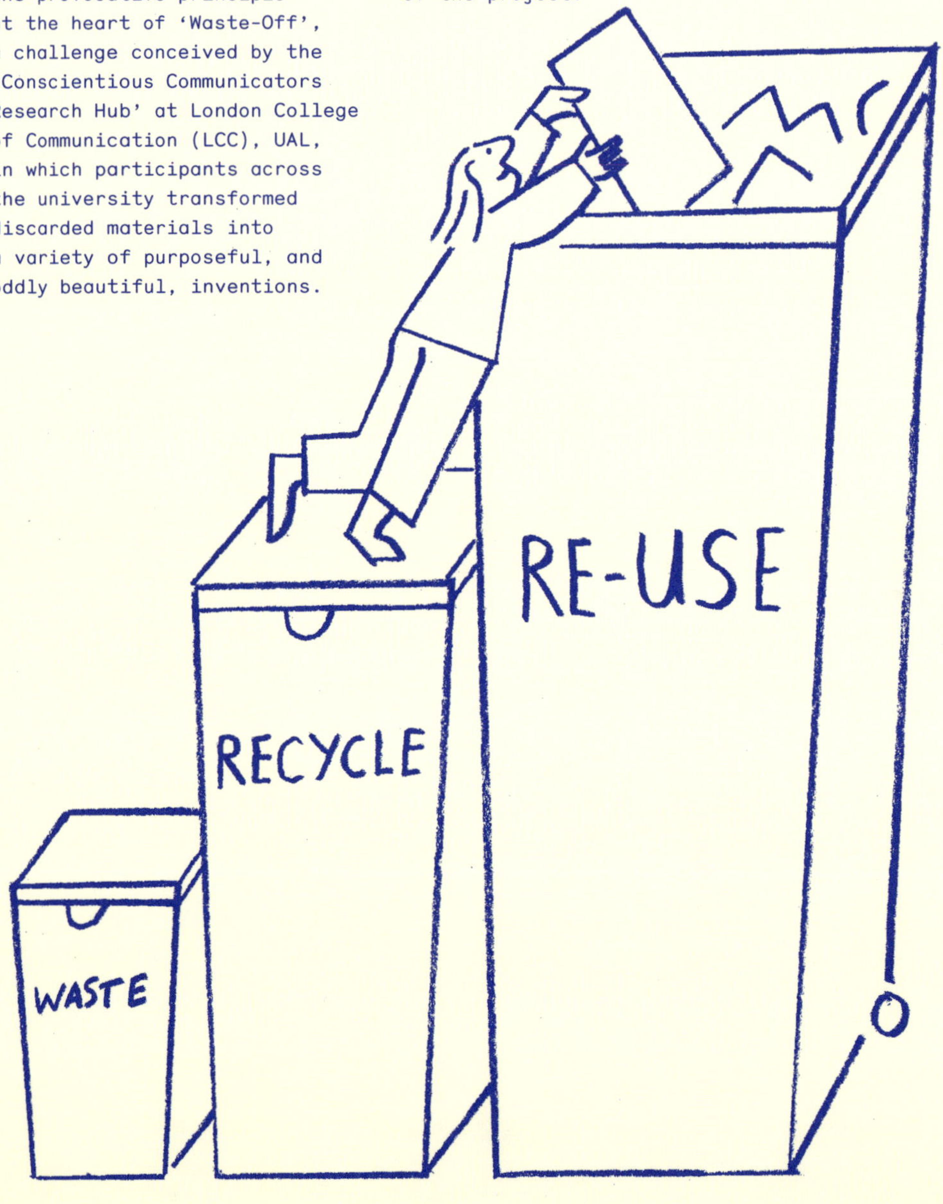

Creative Experience

Sandy Nairne

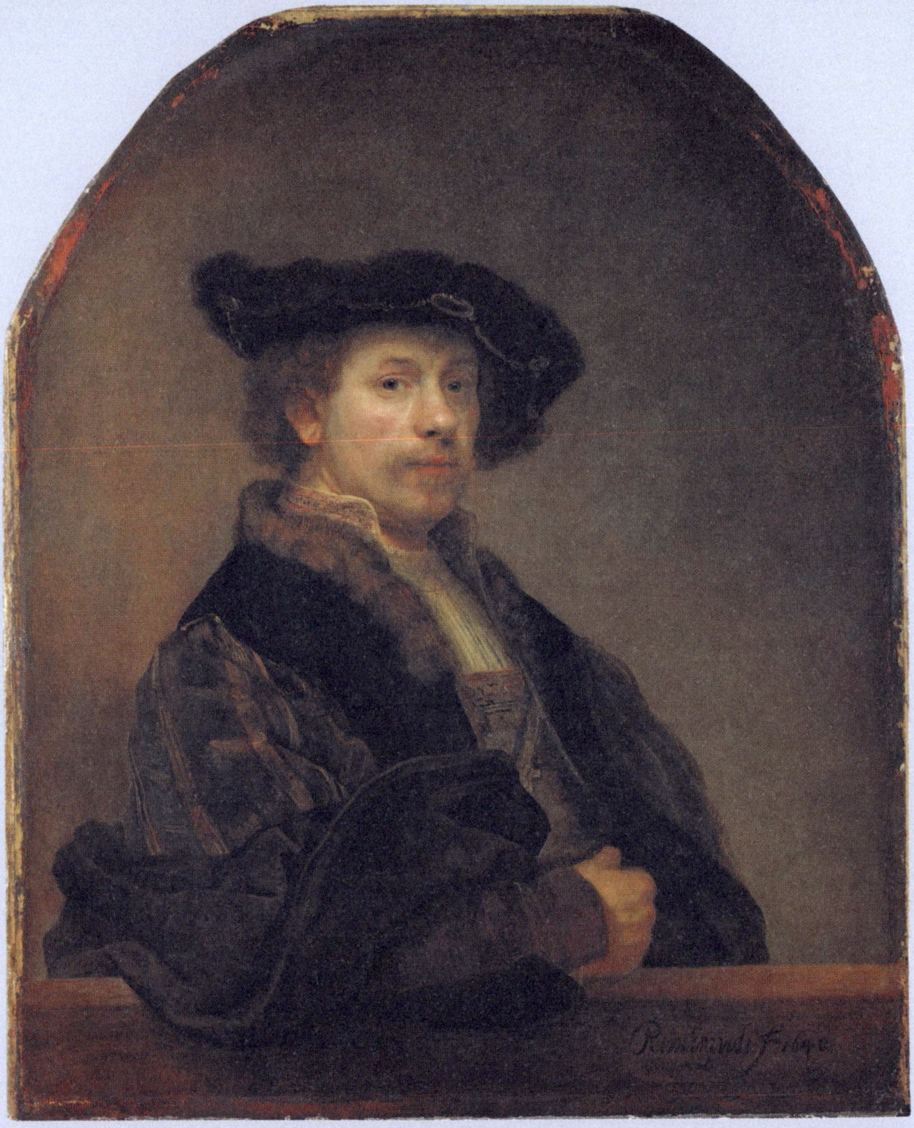

Rembrandt van Rijn, *Self Portrait at the Age of 34*, 1640.
The National Gallery, London.

Time spent with artists, architects or designers invites speculation about their creative processes. But ultimately, as viewers or consumers, we are drawn back to the experience of their work: to the creativity expressed in what they actually make and in their creative effects. In response to the structure of this book, I have chosen to focus on five concepts here - intensity, regularity, economy, identity and connectivity - which relate to creative making and to the experience of creativity in the visual arts as a whole.

Intensity

In 2005, I had the opportunity to hang a painting by Rembrandt in an exhibition at the National Portrait Gallery, London. Technicians were holding up *Self Portrait at the Age of 34* (1640; see opposite) as its exact position was finalised.[1] Rembrandt stared intently - I was under his scrutiny - and, while the overall pose is stolid, his face seemed more vivid than ever. Yet, while close to this real person (albeit 400 years on), I was equally 'lost once more in the unfathomable universe of pure paint', in Simon Schama's memorable phrase.[2]

The occasion might be exceptional, but such intensity of affect - the outcome of creativity - is exactly what artists hope for. Although making people cry may not be their specific purpose, it is one measure of the ways in which works of art can move viewers. In an intriguing book, *Pictures & Tears* (2001), the American art historian James Elkins examines at one point the reactions of those visiting the Rothko Chapel in Houston, Texas, and what causes some people to cry. To which the short answer is, either a sense of emptiness, in which the viewer feels lost, or a sense of being overwhelmed - engulfed by the depth of colour in Rothko's works. Elkins describes how 'Everything conspires to overload the senses: the empty incandescent rectangles of colour, entirely encompassing your field of vision; the sheer glowing silence.' One visitor simply wrote, 'This is where it stops. Depthless.'[3]

Whether encountering historic or modern art, I am struck by David Hockney's assertion that 'all art is contemporary.'[4] It is an important proposition: *when* something was made may be less important than examining what it is and what it does *now*. Not all contemporary artists aspire to produce evanescent 'spiritual' experience, yet there is plenty that is enriching or challenging in terms of their ideas, technical brilliance, politics or sheer chutzpah.

A field in which British artists have made an astonishing creative impact in recent years is cinema. Out of the remarkable writing and directing work of three artists in particular – Derek Jarman, Sam Taylor-Johnson and Steve McQueen – have come extraordinary, and intense, experiences. When asked about the relationship between working in film for cinema and for the gallery, McQueen responded by comparing the two forms: 'the movie is the novel, and art is poetry. Not a lot of people appreciate poetry, and it is the same with art. It is a more specialised form. That's the difference.' He says the two impulses are forever 'expanding and contracting' in his mind; 'It is all about finding what you want to say, and then how you want to say it.'[5]

> An idea comes to you, and you do the first one, and then, after you've done it, you realise what it is that you've done. Do you see? ... you've opened a whole corridor into the darkness; and then you follow it. And then as you go into this dark corridor it begins to light up, and you see things. But it's an adventure, and sometimes a dangerous one, and painful too. And risky. — Paula Rego[6]

Regularity

In 1999, the artist Colin Painter (then Principal of Wimbledon School of Art) proposed collaborating with the Tate Gallery (now Tate Britain) on a project, 'At Home with Art', that might blur the boundaries between art and design. Eight artists, including Tony Cragg, Antony Gormley, Permindar Kaur and Alison Wilding, would be selected to make 'everyday objects', and these would be offered for sale through the Homebase D.I.Y. chain. Tate staged a display and the BBC made a programme about the process.[7] Sales may not have been extensive, but Antony Gormley, for example, created a wonderful set of clothes pegs with polished metal barrels, beautifully chamfered to the centre. I thought these were the perfect expression of William Morris's statement that one should 'Have nothing in your houses that you do not know to be useful, or believe to be beautiful.'[8]

Gormley referred to the work as 'a re-designed nail, basically', but said that he hoped the scheme would change the image of artists. 'We always think of artists as inspired or drunk or recklessly removed from domestic life, but all the artists I know depend heavily on their domestic situation. Maybe we have moved on from the idea of the artist as angst-ridden existential loner to someone more integrated with the conditions of modern life.'[9]

Such an experiment should not be separated from the creative impact made by designers of clothes, furniture, ceramics or domestic objects, appliances or vehicles, or from the huge field of design in communication and the media. Much pleasure in our lives depends, not on the intensity of a special experience, but on the regularity of everyday enjoyment of good design, expressed in the clarity of its look and its utility. It is the touching and holding (recognising good materials put to perfect use), and the looking and learning (seeing ideas wittily conveyed or information concisely expressed), that, if fortunate, one admires and enjoys on a daily basis.

Economy

Taking a broader perspective, the British creative economy is having an increasing impact, nationally and internationally. The most widely used definition of the creative industries includes thirteen sections: advertising, architecture, the art and antiques market, crafts, design, designer fashion, film, interactive leisure software (i.e. video games), music, the performing arts, publishing, software, and television and radio.[10] The astonishing statistics regarding the sector's growth and development are attracting wider political and media attention. The Gross Value Added (GVA) of the British creative industries was estimated to be £84.1 billion in 2014. Between 1997 and 2014, the GVA of the creative industries has increased by almost six per cent each year, compared with the rest of the British economy, which gained an average of only 4.3 per cent a year over the same period. The sector now includes one out of every eleven jobs in Britain (an estimated 2.8 million overall) and is part of an even larger creative economy, comprising creative jobs in 'non-creative' sectors, such as design or marketing within manufacturing.[11]

This is serious business. And it is not just because he loves opera that the former Chancellor of the Exchequer, George Osborne, attended the first anniversary event for the new Creative Industries Federation in 2015. Osborne said, 'It is true that if you do look at the pounds and pence return you get for investing in the arts, it's pretty impressive. You put money in, you get money out as a country.' But, he added, 'Art for art's sake is something I think is very important. And it's not just about reports that say how many people work in that particular sector that I think should sway our decisions. We wanted to put money where it counts ... that I think says a lot about our country.'[12]

Chief Executive of the Federation, John Kampfner, has warned that local-authority cuts and the current threats to arts education within schools could nullify the recent, relatively favourable government settlement for arts funding. In front of the Chancellor he stressed the importance of putting the arts and creative industries at the heart of British life: 'It is the centrality argument – that the arts and creative industries are not something soft you do on a Saturday night. They are the heart of everything we do, of every community and individual's well being. They define our global reputation.'[13] This sense of the creative economy as a serious and real part of Britain today is very welcome, and places even more emphasis on the importance of producing the very best artists and designers for the future.

Identity

> Just because you go to art school doesn't necessarily mean you're going to be famous overnight, and what about all the other qualities that help people to keep going – putting up with disappointment, for instance? If all you've ever had in your life is praise, praise, praise, you're probably not a particularly healthy individual. Phyllida Barlow[14]

The considerable mismatch between the public image of artists – the conception of artists as specially creative people – and the way in which artists and designers actually conduct their working lives, has a history: not only the old stereotype that most artists are male and white, but also in the form of presumptions about attitudes and morals, as much as dress and demeanor. It is exemplified in the modern period by the character of the bohemian painter Gulley Jimson, brilliantly constructed by novelist Joyce Cary in *The Horse's*

Mouth (1944). Jimson's life and work are one step from disaster, so he discourages an earnest young man from becoming an artist: 'If you find life a bit dull at home ... and want to amuse yourself, put a stick of dynamite in the kitchen fire, or shoot a policeman. Volunteer for a test pilot, or dive off Tower Bridge with five bob's worth of roman candles in each pocket. You'd get twice the fun at about one-tenth of the risk.'[15] Films like *Lust for Life* (1956), with Kirk Douglas cast as Vincent Van Gogh, or the 1965 adaptation of Irving Stone's novel *The Agony and the Ecstasy* (1961), in which Charlton Heston plays Michelangelo, have also played a part in popular myth-making about the 'creative genius'.

Mythologies are hard to shift. Despite considerable broadening of the class background of artists, designers and photographers (in part with the opening-up of art schools as the curriculum became more innovative), and their enhanced social profile in the 1960s and 70s, much has *not* changed. Damien Hirst and Tracey Emin are examples of artists whose reputation worldwide is simultaneously enhanced and distorted by their life stories, even when their present-day reality no longer matches the legend. When glowing tributes were paid to the designer Alexander McQueen after his tragic death in February 2010, references were made to his working-class background and how, at sixteen years old, he began work as an apprentice cutter at Anderson & Sheppard on Savile Row. McQueen was described as 'the bad boy of fashion who was beloved by the establishment', as Imogen Fox put it.[16] Although he achieved international recognition through his own brilliance, invention, creative determination and hard graft, the mythic dimension of his story was still thought worthy of comment.

With the greater critical recognition of artists as culturally diverse as Frank Bowling and Rasheed Araeen, both of whom emerged in the 1960s and 70s, or Sonia Boyce, Anish Kapoor or Chris Ofili more recently, it has become clear that successful British artists come from an increasingly wide range of cultural as well as social backgrounds. Yet it is still important that the Black Arts and Modernism (BAM) project at University of the Arts London, led by Professor Sonia Boyce (see pp.159–64), Dr David Dibosa and Professor Paul Goodwin should offer an historical re-balancing by means of which the art world can come to recognise why a wider range of artists might be important and influential.[17]

Artists may not always be revolutionary in the full sense of the word; but they will often jolt, frequently question and occasionally transform. This is what makes them original, exceptional, cherishable and essential.
— John Tusa[18]

Connectivity

35 years ago, I sat at the edge of a field in Oxfordshire and sketched Kelmscott Manor, where, in 1889, William Morris had started to write his great utopian novel *News from Nowhere*.[19] In Morris's vision of life 'after the revolution', individual profit-making is removed and all work becomes creative, and therefore joyful. Making a sketch is a pleasurable form of connecting – to the River Thames nearby, and to Morris's work as a designer and great thinker about art and society.

For many artists, a sketchbook is a valued repository of ideas. Grayson Perry describes it as:

> a place I work through and refine an idea for a good while before I will let it run around the studio, and then the world … A sketchbook for me is a sacred artefact, more so than many of my finished works. The density of thought, the love of art and the sheer number of man-hours in each one load them with huge meaning and memory for me.[20]

Whereas Grayson Perry reconnects directly with his own images and ideas, for many artists a multi-layered connectivity to specific people and places can be equally important. Lucian Freud said he always wanted to 'work from people that interest me and that I care about, in rooms that I live in and know'.[21] One can understand that exactly, and his creative process – in portraying the human condition – was clearly enhanced by these close connections.

Lucian Freud's grandfather, Sigmund Freud, acknowledged daydreaming as a key part of the creative process. No doubt it remains important, but the essays and conversations that follow in this book show a greater emphasis on learning from others, and on critical thinking, hard graft and technical skill. The ways in which these are transmitted (or connected) across the studios of the art school is clearly having great effect, with an impact across Britain and beyond.

Since my career started, I've basically done the same thing over and over again. I mean that in a positive way. I think that's what good art is – the same process and research, but refining your strategy. The reason my work has affected people over the years is because it draws people's attention to their lives and the things in their lives. There's a certain amount of humility that goes with that. — Rachel Whiteread[22]

Notes

1. This was a key work, generously lent by the National Gallery, London, to the exhibition *SELF-PORTRAIT*, curated by Tony Bond and Joanna Woodall at the National Portrait Gallery (20 October 2005 – 29 January 2006).
2. 'Simon Schama on Rembrandt's Late Works', *Financial Times*, 17 October 2014, www.ft.com/cms/s/2/a4230272-552e-11e4-b616-00144feab7de.html#slide0 (all websites accessed before 7 March 2016).
3. James Elkins, *Pictures & Tears: A History of People Who Have Cried in Front of Paintings*, London 2001, p.135.
4. 'All art is contemporary, if it's alive, and if it's not alive, what's the point of it?', Art Quotes, www.art-quotes.com/auth_search.php?authid=50#.VtLud1IWFpk.
5. Steve McQueen, interviewed by Peter Aspden, *FT Magazine*, 3 October 2014, www.ft.com/cms/s/2/5a07b594-49bb-11e4-80fb-00144feab7de.html.
6. Paula Rego, interviewed by John Tusa, in John Tusa, *On Creativity: Interviews Exploring the Process*, London 2004, p.210.
7. Press release, 'At Home with Art', www.tate.org.uk/about/press-office/press-releases/home-art. The project also informed the anthology edited by Painter, entitled *Contemporary Art and the Home*, Oxford 2002.
8. William Morris, 'The Beauty of Life' [a lecture at the Birmingham Society of Arts and School of Design, 19 February 1880], in *Hopes and Fears for Art: Five Lectures Delivered in Birmingham, London, and Nottingham, 1878–1881*, 2nd edn, London 1882.
9. Antony Gormley, quoted in 'Sculpture's Coming Home', BBC News, 28 July 1999, news.bbc.co.uk/1/hi/entertainment/405337.stm.
10. 'What Are Creative Industries and Creative Economy', British Council, creativecities.britishcouncil.org/creative-industries/what_are_creative_industries_and_creative_economy.
11. These figures were published by the Department for Culture, Media and Sport, and then shared by the government and private sector body Creative Industries UK: 'Facts and Figures', www.thecreativeindustries.co.uk/uk-creative-overview/facts-and-figures.
12. 'Chanceller: Public Investment Crucial to UK's Creative Success', Creative Industries Federation, January 2016, www.creativeindustriesfederation.com/news/chancellor-public-investment-crucial-to-uks-creative-success.
13. Ibid.
14. Kira Cochrane, 'Phyllida Barlow: "Just Going to Art School Doesn't Make You Famous"', *Guardian*, 31 March 2014, www.theguardian.com/artanddesign/2014/mar/31/phyllida-barlow-sculptor-tate-britain-interview.
15. Joyce Cary, *The Horse's Mouth*, London 1944, p.18.
16. Imogen Fox, Alexander McQueen obituary, *Guardian*, 11 February 2010, www.theguardian.com/lifeandstyle/2010/feb/11/alexander-mcqueen-obituary.
17. The Black Arts and Modernism project, at University of the Arts London and in partnership with Middlesex University, is funded by the Arts and Humanities Research Council. I am a member of the project's Advisory Board, www.transnational.org.uk/projects/38-black-artists-and-modernism-bam.
18. Tusa 2004, p.7.
19. I come from a family of amateur artists: my father and grandfather painted watercolours, and I enjoy sketching landscapes in pen and ink.
20. Grayson Perry, 'Inside Grayson Perry's Sketchbook', *Guardian*, 19 February 2016, www.theguardian.com/artanddesign/2016/feb/19/inside-grayson-perrys-sketchbook.
21. John Russell, *Lucian Freud*, London 1974, p.13.
22. John Walsh, 'Rachel Whiteread: "I've Done the Same Thing Over and Over"', *Independent*, 2 September 2010, www.independent.co.uk/arts-entertainment/art/features/rachel-whiteread-ive-done-the-same-thing-over-and-over-2068718.html.

Further reading

Books, films, records and more – works that document and inspire creativity, as suggested by our contributors:

A

Hannah Arendt, *On Revolution*, revised edn with introduction by Jonathan Schell, London 2006 [1963]

A Short Film About Killing, Krzysztof Kieslowski, Poland 1988, 84 min, unrated

B

J.S. Bach, 'Cello Suite No.1 in G Major' (BWV 1007) [c.1717–23], recorded by Pablo Casals, EMI Classics, 2011 [1936–9]

Matsuo Bashō, *The Narrow Road to the Deep North and Other Travel Sketches*, trans. by Nobuyuki Yuasa, London 1966

Geoffrey Batchen, *William Henry Fox Talbot*, 55 series, London 2008

The Beatles, *Revolver*, Parlophone, 1966

Walter Benjamin, *Illuminations*, ed. and with an intro. by Hannah Arendt, London 2015

Harold Bloom, *The Anxiety of Influence: A Theory of Poetry*, 2nd edn, Oxford 1997 [1973]

Pierre Bourdieu, *Outline of a Theory of Practice*, Cambridge 2002 [1977]

David Bowie, *Hunky Dory*, RCA Records 1971

Mark Boyle, *Journey to the Surface of the Earth: Mark Boyle's Atlas and Manual*, The Hague 1970

Norman Bryson, *Looking at the Overlooked: Four Essays on Still Life Painting*, Essays in Art and Culture, London 1990

C

Joyce Cary, *The Horse's Mouth*, London 1944

Ed Catmull, *Creativity, Inc.: Overcoming the Unseen Forces that Stand in the Way of True Inspiration*, London 2014

Paul Celan, *Selected Poems*, London 1996

Miguel de Cervantes Saavedra, *Don Quixote*, trans. by John Rutherford, London 2003 [1604–5, 1616], and www.gutenberg.org/cache/epub/996/pg996-images.html, accessed 30 May 2016

Guy Claxton, *Hare Brain, Tortoise Mind: Why Intelligence Increases When You Think Less*, London 1998

D

Day for Night, François Truffaut, France 1973, 115 min, cert PG

Department for Business, Innovation and Skills, *Higher Education: Students at the Heart of the System*, London 2011

Philip K. Dick, *The Transmigration of Timothy Archer*, London 2011 [1982]

Mary Douglas and Baron Isherwood, *The World of Goods: Towards an Anthropology of Consumption*, London 1979

Geoff Dyer (ed.), *John Berger: Selected Essays*, London 2001

E

Umberto Eco, *Faith In Fakes: Travels in Hyperreality*, London 1986

T.S. Eliot, *Four Quartets*, London 2001 [1943, and published individually previously]

Brian Eno and Peter Schmidt, *Oblique Strategies: Over One Hundred Worthwhile Dilemmas* [box of cards], 5th edn, UK 2001 [1975]

Eraserhead, David Lynch, U.S. 1977, 88 min, cert 15

F

Stephen Farthing (ed.), *Art: The Whole Story*, London 2010

Stephen Farthing and Ed Webb-Ingall (with a foreword by Tilda Swinton), *Derek Jarman's Sketchbooks*, London 2013

Professor Stephen Farthing RA and Dr Janet McKenzie (eds.), *The Drawn Word*, New York and London 2014

Grandmaster Flash, *Adventures of Grandmaster Flash on the Wheels of Steel*, Sugarhill Records 1981

David Foster Wallace, 'The Nature of the Fun' [1998], in *Both Flesh and Not*, London 2013

H

'Heaven Sent', *Doctor Who* (series 9, episode 11), Rachel Talalay, written by Steven Moffat, first broadcast 28 November 2015, 55 min

J

Humphrey Jennings, *Pandæmonium 1660-1886: The Coming of the Machine as Seen by Contemporary Observers*, ed. by Marie-Louise Jennings and Charles Madge, London 2012 [1985]

David Jones, *The Sleeping Lord and other fragments*, London 1995

K

Kes, Ken Loach, UK 1970, 110 min, cert PG

Key Words Reading Scheme [Ladybird Books], London 1964–74

Karl Ove Knausgaard, *My Struggle*, trans. by Don Bartlett, 6 vols, London 2012- [2009–11]

Tania Kovats, *The Drawing Book*, London 2006

Alfred Kubin, *The Other Side*, trans. by Mike Mitchell, London 1969

L

Bernard Leach, *A Potter's Book*, London 2015 [1940]

Les Noces, ballet choreographed by Bronislava Nijinska, 1923. Music by Igor Stravinsky, design by Natalia Goncharova

Primo Levi, *The Wrench*, trans. by William Weaver, London 2013 [1978]

Claude Lévi-Strauss, 'The Science of the Concrete', in Claude Lévi-Strauss, *The Savage Mind*, trans. by George Weidenfeld, and Nicolson Ltd, The Nature of Human Society series, Oxford 2004 [1966]

Locke, Stephen Knight, UK 2014, 83 min, cert 15

M

Man with a Movie Camera, Dziga Vertov, USSR 1929, 68 min, unrated

Karl Marx, *Das Kapital*, trans. by Samuel Moore, Seattle 2010 [1867]

Annette Michelson (ed.), *Kino Eye: The Writings of Dziga Vertov*, trans. by Kevin O'Brien, London 1987

William Morris, *News from Nowhere*, Reeves & Turner, 1891

Grant Morrison, Mark Millar and Steve Parkhouse, 'Big Dave', serialised in *2000 AD*, nos. 842–907, 1993–4

N

Harry Nilsson, *The Point*, RCA Victor, 1971

P

Victor Papanek, *Design for the Real World: Human Ecology and Social Change*, New York 1971

R

Alice Rawsthorne, *Hello World: Where Design Meets Life*, London 2013

Eric Ries, *The Lean Startup: How Constant Innovation Creates Radically Successful Businesses*, London 2011

Andrei Rublev, Andrei Tarkovsky, USSR 1996, 174 min, cert 15

S

Edward Said, *Orientalism*, London 2003 [1978]

W.G. Sebald, *Austerlitz*, trans. by Anthea Bell, London 2001

Muriel Spark, *The Ballad of Peckham Rye*, London 1999 [1960]

Spirited Away, Hayao Miyazaki, Japan 2001, 124 min, cert PG

Wallace Stevens, *The Collected Poems: The Corrected Edition*, 2nd edn, New York 2015 [1954]

T

Junichirō Tanizaki, *In Praise of Shadows*, trans. by Thomas J. Harper and Edward G. Seidensticker, London 2001 [1933]

The Dhammapada: The Sayings of the Buddha, trans. by Thomas Byrom, London 2008 [200–300 BCE]

The Face (magazine), May 1980 – May 2004

Paul Thek, *Teaching Notes: 4-Dimensional Design*, teaching notes, 1978–81, www.brookechornyak.com/files/paulthekteachingnotes.pdf, accessed 15 June 2016

Eckhart Tolle, *The Power of Now: A Guide to Spiritual Enlightenment*, London 2005 [1999]

Lisa Tickner, *Hornsey 1968: The Art School Revolution*, London 2008

'Eckhart Tolle, Dalai Lama, Desmond Tutu & Authors: Educating the Heart and the Mind - Creativity', YouTube, 2015, www.youtube.com/watch?v=Zb3_wqX7yNE

Toy Story, John Lasseter, US 1995, 77 min, cert PG

Toy Story 2, John Lasseter, US 1999, 88 min, cert U

John Tusa, *On Creativity: Interviews Exploring the Process*, London 2004

W

Amy Whitaker, *Art Thinking: How to Carve Out Creative Space in a World of Schedules, Budgets, and Bosses*, ebook 2016

Z

Zen teahouse, Kōtō-in, Daitoku-ji temple complex, Kyoto

Author biographies

Sophia Al-Maria

Sophia Al-Maria is an artist, writer and film-maker. Her first book, *The Girl Who Fell to Earth* (2012), was published in Arabic in 2015, by Bloomsbury Qatar. Al-Maria's most recent solo exhibition, *Black Friday*, was staged at the Whitney Museum of American Art, New York, in 2016. She lives and works in London, where she writes screenplays for a living.

Phil Baines

Phil Baines is subject leader for Typography on the BA Graphic Design course at Central Saint Martins (CSM), UAL. He is also a freelance designer and the author of four books on design, including *Signs: Lettering in the Environment* with Catherine Dixon (2003) and *Penguin by Design: A Cover Story 1935–2005* (2005). With Catherine Dixon, Baines currently curates the Central Lettering Record, part of CSM's Museum and Contemporary Collection.

Sonia Boyce

Sonia Boyce MBE RA is a visual artist, a Professor of Black Art and Design at University of the Arts London, and Professor of Fine Art at Middlesex University. She is the principal investigator of 'Black Artists and Modernism', a major study of the influence of Black British artists on modern art.

Nigel Carrington

Nigel Carrington has been Vice-Chancellor of University of the Arts London since 2008. An advocate for creative education and the creative economy, he is Chairman of the Henry Moore Foundation, a director of the Creative Industries Federation, and a member of the Board at Universities UK. He holds a Graduate Diploma in the History of Art from the Courtauld Institute.

Marvin Gaye Chetwynd

Marvin Gaye Chetwynd is an artist whose practice intertwines performance, sculpture, painting, installation and video. Her work incorporates elements of folk plays, popular culture and Surrealist cinema; her performances and videos often employ troupes of performers – friends and relatives of the artist – and feature handmade costumes and props. She has performed and exhibited internationally, and was shortlisted for the Turner Prize in 2012.

Neil Cummings

Neil Cummings is Professor of Theory and Practice at Chelsea College of Arts, UAL; a member of the Critical Practice research group; and sits on the editorial board of the 'Documents of Contemporary Art' book series (Whitechapel/MIT Press). All of his work consistently engages with the cultural institutions that designate and exhibit art, and the increasingly devolved experience of art, to its publics.

Siobhan Davies

Siobhan Davies CBE is a renowned British choreographer who rose to prominence in the 1970s. She founded Siobhan Davies Dance in 1988 and works closely with collaborating artists. By 2002, she had moved away from the traditional theatre circuit and started making work for gallery spaces, applying choreography across a wide range of creative disciplines. In 2006, the RIBA award-winning Siobhan Davies Studios opened in London, establishing a permanent base for the organisation and for independent dance artists.

Richard Deacon

Richard Deacon CBE is a leading sculptor. His work was the subject of a large-scale survey at Tate Britain, London, in 2014, while a ten-year survey - *On the Other Side* - toured to museums in Switzerland, Azerbaijan and Germany in 2015–16. A collected edition of Deacon's writings, *So, If, And, But*, was published by Richter Verlag in 2014. In 2015 he retired from his post as Professor at the Kunstakademie Dusseldorf, ending thirty-eight years of teaching at art schools in Britain and abroad.

Fred Deakin

Fred Deakin runs the studio Fred & Company, which specialises in collaborative, social and interactive projects. As half of the band Lemon Jelly, Deakin has been Mercury Prize- and Brit Award-nominated and has headlined stages at Glastonbury and Bestival. Deakin was co-founder and director of groundbreaking London digital design agency Airside, which won and was nominated for two BAFTAs, nine D&ADs and a Webby, among many others. He is currently Professor of Interactive Digital Arts at University of the Arts London.

Edmund de Waal

Edmund de Waal OBE is best known for his large-scale installations of porcelain vessels, informed by his passion for architecture, space and sound. His work has been exhibited internationally, and recent public installations include *Lichtzwang* in the Theseus Temple, Vienna (2014), and *another hour* at Southwark Cathedral, London (2014). De Waal's memoir, *The Hare with Amber Eyes* (2010), has won literary prizes including the RSL Ondaatje Prize and been translated into over thirty languages. His second book, *The White Road*, was published in 2015.

Mark Dunhill

Mark Dunhill is Dean of Academic Programmes at Central Saint Martins, UAL. He is an executive board member of European League of Institutes of Arts (ELIA), and serves on a number of advisory boards for arts organisations. Since graduating from the Royal College of Art in 1977, Dunhill has exhibited internationally, and with Tamiko O'Brien from 1998. Rooted in the traditions of sculpture, Dunhill and O'Brien's work is concerned with the tools and procedures of making, collaboration, its motivations, issues and dilemmas. A recent publication, *In this Point of View*, documents a series of projects undertaken in Japan since 2007.

Sonya Dyakova

Sonya Dyakova is a Russian graphic designer living in London, where she runs her multi-disciplinary studio, Atelier Dyakova. After studying in San Francisco, Dyakova worked with Vince Frost and KerrNoble, before joining Phaidon Press in 2005. She is the art director of *Frieze Masters* and *Guestbook* magazines. Dyakova was *Frieze* magazine's art director 2011–16. In 2011 she received a Grand Prix from the Tokyo Type Directors Club. In 2013 she became a member of AGI, Alliance Graphique Internationale.

Cécile B. Evans

Cécile B. Evans has recently participated in the 20th Biennale of Sydney and the Berlin Biennale, as well as other group exhibitions. Her films have been screened at the British Film Institute (BFI), London; Hamburg Film Festival; and Art Basel Miami. She is recipient of Frieze Art Fair's Emdash Award (2012) and Palais de Tokyo/Orange's Push Your Art Prize (2013).

Stephen Farthing

Stephen Farthing RA is the Rootstein Hopkins Chair of Drawing at University of the Arts London; Honorary Curator of the Collections at the Royal Academy, London; and an Emeritus Fellow of St Edmund Hall, University of Oxford. Farthing has exhibited extensively since his first solo exhibition at the Royal College of Art Gallery in 1977. His work represented Britain at the São Paulo Biennale in 1989, leading to many further solo shows around the world. He is currently writing *Living Color* for Yale University Press with David Kastan, and researching *Leonardo: The Corpus* with Professor Michael Farthing MD.

Roger Hiorns

Roger Hiorns is a sculptor. His work has been exhibited at institutions throughout Europe and the Americas and is held in institutional collections such as those of the Museum of Modern Art, New York, and Tate Modern, London. In 2009, Hiorns was nominated for the Turner Prize for his critically acclaimed work *Seizure*, a massive crystallization of a bedsit interior in a condemned South London council estate. In 2011, *Seizure* was acquired by the Arts Council Collection, and is currently on a ten-year loan to the Yorkshire Sculpture Park.

Mary Katrantzou

Mary Katrantzou's first ready-to-wear collection debuted at London Fashion Week in Spring/Summer 2009, with the support of the British Fashion Council and the NEWGEN Scheme. Despite having a small collection of nine dresses, Katrantzou picked up fifteen prestigious stockists; she now boasts over 250 stockists in sixty countries. She was named Designer of the Year at the Glamour Awards 2015, and Breakthrough Designer at the Harpers Bazaar Women of the Year Awards 2015.

Scott King

Scott King was art director of *i-D* magazine and creative director of *Sleazenation* magazine. He has produced work for many influential figures, including the Pet Shop Boys, Malcolm McLaren and Suicide. King's work has been exhibited worldwide in commercial galleries and institutions; he has also produced several books, including *Anxiety & Depression* (2009), *Art Works* (2010), *Anish & Antony Take Afghanistan* (2014) and *Public Art* (2016).

Tom Morton

Tom Morton is a writer, curator, lecturer and Contributing Editor for *frieze* magazine, based in Rochester, UK. His recent exhibitions include *Panda Sex* at State of Concept, Athens (2014), and *Äppärät* at The Ballroom Marfa, Texas.

Sandy Nairne

Sandy Nairne CBE FSA is an historian and curator and was director of the National Portrait Gallery, London, from 2002 to 2015. Formerly Director of Visual Arts at the Arts Council (1987–93) and Director of Programmes at Tate (1994–2002), where he supported the development of Tate Modern and led the Centenary Development of Tate Britain, Nairne also developed the Channel 4 series 'State of the Art' and is the author of *Art Theft: and the Case of the Stolen Turners* (2011).

Nils Norman

Nils Norman is an artist working across the disciplines of public art, architecture and urban planning. He has exhibited in museums and biennials worldwide and has developed commissions for Tate Modern, London; SculptureCenter, New York; and London Underground, among others. Norman is the author of four books, including *Edible Park* (2012) and *The Contemporary Picturesque* (2000). He is also a Professor at the Royal Danish Academy of Art and Design, Copenhagen, where he leads the School of Walls and Space.

Lucy Orta

Lucy Orta is a curator and visual artist working across media including drawing, couture, sculpture, performance, video and photography. Since 2002, she has held the title of Professor, and Chair of Art and the Environment, at University of the Arts London. Orta also collaborates with her husband, the Argentine artist Jorge Orta, under the co-authorship Lucy + Jorge Orta. Their work has been the focus of many major solo exhibitions and biennale events worldwide.

Grayson Perry

Grayson Perry RA CBE is one of Britain's best-known contemporary artists. His hard-hitting and exquisitely crafted works in a variety of media reference his own childhood and life as a transvestite while engaging with wider social issues. Perry won the Turner Prize for Contemporary Art in 2003 and has had major solo exhibitions nationally and internationally, including the critically acclaimed *Tomb of the Unknown Craftsman* at the British Museum, London. He is currently Chancellor of University of the Arts London.

William Raban

William Raban is an artist film-maker who has exhibited worldwide in both art and film contexts. Initially known for his landscape and expanded cinema films of the 1970s, Raban's landscape interests were framed in the 1980s within a historical and socio-political context: the history of London and the Thames. Reminiscent of Humphrey Jennings's wartime films, Raban's films from the 1990s onwards look at the island of Britain and its people in the context of the global economy and the effects of urban change.

Jane Rapley

Jane Rapley OBE MA RCA FRSA is Professor Emeritus of the University of the Arts London. She has extensive experience of design, management and wholesale and retail operations in the fashion industry and has been involved with education for the last 46 years, leading the School of Fashion & Textile Design at Central Saint Martins (CSM) as its Dean for nineteen years from 1989. In 2006, she became Head of CSM and, in 2012, became Pro Vice-Chancellor of University of the Arts London. Since retiring in late 2012, she has undertaken consultancy work in Britain, China, Sri Lanka, Hong Kong and Italy.

Pratap Rughani

Pratap Rughani's documentary practice ranges across modes, from broadcast (with 25 films for BBC2 and Channel 4) to commissions for galleries such as Modern Art Oxford. Several of his award-winning films connect people of radically different perspectives and politics, for example with the Truth & Reconciliation Commission of the new South Africa. Rughani is Reader in Documentary Film at London College of Communication, UAL, and Director of Lotus Films. He is Deputy Chair of the UAL Professoriate and of the UK's National Teaching Fellows Association.

Bob and Roberta Smith

Bob and Roberta Smith RA see art as an important element in democratic life. Central to Bob and Roberta Smith's thinking is the idea that campaigns are extended artworks, which include a variety of consciousness-raising artefacts. Bob and Roberta Smith studied at Goldsmiths from 1991 to 1993. He was an Artist Trustee of Tate between 2009 and 2013 and is currently a trustee for the National Campaign for the Arts, and a patron of the NSEAD.

Helen Storey

Helen Storey MBE RDI is an award-winning British artist and designer. She is Professor of Fashion and Science at the Centre for Sustainable Fashion, London College of Fashion, UAL, and Co-Director of the Helen Storey Foundation. In 1991, Storey won Most Innovative Designer of the Year and was nominated for British Designer of the Year by the British Fashion Council. She holds a number of honorary degrees and was awarded a Royal Designer for Industry in 2015.

Susanne Tide-Frater

Susanne Tide-Frater is a Brand Consultant specialising in innovative fashion and retail projects. After working as Creative Director for both Harrods and Selfridges, she was involved in building the Victoria Beckham label as Fashion Director between 2008 and 2016. In 2010, she joined Farfetch as Brand and Strategy Director. Tide-Frater sits on the NEWGEN Advisory Panel of the British Fashion Council and the Vogue Fashion Fund Panel. She is a Director of the Venture Board, Whitechapel Art Gallery.

Teal Triggs

Teal Triggs is an educator, historian and writer, whose research focuses primarily on graphic design history, design research methods, self-publishing and feminism. At the Royal College of Art, London, Professor Triggs is Associate Dean in the School of Communication. In addition to her work as an educator and researcher, Triggs co-founded the Women's Design + Research Unit (WD+RU), whose main intent has been to raise awareness about women working in visual communication and design education.

Lawrence Zeegen

Lawrence Zeegen is Dean of the School of Design at Ravensbourne, where he leads courses and research in Communication and Product Design, Fashion and Architecture. A practising illustrator since graduating from Camberwell College of Arts (1986) and the Royal College of Art (1989), Zeegen has worked for clients that include international newspapers, publishers and advertising agencies. He is the author of nine published books since 2005, the latest of which are *Fifty Years of Illustration* (2014) and *Ladybird by Design* (2015).

Acknowledgements

We would like to extend our warm thanks to all those who have contributed to *The Creative Stance*, including those who were involved in the earliest research and planning stages: Monica Alcazar, Adeeb Ashfaq, Karin Askham, Peter Austin, Tricia Austin, Oriana Baddeley, Paul Bailey, Alenka Banic, Heather Barnett, Graham Barton, Hilary Baxter, Stephen Beddoe, Nick Bell, Luc Bernay, Simon Betts, Sarah-Louise Bingley, George Blacklock, Rebecca Brammall, Natalie Brett, Caroline Broadhead, Kellie Bryson, Elliott Burns, Sophie Chapman, Hannah Clayton, Rachel Clowes, Shaun Cole, Carole Collet, Jane Collins, Julie Coombes, Frances Corner, Daniela Davies, Catherine Demoisy, Paul Dewis, Mel Dodd, Rebecca Earley, Anne Eggebert, Patricia Ellis, Lizzie Finn, Terry Finnigan, Angela Flanagan, Chris Follows, Fiona Fung, Lorraine Gamman, Darla Gillroy, Beatrice Giovannini, Kate Goldsworthy, Nick Gorse, Alison Green, Chloe Griffith, Silvia Grimaldi, Tara Hanrahan, Jenny Hayton, Dan Henderson, Simon Hinde, Jane Holt, Andrew Hughes, Monica Hundal, Michael Hurley, Sadhna Jain, Amanda Jenkins, Jonathan Kearney, Mark Lebon, Judy Lindsay, Paul Lowe, Anne Marr, Jonathan Martin, Sarah McLean, Fred Meller, Clare Mitten, Janet Mowbray, Rebecca Munro, Karla Newell, Martin Newth, Alistair O'Neill, Susan Orr, Jo Ortmans, Sara Ortolani, Jane Penty, Fabio Piras, Kay Politowicz, Malcolm Quinn, Dai Rees, Jake Charles Rees, Richard Reynolds, Naomi Richmond-Swift, Christopher Roberts, Rebecca Ross, Elizabeth Rouse, Lois Rowe, Linda Sandino, Alex Schady, Benjamin Schmechel, David Scothron, Adrian Scrivener, Jacqueline Sealy, John Seth, Anne Smith, Michael Spencer, Nina Stevenson, Sian Stirling, Patrick Sutherland, Claire Swift, Anne Tallentire, Sarah Temple, Ian Thompson, Adam Thorp, Mo Throp, Georgina Tibbott, Jeremy Till, Anna Tsekouras, Jennifer Tuckett, Athanasios Velios, Edward Venning, Christopher Wainwright, Willie Walters, Ken Wilder, Rosie Willatt, Judy Willcocks, Anne Williams, Dilys Williams, Amanda Windle, Rebecca Wright, Joshua Y'Barbo.

Credits

common-edition no. 8
The Creative Stance
common-editions and University
of the Arts London

Published in 2016 by common-editions
110 Stoke Newington Church Street
London, N16 0JX
common-editions.com

University of the Arts London
272 High Holborn
London, WC1V 7EY

Publisher: Nadine Monem
Editor: Faye Robson
Editorial assistance: Ruby Lawrence
Designer: Sarah Boris
Illustrator: Jay Cover
Image research: Vicky Haverson
Colour management by Dexter Pre-media
Printed in China by Toppan Printing Co. Ltd

British Library Cataloguing-in-Publication Data:
A full catalogue record of this book is available from the British Library.

ISBN 978-0-9931563-1-1

Distributed by:
Cornerhouse Publications Ltd
HOME, 2 Tony Wilson Place
Manchester, M15 4FN
England
+44 (0)161 212 3466
publications@cornerhouse.org
www.cornerhousepublications.org

Endpapers (front): Bushra el-Turc (composer), Miranda Fulleylove (violin), with Philippine Laureau, Jack Irving, Sylvana Lautier and Tracy Ting (performance designers), *Tanit*, Queen Elizabeth Hall, London, 2013; Sarah-Louise Bingley, Maria Hamer, Freya Smith and Karina Stolf, artwork from 'What Not To Say', part of 'Critical Mass' (see p.183), 2014. Photo courtesy and © Sarah-Louise Bingley, Maria Hamer, Freya Smith and Karina Stolf; Luc Bernay, *ABC Juxtaposed* (installation view), *Ladybird Books Reimagined* (see pp.154–5), London College of Communication, UAL, September 2015. Photo courtesy Ana Escobar. Original archive illustrations all © Ladybird Books Ltd, 2015. Used under license from Ladybird Books Ltd; Will Shannon, 'Shoe-Dip' (installation view), VF Corporation 'Futurewear' summit (see p.86), Winston-Salem, NC, March 2012. Photo courtesy and © Giles Price; Neus Torres Tamarit responds to 'Slavery | Interviewing | Plastic' for 'Matter | Method | Material' (see p.57), Central Saint Martins, UAL, 2015. Photo courtesy Heather Barnett; Isabella Bagwell, Hannah Foster, Xuaogen Li, Helen Milne, Danny Olashore, Suwun Park and Suolonga Wang, hanging baskets, part of 'Waste-Off' (see p.186), Central Saint Martins, UAL, February 2015. Photo courtesy and © Helen Milne; Pui Yee Tong (dress) and Daniela Deiana (clutch), costumes designed for the English National Ballet, 2010. Photo by Sean Michael; Beatrice Giovannini, Jennicka Sapigao and Thiery Nahayo, 'The Face', a game made for *Ladybird Books Reimagined* (see pp.154–5), London College of Communication, UAL, September 2015. Photo courtesy and © Beatrice Giovannini.

Endpapers (back): Anna Cennamo and Martina Giulianelli, natural dye swatch-book (detail), part of 'Waste-Off' (see p.186), 2011. Photo courtesy and © Ted Mendez; Alenka Banic, '101 Things to do in an Empty Swimming Pool' (see p.130), 2013. Photo courtesy and © Alenka Banic; Philippa Brock and Kay Politowicz, 'Long-Life' Denim: 'Cherish' (jeans textile design), presented at VF Corporation 'Futurewear' summit (see p.86), Winston-Salem, NC, March 2012. Photo courtesy and © Giles Price; 'M-stand' on the street, 2008. Courtesy the Design Against Crime Research Centre (see pp.84–5); (top) Lorenzo Davitti and Sara Ortolani, *The Essence of Ladybird* (animated film, installation view), *Ladybird Books Reimagined* (see pp.154–5), London College of Communication, UAL, September 2015. Photo courtesy Ana Escobar; (below) Patrick Ward, *The Year Above* (2013–15), at 'Acts Re-Acts 2' (see p.108), Wimbledon College of Arts, UAL, May 2015. Photo by Student Documentation Team; Yu Ji responds to 'Hearing | Drawing | Projector' for 'Matter | Method | Material' (see p.57), Central Saint Martins, UAL, 2015. Photo courtesy Heather Barnett; Sarah-Louise Bingley, Maria Hamer, Freya Smith and Karina Stolf, artwork from 'What Not To Say', part of 'Critical Mass' (see p.183), 2014. Photo courtesy and © Sarah-Louise Bingley, Maria Hamer, Freya Smith and Karina Stolf.

COMMON-EDITIONS ual:

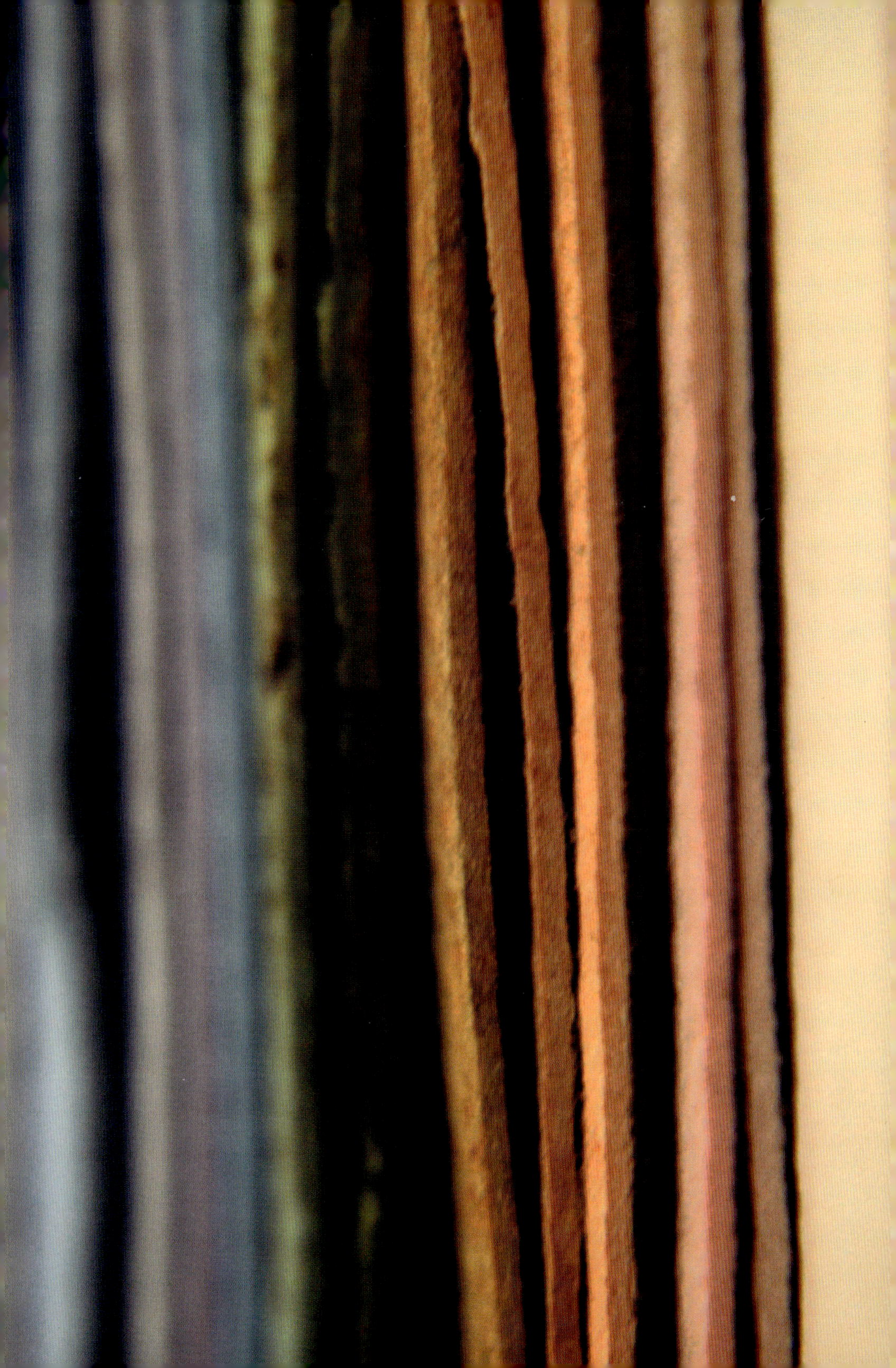

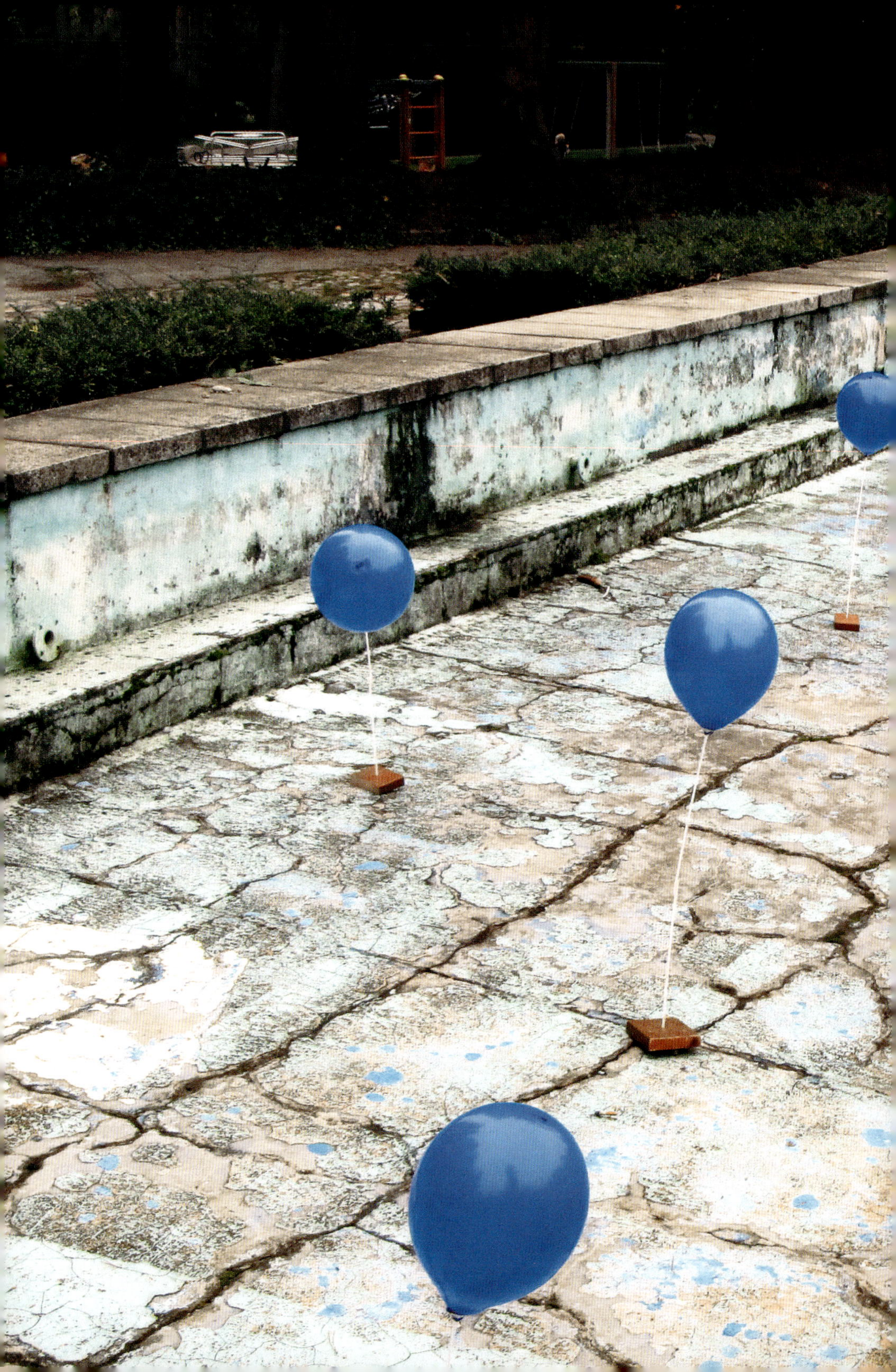

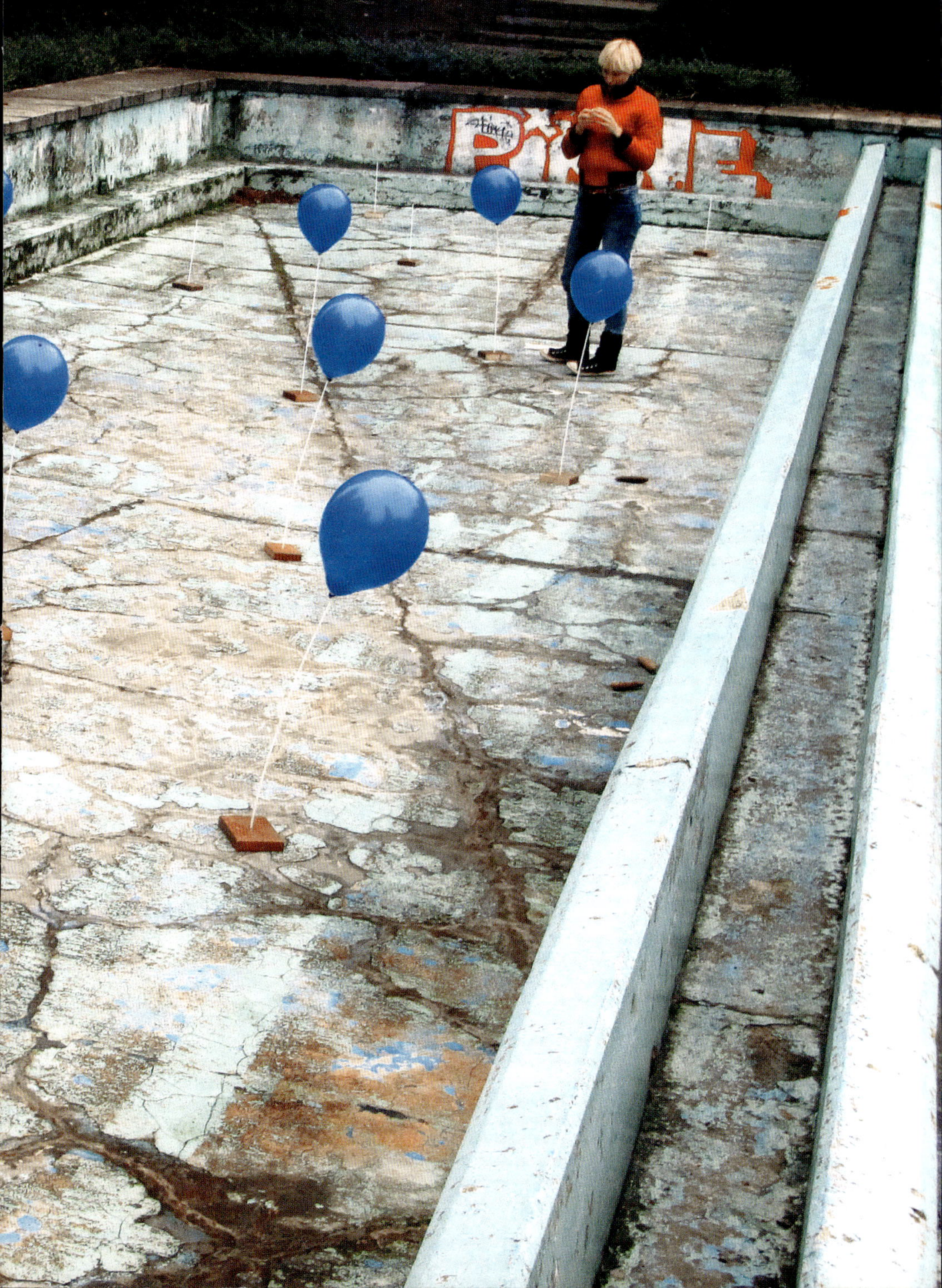

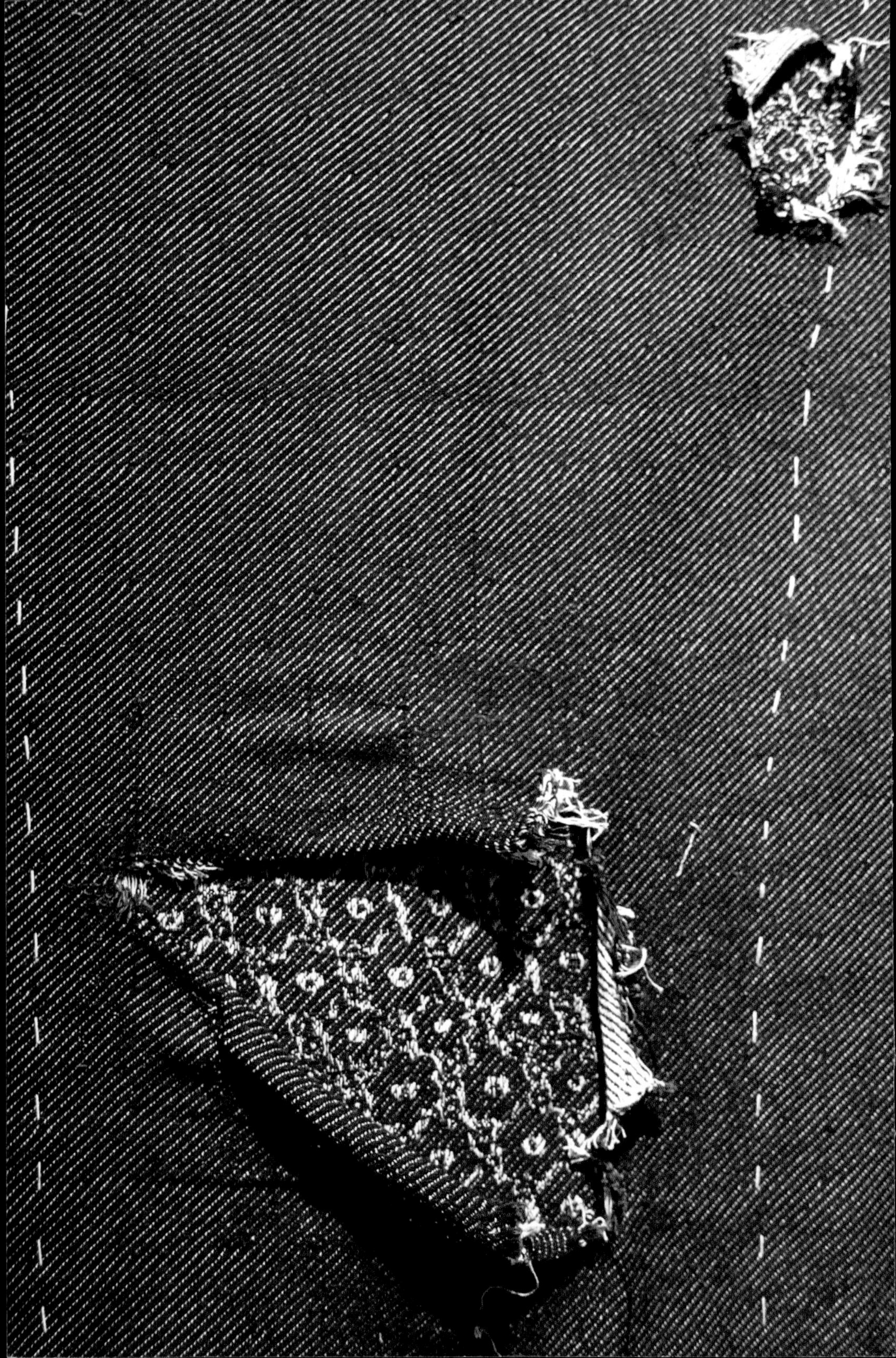

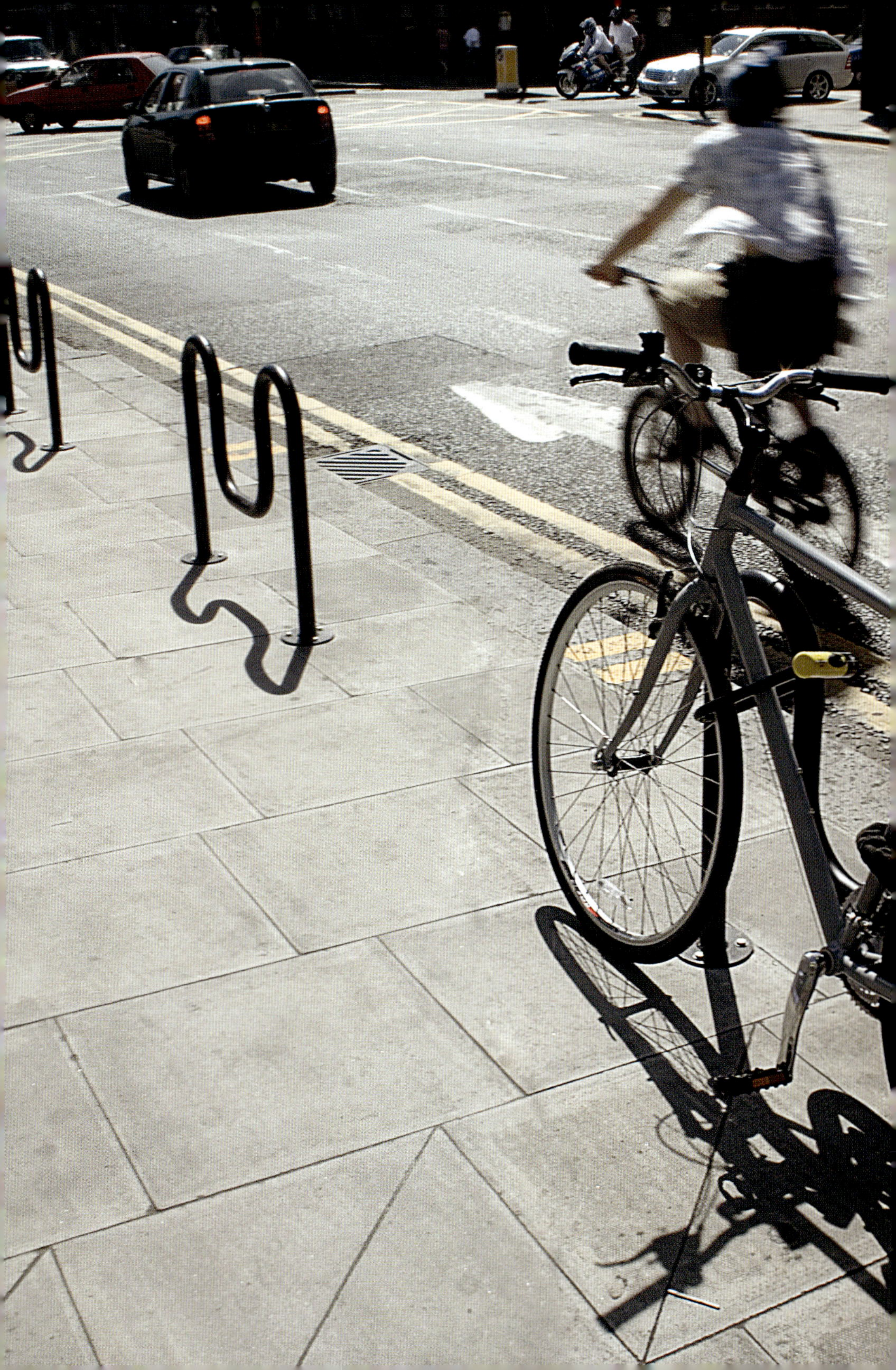

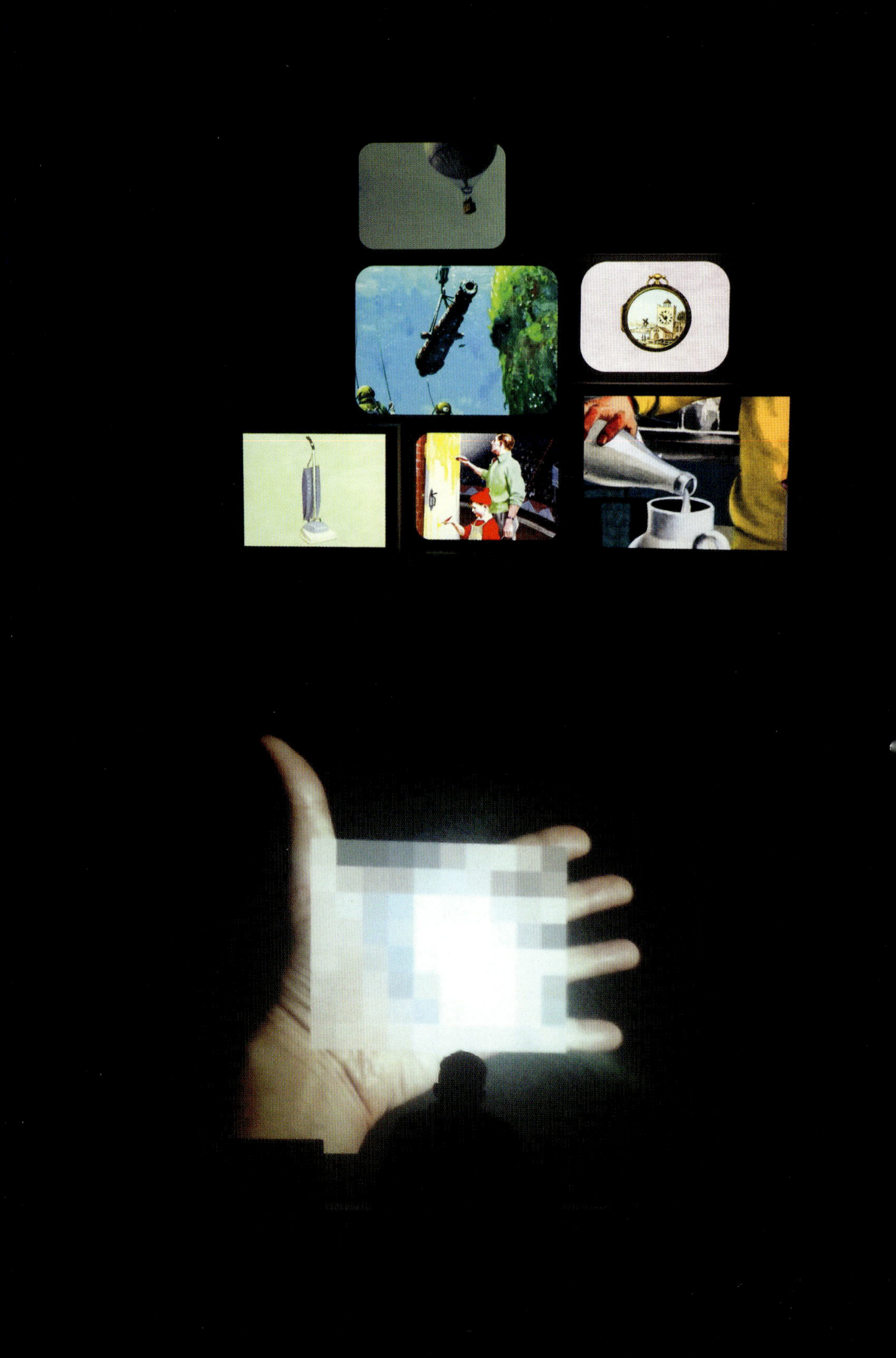

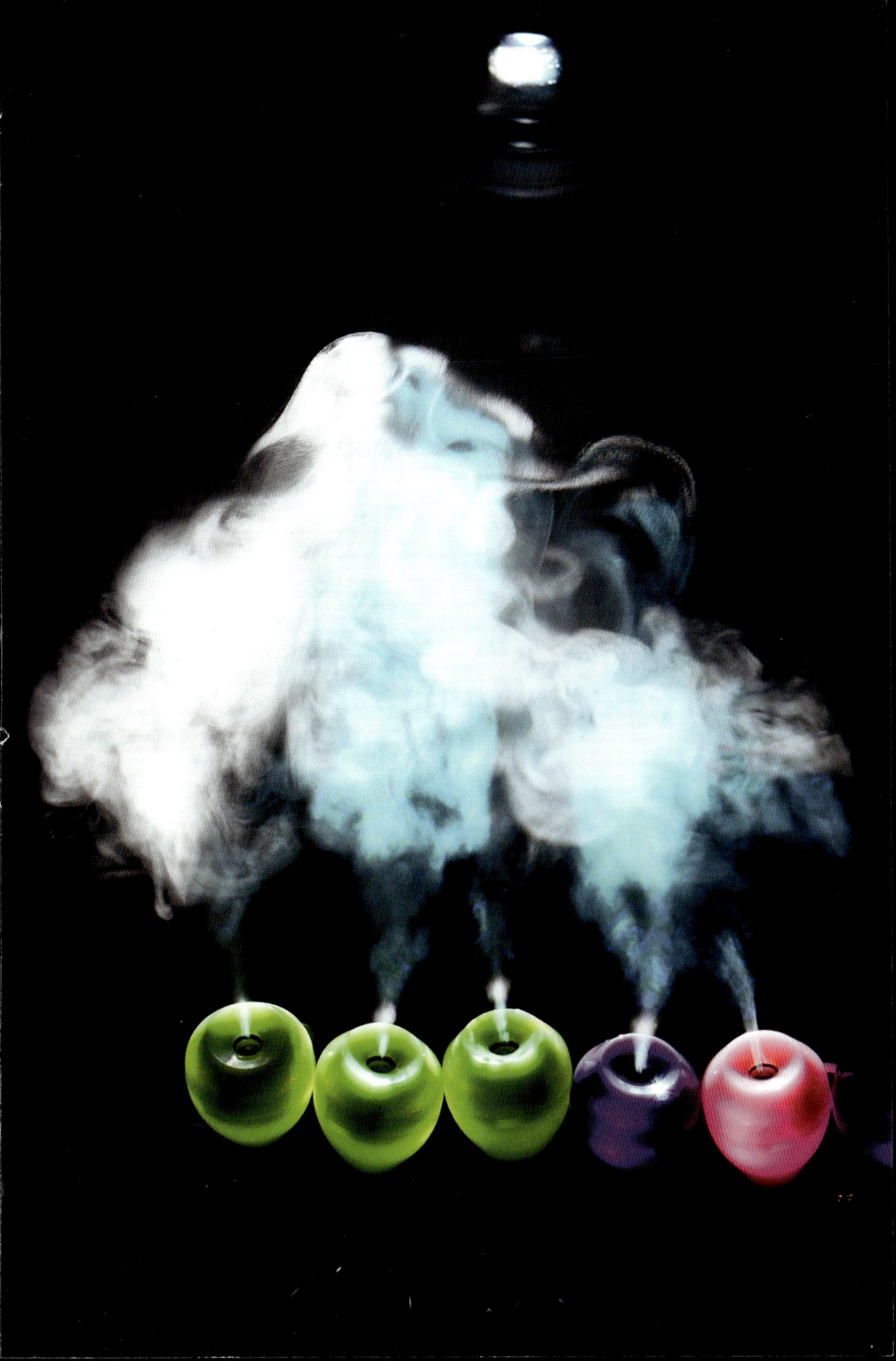

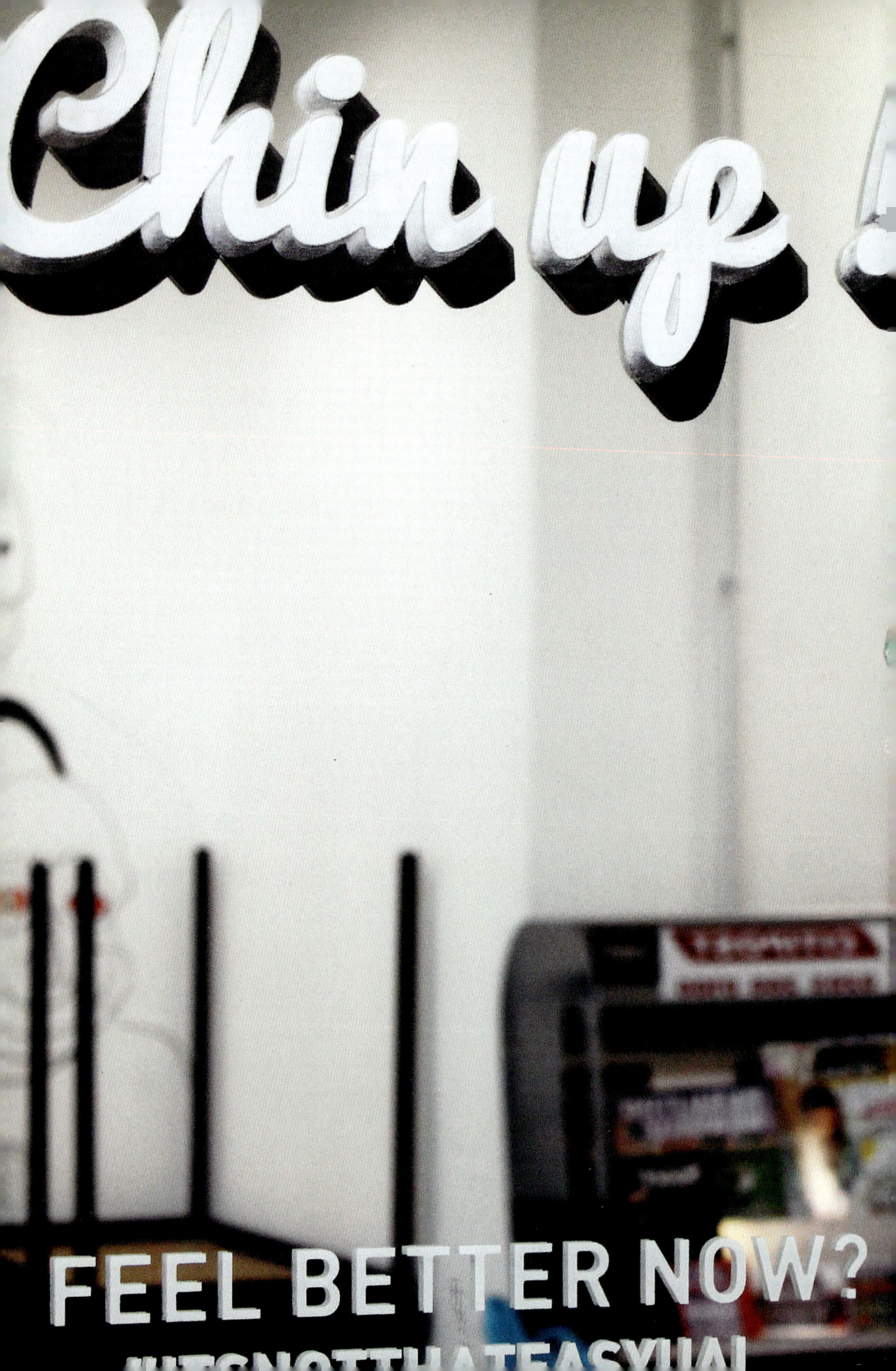
Chin up!
FEEL BETTER NOW?